My Life
on Mountain Railroads

The Utah Railway 200. Photo by John Lawson from the W. J. G. Gould collection.

My Life on Mountain Railroads

William John Gilbert Gould

edited by
William R. Gould

Utah State University Press
Logan, Utah
1995

Cover painting, "Water Stop at Gilluly," showing Gilbert Gould and his son Bill alongside the Utah Railway 108, by Howard Fogg

Typography by WolfPack
 Cover design by Michelle Sellers

Library of Congress Cataloging-in-Publication Data

Gould, William John Gilbert, 1888-1961.
    My life on mountain railroads / William John Gilbert Gould, edited
by William R. Gould.
    p. cm.
    Includes index.
    1. Gould, William John Gilbert, 1888–1961. 2. Mountain railroads—
Utah—History. 3. Mountain railroads—Utah—Employees—Biography.
I. Gould, William R., 1919– . II. Title.
HE4071.U49G68 1995
385'.092--dc20[B   95-4427
                                                                        CIP

Contents

Illustrations

Foreword

*M*y father followed the railroad as a boyhood preoccupation and an adult profession. It was an era when railroading was at once a hazardous and a romantic occupation. In fact, it was more than an occupation; it was a complete and distinct way of life—a culture separate from that of those whom the railroader considered lesser men.

The true adherent did not merely get a job on the railroad. He (at the time, it was an exclusively male profession) "went railroadin'." Usually it was a lifetime commitment. But his attitude toward the rail was often a contradiction. He would complain incessantly about what a hard life it was, lamenting the long hours and difficult working conditions in wind, rain, sleet, and snow. He would sternly counsel his sons to avoid the rigors of such a life and to better themselves by pursuing other occupations. Yet if he was himself for a time out of a job, he would instinctively and determinedly drift back to the rail and would sigh in contentment when he was again within that strange and exclusive world of the roaring road.

Railroading and railroads long dominated the industrial, financial, and commercial sectors of society. Rails led everywhere and anywhere. Brave young railroad engineers became heroic figures. This was the milieu of my father's adult life. He spent fifty years and eight months in the cabs of locomotives—mostly steam locomotives. At the age of seventy the law of the land told him it was time to retire. He did so somewhat reluctantly and immediately mired down in a morass of idleness that threatened his health.

To keep his mind active, I wrote to him asking pointed questions about some of the more lurid tales he had told me when I was a child. This was a natural thing for me to do: my own romance with the steam locomotive had never abated, although I had come along in time to share in only its afterglow. He responded directly to my questions with a series of vignettes that are separate from the longer narrative here, although I have integrated a few of them into it. Eventually the writing itch took possession of him, and on his own initiative he began to write his life story. This was precisely what I had wanted to occur, and I encouraged him at every turn.

This memoir was first written in soft pencil on pulp paper tablets, which were sent to me one by one as they came from under his hand. Later I had a typist prepare an exact transcription of his text. I then undertook a first effort to edit it, making only essential corrections of his grammar, punctuation, and spelling and adding a word here and there solely to clarify some passages for readers from a later generation. I earnestly sought to preserve his distinctive literary style and his great skill as a storyteller, hoping to lose nothing of the natural narrative flow of the Welsh bard.

My father was a Welshman—a Welshman with the name of an early English ancestor. He was born into a family of coal miners and ironmongers who were rather poor, never affluent. They came from the lush green valleys of South Wales. Anciently this region was known as Dyfed. The family came at last to live in the village of Merthyr-Tidfyl in Glamorgan. In Welsh this meant the place of the martyr, for there a woman, later known as St. Tidfyl, was martyred as an early Christian. The town lay alongside a small stream, the Taff River, from which the valley took its name.

The place was home to the ancient industry of ironmongery, which probably located there because of the abundance of good Welsh coal at minable depths beneath the green hills. During the industrial revolution the mining of coal became more important than ironmongery. In ever larger quantities, coal flowed down the valleys, first on horse-powered trams and later on rickety early railroads, to the little Welsh seaports on the Bay of Bristol. From there it was shipped by sea to fuel the burgeoning industries of Britain.

It was coal that brought the Gould family into Wales from nearby Somerset several generations prior to the birth of my father. A few Goulds recorded the occupation of ironmonger on their marriage and death certificates, but most dug coal from dirty dank coalpits. Marrying Welsh natives and adopting the language, they and their progeny became Welsh, steeped in the folkways of the land and seemingly enslaved to the pits. Boys and girls alike would enter the mines at eleven or twelve years of age. The women left upon marriage or childbearing; usually only death or disease released the men.

A temporary respite occurred in the case of my grandfather, Richard John Goold (called "Dick the Devil") who as a young man ran away to the army. After several years as a foot soldier in colonial India, he came back to the valleys to dig coal. Upon his return he married Sarah Perrin. They had two children, Ellen and Christina. But life in those mining towns overwhelmed Sarah Perrin Goold, and she died, leaving two tiny daughters in the care of Dick the Devil. Shortly thereafter Dick married my grandmother, Elizabeth Lewis, the daughter of William Lewis, who had relocated from his native Pembroke to work in the mines of Glamorgan.

Elizabeth Lewis Goold took Ellen and Christina as her own, and shortly thereafter Elizabeth, a determined woman who could read and write both English and Welsh, recorded the birth, in December 1888, of her first son in the registrar's office in Merthyr. In a bold clear hand she wrote his name, William John Gilbert Goold (later changed to Gould). William was for her father; John was for his father; and Gilbert was from a source known only to the Lord and to Elizabeth Lewis. All his life the boy preferred to be known as Gilbert. It was the only name, except some nicknames he acquired on the railroad, I ever heard his mother or anyone else apply to him.

About the time Gilbert was born, a new influence was at work in the Goold family. This was the Mormon Church, more properly the Church of Jesus Christ of Latter-day Saints. I do not know who was the first of the Goolds to join this church, but I do know that my great grandfather, John Gulliford Goold, was a member, as were his children, including Dick the Devil. I assume that Elizabeth Lewis Goold was converted by virtue of her marriage into the family because there is no record of her father, mother, or siblings joining. Nevertheless, she was to be among the most faithful of the Goold clan.

Mary Goold, my grandfather's sister, was the first of the clan to respond to the Mormon call to "gather unto Zion." Family tradition, oral history, says that she immigrated to Salt Lake City in the 1880s when she was in her late teens. There she found employment as a domestic in the home of President John Taylor, where she met George Reynolds, a member of the First Quorum of the Seventy and secretary to the president of the church. Elder Reynolds was also something of a scholar and an early Mormon scriptorian. She subsequently became his wife in a polygamous marriage performed near the end of the period in which the institution was practiced.

It is my impression that after Mary Goold came over the men were the next to come. They included John Gulliford and his sons Brigham Mon Victor and Richard John, my grandfather. It could be that women of the family, other than my grandmother, were also in the party. I have the distinct impression that my grandmother came over later with the children, including my father.

Upon arriving in the United States the family proceeded directly to Utah. Once there, the first order of business was to obtain employment. The basic skill of the male members of the family was mining coal; they knew little else. However, there were coal mines in Utah, most of them in Carbon County, some one hundred and twenty miles southeast of Salt Lake City. To these mines they took themselves, arriving at a dreary little place called Castle Gate. This name derived from two towering parapets of rock in the canyon of the Price River. The town, what there was of it, clung to the canyon walls and consisted of rude cottages, scattered randomly and punctuated by a company store, a mine office, a boarding house, and what passed for a depot, or station, on the narrow gauge railway that threaded its tortuous path through the Castle Gate and on up the canyon to cross the Wasatch range at Soldier Summit.

At the beginning of some fine work day in 1890, John Gulliford, Brigham Mon Victor, and Richard John presented themselves at the mine office. Luck was with some of them because the mine was hiring. John Gulliford and Brigham Mon Victor obtained jobs. Richard John was not hired. Being the runt of the family, he was told to come back tomorrow. Somewhat dejected, he went out of the office and sat down on the wooden steps fronting the narrow gauge mainline of the Rio Grande Western Railway. No doubt he was reflecting on the fact that life is unfair—as it always is.

But Lady Luck smiled on Dick the Devil and his descendants as well. He may not have deserved it, but I did! Along that crooked streak of narrow gauge rust that passed for a railroad came a section gang. On their pushcar they had long ties and heavier rail ready for the broad gauging of the Rio Grande.

Whatever else Dick the Devil may have been, he must have been, if even for one brief moment, resourceful. He got himself off those porch steps and went down and asked the section boss for a job. And he was hired on the spot. As he went trundling off after that pushcar, the entire horizon for my father, for me, and for my children was immensely altered. After generations of our family being in those dirty old coalpits, we were now out in the sunshine and the weather, on the railroad, which could lead to anywhere. My father was fond of saying that this was the most single important event in the history of our family. In my adult life as a director of Kaiser Steel, I visited numerous coal mines in Utah and elsewhere. It was not uncommon even in the latter part of this century to find third- and fourth-generation coal miners. But for the grace of the good Lord and a railway section gang, I could have been one of them.

When musing on this, I always remember a warm experience I had with my father when I was about fourteen. Like so many of my incidents of learning, it happened on a railway locomotive, one of the ungainly mallets of the Utah Railway. Mallets were articulated locomotives which embodied two engine mechanisms, such as 2–6–0s or 2–8–0s, set under the same boiler. The two mechanisms were hinged or articulated in order to traverse curves easily. This configuration produced power at lower speeds and fuel economy, but the locomotives were difficult to maintain. The Utah Railway used mallets in mainline helper service on the westward ascent of the Soldier Summit grade and in the tramp mine runs from Martin to the various little mining towns in western Carbon County.

On this day we were on the mine run up the branch to National. We had brought a train of empties to be distributed to the various mines. Loaded cars then would be collected and assembled into a train for return to Martin.

These switching operations consumed most of two to three hours. Empty cars, hoppers, gondolas, and even boxcars to be side loaded would be positioned above the mine tipple. On a given trip to the mine the railroad tramp crews would try to place a two- or three-days' supply of cars in that position. Workmen called by the likely name of "car droppers" dropped the empty cars from their stored positions above the mine down a slightly descending grade, releasing the brakes of the cars by means of a three-foot hickory club applied through the spokes of the hand brake wheel. Riding a car slowly down the grade, controlling it with the hand brakes, a workman let it drift slowly under the tipple where the newly mined and sized coal poured in until evenly loaded. Once filled, the cars were dropped further downgrade to storage tracks where they were spotted with dogged-down hand brakes until picked up and assembled into a train by the rail crews. This was precisely what my dad and his crew were doing on this day.

These car droppers were usually well-built, husky young men. They carried their long hickory brake clubs as a badge of office. It was a form of unskilled labor, probably paying somewhat less than the underground miner was paid. But I always thought it was a better job because it was above ground and in the unconfined world. I remember them as a jolly lot who called back and forth to each other in camaraderie and friendly derision as they dropped their cars down from the tipple on the adjoining tracks.

The aspect of this operation that I considered discouraging was that it was never done. As fast as the upper tracks were emptied of cars going to the tipple, some train crew would shove a new batch up the line to take their place. And as rapidly as the lower tracks accumulated a number of loads, they would be assembled into a train and taken off down the mountain. But this was the business of mining—and railroading.

While Dad and the train crew were engaged in these switching operations, I would drop off the engine with a .22 rifle in my hand and disappear into the wilderness above the mines. I never quite knew what kind of game I was pursuing. The train crew would good-naturedly kid me about the buckskin I failed to bring in, but that didn't really matter. It is the joy and freedom of roaming those sun-drenched hills without a care in the world that I remember. I don't believe I could have shot with intent to kill any of God's gentle creatures, although a few lizards and bull snakes fell victim to my marksmanship. Mostly I was rewarded only by the sound of a shot ricocheting off a rock and the echo reverberating across the hills. Toward sundown I would hear the whistle from Dad's engine in prearranged tones and sequence telling me that the switching operations were drawing to a close and it was time to come back to the train.

On this particular day as I climbed up the gangway on Dad's engine the valleys were taking on the twilight gloom and misty chill of an early autumn evening. The mood of the scene changed. The mine buildings looked dingy and shabby. The cars rolling down from the tipple seemed ominous and foreboding. I remember shivering a little as I entered the warm cab of the engine and stood my rifle in the corner behind Dad's seatbox.

The switching process had proceeded to the point that the train of cars had been assembled and the air brake test was in process. In this procedure the engineman made a full application of the air brakes while the trainmen walked the length of the train and checked the brakes on each car. It would be foolish to descend that four percent grade without the assurance that the brakes on every car were working properly. Once the train had been inspected, the brakemen would release the few hand brakes that had been set to hold the cars. They would then signal the "highball" to the engineer who would whistle-off, and the train would proceed down the mountain.

On this day the head-end brakeman was a man named Speedy Martin. His Christian name was probably known only to the payroll department. Along the entire railroad he was known as "Speedy" because of the slowness of his movements. Tonight as he ambled along the train of cars toward the engine my dad became increasingly irritable. He threw open the cab window and urged Speedy into a faster gait by certain rude references to his agility and intelligence.

This action was totally out of character for my usually jovial father and prompted me to inquire, "What's wrong, Dad?"

Closing his window and turning to the inside of the cab he said seriously, "Son, our ancestors spent too many generations in those dank dark holes known as coal mines. When the sun goes down in a coal camp I become very depressed and melancholy. I realize that except for a quirk of fate you and I could be down there now! When darkness falls in a coal camp I want to be rolling down the mountain towards God's country!"

About that time he got the highball and whistled-off with two blasts. The cab was filled with the screech of hissing air as the brakes were released and the train lurched into motion downgrade and into the autumn twilight. As we slowly threaded the tortuous turns of the canyon I reflected on that quirk of fate that had brought my dad and me out of the pits. I have had occasion to reflect on it more soberly as the years unfolded the course of my life and that of my family. Somehow it causes me to think more kindly of my much-maligned grandfather, Dick the Devil, as he got off the steps of the mine office at Castle Gate those many years ago.

This history begins with my father's account of growing up as an immigrant boy, first in the several rural locations of 1890s Utah where his father's work as a section hand or boss took the family, and later as a streetwise newsboy observing life in Salt Lake City in the early years of this century. During this time the influence and pull of railroads remained strong, becoming the consuming interest of his life. He achieved his ambition and became first a fireman and then an engineer. The greater part of his book tells of life on the railroad: its hazards and adventures, the fascinating characters who lived it, its traditions and skills, and the changes technology brought to it during his lifetime. I am aware of no written work that captures as well the culture, atmosphere, and ambience of the high noon of steam railroading as I knew it.

WILLIAM R. GOULD
LONG BEACH, CALIFORNIA

Publisher's Note

My Life on Mountain Railroads is both the memoir of one experienced engineer (an "old head" in the argot of the rails) and a rich primary source for the occupational folklore of railroad culture during the last days of steam. The story is largely written in the vernacular of that culture, and thus it contains much railroad jargon and many technical terms. In consultation with the editor, William R. Gould, we concluded that most of these are comprehensible in context. Here and there, definitions have been added for those that were not; these are at the first or another early appearance of the word or phrase. Entries for such definitions or explanations are highlighted in the index, which readers should consult if they do not understand specific terms. Although a reader can learn much about the operation of steam locomotives from this book, it is not meant to be a technical guide to running such engines, and thus some of the technical terminology may remain obscure or difficult even as defined.

We have, in addition to adding a few definitions and lightly editing the text, reorganized it into chapters that proceed in roughly chronological order. Otherwise, we have altered little and have instead preserved Gilbert Gould's writing with all its rich character. We hope the result will both entertain and inform while providing a unique glimpse of life on a steam engine.

Youth

I remember a little-used passing track at mile post 15. It meandered away from the mainstem of the Tintic branch of the Oregon Short Line (OSL) railroad to skirt the edge of a wheat field and further on it wound back to connect with the main again. Between the main and passing tracks, about halfway along, stood a very leaky old water tank where the engines of eastbound trains always came to a stop to replenish their water supply before tackling the rising grade that lifted sharply after leaving the tank. To the right of the passing track going east, a pump house labored throughout the day to keep the leaky old tank from going dry. To the left of the mainline stood a large red section house with a wooden platform leading from the front door to the rail's edge.

That's all there was at mile post 15 except a crossboard that proclaimed the place, "Cedar Fort." In order to see the town, you would have to direct your gaze up toward the foothills. That lush green spot against the mountain, two and a half miles away, was the town—Cedar Fort.

Once in a great while a resident or two of that community would find it necessary to come down to the section house, or station, as they called it, to flag a westbound passenger train in order to ride to the city around the mountain.

That section house, call it what you like, was the home of my parents and a half dozen of us kids. My dad was section boss at mile post 15. Follow the mainline east, up the grade and at mile post 21 you came to a junction town called Fairfield. It derived the appellation of junction from the fact that a mining company, high up in a canyon to the right, owned a railroad of their own. This railroad ran down to meet the Oregon Short

Line at Fairfield. The motive power on the mining company's railroad consisted of slow moving, but very efficient and busy, little cogwheel, or shay, engines. Cogwheels were locomotives which used shafts and reduction gears to drive the wheels. This configuration permitted greater power to be delivered to the wheels at a sacrifice of speed. The shay was a type of cogwheel where the cylinders were in vertical alignment and the geared shafts ran along the length of the right side of the locomotives and tenders.

The big OSL railroad would set out empty cars and passengers and whatever else was to be transported to the mining town, at Fairfield. Westbound OSL trains would pick up these cars, now laden with precious ore, to be delivered to the smelters around the mountain.

Fairfield, being a junction of the two railroads was a small town in itself. There were a dozen or more homes, a grocery store, a post office, a schoolhouse, and last but not least, a large frame building that from the sign over the doorway proclaimed itself a saloon.

It was shortly after a regular pay day. Dad had received his monthly check of sixty dollars—that being the magnificent sum doled out to the section bosses in those good old days. Being in need of cash to meet monthly bills, mostly mail-order, he had to get the check converted into currency. There being no place at mile post 15 or at the community at the foothills to oblige him, he must therefore journey to Fairfield.

Mother was in the habit of accompanying him, but on this night she didn't feel up to it. My younger brother Pat, being about six or seven at the time, and myself, being about eleven, went along to keep Dad company and to help him pump the old hand car up the grade.

We started out bravely, Pat and I, throwing our combined weight upon the pump handles to help make the car go. Our enthusiasm was dampened considerably upon reaching the grade. From there on, it was pump, push, and rest, pump, push, and rest. After numerous periods of this we finally arrived at Fairfield.

After detracking the hand car, Dad was all for getting to the business at hand, which was to get the check cashed. After which, he intended to stock up on a few groceries before that large frame building closed it's doors for the night. As it turned out later, those doors could be closed right then for all the good they were to do us.

Dad proceeded to the saloon with Pat and myself trailing along. That is usually the one place a railroad man selects to cash his paycheck—Rule G, the rule prohibiting employees from using alcoholic beverages, notwithstanding. I do not wish to intimate that my Dad was a drinking man, far from it. But temptations do arise.

Dad met a man at the saloon named Murphy. Murphy was the section boss at mile post 21—Fairfield. This man Murphy, being section boss at

Fairfield, and Dad being the same at Cedar Fort, found a lot to talk about, between the times they found nourishment gazing at the bartender's diamond stick pin through the bottom of a beer glass.

The talk grew too technical for Pat and I to follow closely, but we realized it dealt mostly with low joints, high centers, and curve elevations. Also how in times past, they had each put the roadmaster in his place. All the time the bartender was busy keeping the foam on the top of their glasses.

Pat and myself, although we were greatly interested, began to get sleepy. After a while it developed that these two kingsnipes had found something else in which they were on common ground. This was the fact that both, in their wild and distant pasts, had been soldiers in the armies of Her Gracious Majesty Queen Victoria of Great Britain.

This called for more of the same, and the friendship grew apace. Soon the large interior of the drink emporium was resounding with the shouted commands of the British army. One would think they had both been sergeants. Then came criticism: Lord Roberts was a very strict disciplinarian. He kept Dad standing at attention for a considerable length of time for some slight infraction of the rules. Kitchener was a butcher. Others, whom I have forgotten, came in for their share.

Finally the talk turned to the manual of arms as it was done in Her Majesty's armies. Dad was eager to demonstrate his ability in performing the manual of arms. So picking up a broom that stood in a corner and with Sergeant Murphy calling the commands, the show began.

It was soon evident that a broom could not take the place of a gun in these maneuvers, so Murphy must step across the tracks to his home to get a shotgun, which he used to shoot jackrabbits, and substitute it for the broom. Spying Pat and myself dozing behind the stove, he invited us to go along to his home. We were all for staying to see the fun, but we were urged to go by Sergeant Gould.

Upon arriving at Murphy's home we were served a bit to eat, and Murphy left with the shotgun—much to the annoyance of Mrs. Murphy. As time drifted on we fell asleep, only to be awakened in the middle of the night for the homeward trip.

After long deliberations and great effort they finally got the hand car back on the track. Then after numerous manifestations of undying friendship and many exclamations favoring long life to the Queen, the two ex-sergeants loudly bid each other Godspeed.

In the usual case, if a hand car was to drift down a long grade, there was no need to exercise the pump handles. They were just a nuisance and a source of danger to those riding the car, so the usual procedure was to knock out the key holding the small pinion in place on the axle and disengage it from the large cogwheel. This put the car in free wheeling.

Tonight no one thought of this, and we went down into the black night with the pump handles flapping up and down at a dangerous tempo. Dad stood upright on one side of the superstructure with Pat and me grasping the iron handhold on the other. Down into the dark night we went with ever increasing speed—the pump handles battering the night air savagely. The flanges whined as the car swung around the curves, and the wheels sang a song of ever increasing speed as they smashed over the rail joints. It was soon evident that Dad had no intention of checking the speed of this wildly pitching vehicle.

We were surely going home in a hurry!

Dad, who hadn't uttered a word since bidding Murphy that boisterous adieu, now suddenly groaned and slumped to the floor of the car to lay prone with eyes gazing up into the starless night. How he missed coming in contact with those murderous pump handles is a mystery. He lay there staring up into the blackened sky as the car rocketed down the grade. We were sure making miles per hour, plenty of them!

Thoughts of meeting an opposing train never entered my mind, and I'm sure it concerned Dad very little. I shudder to think what would have resulted if a roaming cow should have stepped on the track ahead of us. Our worries would have been all in the past.

When it seemed that the momentum would take us clear off the right of way, my foot accidentally came in contact with the brake pedal protruding up along the side of the car. I recognized it for what it was, having seen it in operation many times previously. So with my full weight of seventy pounds or more bearing down on it I was able to slow our speed slightly. But what kid wants to slow down a fast ride? Wouldn't this be something to tell the kids at school the next day? Wouldn't they be envious, though?

With all these thoughts surging through my mind is it any wonder that the section house, our home, loomed up out of the black night all too soon? With all my weight on the brake pedal the speed gradually lessened. The song of the flanges, the clicking of the wheels over the rail joints, muted. The slashing pump handles were stilled.

Dad still lay prone on the car floor after everything else was silent. His groans and sighs were the only evidence that he still lived. Our efforts to arouse him only produced more sighs and groans. These manifestations of distress finally brought Mother to the door. She recognized conditions at a glance. She closed the door and soon reappeared dressed more suitably for the task at hand—that of getting Dad off the car and into the house. This took some doing. It seemed that for some reason Dad was unable to stand on his feet.

After we had finally gotten him into the house, our next job was to get the hand car off the track and into the toolshed before some speeding westbound extra came along and demolished it. This was no easy task for two small boys, but with Mother's help, we finally got the car tucked away for the night.

When we re-entered the house we could hear Dad crying and bawling. Crying in his cups! It at last dawned on me that my Dad was drunk—dead and sick. In his efforts to lay the blame for his condition on someone else he cried out, "Liz, Liz, will you ever send me to Fairfield again?"

Mother was trying to silence him and get him to bed. All the time Dad kept muttering sorrowfully, "Liz, will you ever send me to Fairfield again?" Mother's assurance that she would not hardly seemed to placate Dad, but at last he finally drifted off to sleep.

You can bet that mother never did send Dad to Fairfield alone again. She went with him! For days after that if we knew Dad was in a good frame of mind, we plagued him by crying out, "Liz, will you ever send me to Fairfield again?"

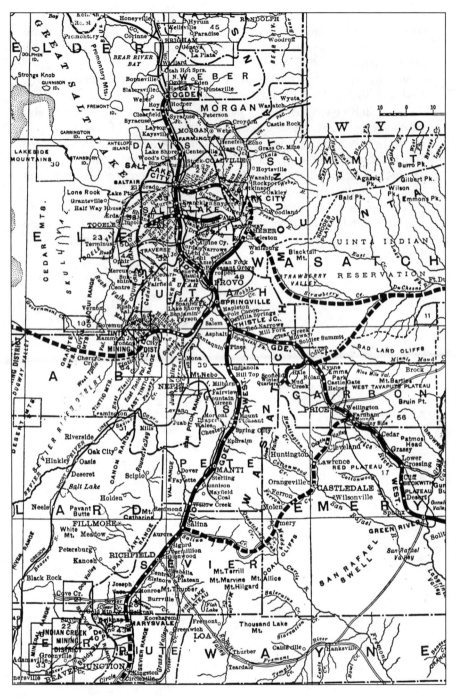

Central Utah showing Rio Grande Western Railway trackage in the early twentieth century. From "Prospectors' Map of Utah," Utah State Historical Society.

Trackside Childhood

The first recollection that I have deals with the little town of Sandy, about twelve miles south of Salt Lake City. It was there that I first started my meager education. It was also there that I first fell in love. The object of my childish affection happened to be my school teacher. I have long since forgotten her name. But I well remember my anguish at the end of that first term of school when I realized that it would be a long time before I would be able to see her again. But I guess I was of a very fickle nature, as I seem to have survived very well.

It was also at Sandy that I first developed a wanderlust. This was brought on by my natural curiosity. From where we lived I could look down across the slanting landscape and note the progress of the trains that smoked up the valley as they wended their way into a wondrous unknown. Sandy at that time had not developed into the small city that it is today. There were hardly any dwellings between our house and the faraway tracks of the Rio Grande Western Railway.

On that day I was only about six years old. I had decided to look into certain things that had long bothered me. I wished to satisfy my curiosity and see for myself where those distant trains came from and just where they were going. How I ever made it down across State Street, over the numerous fences, and through the many fields and pastures to the railroad right of way is something to think about.

William J. G. Gould at a young age. Photo from the W. J. G. Gould collection.

When I arrived at that place I must have been lost. I started walking along the tracks. I must have had divine guidance, because my feet brought me to the town of Bingham Junction, now called Midvale. There again my feet propelled me in the right direction, and I followed the rails that curved to the right toward State Street. It was starting to get dark now, and I knew I was hopelessly lost. I was tired, and I was crying, but my weary feet kept dragging me onward.

Little did I know that the larger part of the population of Sandy was out looking for a small lost boy. Then, when things began to look darkest, and I had just gone over the crossing at State Street, a horse and buggy stopped and a voice called to me. I knew that voice! A lady was hurriedly climbing down from the buggy. I recognized her instantly! It was my mother!

What guiding power finally brought us to that spot at the same time I will never know. Another few moments and I would have been trudging along on my weary way, and Mother would have missed me.

My Dad worked as a section hand for the Oregon Short Line Railroad. One day a boy, much older than I, told me that my dad had been killed by a train. I ran home crying to Mother. I remember how she hurriedly dressed in her best frock and we proceeded to where the gang was working. Dad was unhurt but very angry. That boy avoided me in the future.

There was a time at Sandy when I saw a man die with his head in my dad's lap. This man was the section boss. He had only been on the job a few days. His wife and small daughter were staying at our house until they could get located. As was my habit, I drifted down to the tool shanty about the time the section gang tied up in order to walk home with Dad. They had got in and had run the push car into the shed. My dad was sitting on the end of the car. The dying man was laying on his back with his head in Dad's lap. He was screaming and cursing. I had never heard a man curse so in my young life. He was a foreigner of some kind. He would scream, "I'm die! I'm die!" And then he would curse. I thought that it was an awful way for a man to go to meet his God. He shortly died right there on the section car. I understood it was a heart problem.

There came a time when the section gang at Sandy was abolished. Dad was sent to Salt Lake to work on a gang there. Every morning he would get up and walk to Murray where he would catch the street car to ride into Salt Lake. Murray was as far south as the street cars ran at that time.

We moved to Ironton about 1895. Ironton is not on the map anymore. It was about a mile and a half straight down the grade from Silver City Junction. This was about the same distance from what is now Tintic Junction on the present day Union Pacific Railroad (UP). Dad left Salt Lake first. As soon as it could be arranged Mother and the family followed.

All there was at Ironton was a wye track configuration for turning railroad engines in the opposite direction, the section house where we lived, and a corral and loading chute for loading cattle and wild horses. There were lots of wild horses in the surrounding country at that time. After passing the switch at the west leg of the wye the rails continued for about five miles further down to what was known as McIntyre's Ranch. I was never at the ranch, but from all accounts it must have been quite an outfit.

A freight train used to come out from Salt Lake every morning. The crew would leave their caboose standing in front of our section house while they distributed their train around the different mining camps. This seemed to be the procedure during times when activity was slack at the mines. When business was good, the crew would tie up at Ironton, and the mine-run job would distribute the freight and make up the returning train.

A platform surrounded our section house just high enough to step off and onto the caboose platforms. One day when the crew was up working the mines, my younger brother Richard (who several years later acquired the nickname of Pat) climbed over and sat down on the forward platform of the caboose. He had a little hatchet in his hand and was hammering away at anything that struck his fancy. He started pounding on the "dog," as it is called, that fits into the teeth of the brake staff ratchet. This holds the hand brake set when it is applied. Apparently Pat's hammering knocked the dog loose.

I saw the caboose start to move slowly down the track. Pat was sitting there on the platform quite unconcerned. I screamed for Mother, and she came running out, reached over and lifted Pat off the platform. I wanted to get a piece of wood and put in front of the wheels, but Mother told me to stay away. We stood there and watched that caboose gather speed as it went rattling down through the open country. About one-half or three-quarters of a mile further down the grade the track curved sharply to the left and ended up against a low foothill.

It seems that the track ending as it did against the mountain comprised sort of a derail to catch anything that may have gotten loose in the mining camps above. It had been installed before those camps had started to boom. There had been no time when it had been used so the switch had been neglected and left lined for the mainline, but that morning as Dad and the crew started for work, he sent one of his men down to line the switch for the derail.

I believe that sometimes we Goulds have some sort of second sight. It seems the crew had seen the caboose get loose from where they were working up around Mammoth or Silver City. It wasn't long before they came on down to the section house. On the way they picked up Dad and his section gang. They also had a ten gallon keg of beer.

When they arrived they all went into a conference. They wanted to know what had caused the caboose to get away. Mother told them how it happened, that Pat had climbed on with his little hatchet and had knocked the brake loose. The train crew didn't want to believe that a little kid the size of Pat with a toy hatchet could hit the dog hard enough to release the brakes. The conductor, a big fierce-looking fellow with a long mustache, glared at me and wanted to know if it wasn't me that turned the caboose loose. We had a hard time trying to convince him that Pat was the guilty one. These many years later I think that the brake wasn't set very tight when Pat hit the dog. Since going railroading myself I can easily see what happened.

The brakeman that set that hand brake claimed he set it up really tight. Maybe he did. But did he also take time to drain the auxiliary reservoir? If he didn't, failure to do so caused the brake to loosen. He may have set the hand brake tight, but after a while the air leaking out of the train line set the brake a little tighter and tighter still, until it loosened the dog from the ratchet. Then the air finally leaked out of the brake cylinder. That loosened and moved the dog away from the ratchet so that any little tap let the brake loose. After a little while all the tension in brake and rigging let go. About the time that Pat hit the dog, the brakes were nearly released anyway and the caboose was ready to move.

Air brakes were new about that time, and the crews were not up on all the tricks as they are now. Nowadays you wouldn't see an informed brakeman leaving a car on a grade with the hand brake set without draining the auxiliary reservoir.

That ten gallon keg of beer was brought onto the platform, and everyone proceeded to get real friendly. When the keg was about empty they decided it was about time to go to work, so they all proceeded down to the derailed caboose. After two or three hours that caboose was finally pulled back on the rails.

The freight train bound for Salt Lake left Ironton about six hours late. There was no report made of it, and nobody was censured. That's what a keg of beer will do—sometimes. Can you imagine getting away with anything like that nowadays?

We were not at Ironton very long. It seems there was a derailment at Mammoth Junction—the engine of the mine-run crew turned over at the stub switch on the mainline. For this the section boss at that place was fired. Dad was sent to Eureka to take his place. In a few days we followed him.

We lived in a little frame house in Dutchtown. Across the canyon on the mountain side lived a family by the name of Faser. There was a girl in the family named Pauline—Pauline Eva Faser. Although I never remember meeting her in those locations, about ten or twelve years later she became my wife.

Dad's section included Eureka, Mammoth, Silver City, and all the connecting trackage. I have heard Dad say that his first official act on taking charge was to fire one of the hands and order him to get clear off the right of way. It seems that this action concerned the wreck at the stub switch which derailed and turned over the 518 at Mammoth Junction. Dad had heard this man remark that he could have prevented that happening if he had chose to do so. He had noticed a lip on that stub switch at quitting time that night, but being in a hurry to get home he had not called it to the attention of the foreman. Dad told him no man who so neglected his duties could work for him ten minutes.

We were at Eureka when the Spanish-American War broke out. There was considerable excitement and much patriotism around town. Every young buck wanted to go to war. Everything was subject to the war. I remember the newsboys screaming about it. Across the front page of the newspaper was the caption, "War Begins at Eight P.M." Bulletins posted in store windows screamed the same tidings: "War Begins at Eight P.M." Of course I was just as patriotic as anyone in town. I had an air gun and was busy shooting imaginary Spaniards.

I remember there was much weeping and lamenting among the young women. I recall my mother and her women friends speaking in hushed tones of a certain girl who had tried to commit suicide by throwing herself in front of the train that carried her sweetheart away to war. Apparently the attempt was not successful.

The Rio Grande was in the habit of running excursion trains out of Salt Lake to Eureka, Mammoth, and Silver City almost every Sunday during the summer months. They usually had a couple of Rome engines double heading six or seven coaches. Romes were little ten-wheelers (4–6–0 wheel configuration) built in Rome, New York. Eureka is built in a canyon between two mountain ridges. The Rio Grande comes in high up on the mountain slope on one side. The Oregon Short Line, now the Union Pacific, comes in from the other direction and follows a course along the bottom of the canyon.

Residences used to be scattered all over the sides of the mountain. The business district was located in the lower levels of the canyon. About halfway up the mountainside near the Rio Grande tracks was the Mormon chapel. It was directly across the canyon and about the same level as the Rio Grande depot. A long flight of stairs led high up the mountain to the Mormon church house.

On the other side, just before passing the Rio Grande depot, a spur track took off from the mainline and circled around the depot. The switch controlling this spur was of the new-fangled split-rail type. All switches on the OSL at the time were still of the stub-rail type. The Rio Grande was just beginning to install this new split switch—the "deadly split," it was called for a long time.

One Sunday morning one of those excursion trains was coming into town. On the other side of the canyon Sunday School was just being dismissed. As I came out of Sunday School I looked across the canyon. Two little Romes on the head end of that passenger train were gliding majestically down toward the depot. A train anywhere always held my attention.

As I watched those two engines start to fade behind the depot I noticed something wrong three coaches back in the train. The third or fourth coach seemed to slither out of line with the rest of the train. It seemed to be inclined to turn at right angles to the track. Then with a scraping, dust-clouded crash, that coach turned over on its side and slid a little ways to a stop.

I didn't wait to find out what it was all about. I scrambled down that long, steep stairway and raced home as fast as I could go. My dad was lying down taking a Sunday nap. I woke him up and told him what I had seen. He hurriedly dressed, and we both took off up the mountainside to the Rio Grande depot. That coach was lying on its side. Half of the people of Eureka were there. They were helping the injured passengers get out of the coach.

It was later determined that the split rail (or point) on that switch was partly open. The two engines and the first two coaches followed the mainline. The front truck on that third car also took the main track toward the depot. But the rear truck on the same coach split the partly open point and decided in favor of the side track. You can imagine the mess that resulted from this difference of opinion.

Those split-rail switches were considered to be dangerous when they were first coming into favor. In this case it was the opinion that some train or engine had run through this switch in the reverse direction and failed to report it. This is still a common occurrence. They don't censure a crew very much now if they run through a switch, but it's almost a dischargeable offense to leave without reporting it.

Several years later I was firing the Eureka switch engine. The crew and I were in the depot shooting the breeze. I told the gang about this wreck I had witnessed from the steps of the church that Sunday morning. When I finished the tale that station agent swung around in his swivel chair and looked at me. He asked me who I was. I told him. He confirmed my story. He was the agent on duty that Sunday morning.

This wreck didn't discourage the Rio Grande. The next Sunday morning another excursion train came into Eureka, this time with better luck.

In those days the railroad would, on the slightest pretext, run excursion trains at reduced rates. There were no automobiles, and so this was the only way people had of seeing something different from their daily scene.

During the summer months the Rio Grande would advertise moonlight excursions. Late in the afternoon a train of coaches would drift into Silver City. Just before dusk that train would leave partly loaded. It would go to Mammoth and pick up passengers. Then at Eureka they would board more excursionists. I never knew where those trains were headed until I started firing on the Rio Grande. I asked an old-time engineer about it. He told me those trains would go to Castella, a hot spring resort in lower Spanish Fork canyon, or to Geneva, the present site of the Geneva Steel plant. Both of these locations were resorts at that time. The people would dance until midnight, and then the trains would return them to their destinations. "There just ain't no fun no more!"

I remember one other thing from those days at Eureka. Someone had given me one of those dollar Ingersoll watches. I was very proud of my watch as I carried it to school. But if my dad and his gang happened to be working close by he would usually contrive to meet me on my way to school: "Let me take your watch, Siree, I got a job that has to be finished before that passenger train is due. Come on now, Siree, you can have it back again before tonight." And so I would go on to school brokenhearted and without my watch.

The railroads serving the mines in the Tintic area were a prominent feature of community life. They were the connecting link to the outside world in that they carried people to and from those little mining towns. They carried ore produced in the mines to the smelters to be processed. They moved all other freight and commerce necessary to sustain life.

I have the feeling that my life must have been dedicated to the railroads from the very beginning—even before my actual appearance on the scene. As far back as I can remember railroading has been a dominant part of my world. The sound of a locomotive working, the chime of its whistle, the blast of exhausted steam erupting from its stack, the black clouds of smoke rolling back over the train, or the clang of the bell always would unfailingly attract my attention—so much so that I had little or no time for other interests. From those days of early childhood in and around Tintic the course of my life seemed to have been set.

The territory of the Oregon Short Line Railroad included Eureka, Silver City, Mammoth, and all connecting and yard trackage. The railroad company decided a more central location for the section gang would be at Silver City Junction, so they hurriedly rehabilitated an old run-down log house at that point, and we moved into it, my father being the section boss. This whitewashed old log house was the only habitation for two to three miles in any direction.

Silver City Junction was where the branch line to Silver City came down to connect with the mainline by way of an old stub switch. There was also a wye at that point and off to the side an abandoned pump house that had been used to pump water up into Mammoth. Other sources of water had been found and so the pump house had been boarded up. The reservoir was still there and was used occasionally as a swimming hole for kids who came down from the mining camps.

I was in the second or third grade at school, but owing to the distance to the nearest schoolhouse I had to forego my chances for a higher education while we were there. There was no law at that time compelling a child to attend school, and there were no busses to haul him there. I spent my time mostly roaming through the cedars that surrounded our house or sitting on that knee-high porch gazing up into Mammoth and Silver City.

A mine-run crew worked the mines and connected with the freight crew that tied up at Ironton, a mile and a half below Silver City Junction. It was a panorama of action thas was interesting to me, because at almost all times I could see an engine working somewhere on the scene.

Many times I sat on the porch of that log section house and watched that little diamond-stacked eight-wheeler hammer its way up those grades with the two or three coaches that made up the morning passenger train out of Salt Lake. Invariably it would be a combine and one coach, but there were special occasions when there would be a second coach making a three-car train.

That extra coach demanded more power, so the 518 would meet them at Ironton. The 518 was a low-wheeled mogul, a diamond-stacker. A mogul was a class of locomotive with a 2–6–0 wheel configuration. The 518 had an old style smoke or exhaust stack which in profile had a diamond shape. The train backed up from Ironton into Mammoth, then headed down to the mainline, only to reverse direction and back up into Eureka. From there it headed down to Silver City Junction from which point it backed up again into Silver City.

What a sight it was to the eyes of a small boy to see those two wonderful engines blasting up the grade with huge volumes of black smoke belching from their diamond stacks! It was truly something that will never be seen again.

Here is a rustic plan of the track configuration:

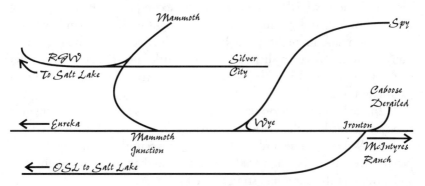

There was another railway in my sight as I sat on that porch. It was owned by the Mammoth mines and mills. It circled the mountains

The Tintic loop on the Rio Grande Western in the early 1900s. Four trains are shown. Photo by R. H. Kindig.

between Upper and Lower Mammoth. Its motive power consisted of a single shay engine.

The Rio Grande Western also entered the area. Their trains came in from the other direction. Those Rio Grande engines sounded a mournful whistle down into our valley as they screamed through the deep cuts and roared across the high fills clinging to the mountainside.

The night passenger train of the Rio Grande Western came around the mountain at a time when I had usually been hustled off to bed. How mournful those whistles sounded to the accompaniment of a pack of coyotes howling and yelping, as it seemed, right under my window. Two coyotes on a moonlit night can make more noise than a dozen dogs! I would pull the covers up over my head and shiver. I little knew then that in another dozen years I would be the fireman on that little Rio Grande Western passenger train.

In the limited horizon that screened my boyish mind there were only two real railroads in the world: the Oregon Short Line (OSL) and the Rio Grande Western. The only difference between them in my limited perspective was in the engines. The former had diamond-stacked engines, while those of the latter had straight stacks.

The passenger train of the Oregon Short Line came out of Salt Lake in the morning and tied up at Silver City about 10:30 A.M. Its movement was plainly visible to me as I watched from that porch down in the valley. Due to the alignment of the road the passenger train would be backing up when it entered Silver City, its laying-over point. I could watch it as it stopped at the depot to unload the last of its passengers. Then it would slowly back up beyond the ash pit. The engine would then be cut off from the train to stand over the pit, where it would remain until about 2:50 P.M. At that time it would be moved back to a coupling with the train, after which it would move ahead to the depot.

Promptly at 3:10 P.M. two white puffs of steam would appear above the whistle. If there was no adverse wind, the sound of the two blasts would drift down into the valley. Then that old diamond-stacker would start throwing out black rings of smoke as it moved ahead with increasing speed. Pretty soon it would be lost to view as it sank behind a forest of cedars. Presently it would come charging out of those cedars where the rails ran in a straight line for about a mile pointing directly at where I sat on that porch.

I have often likened the appearance of the front end of that train to the frightening charge of some monstrous, indescribable wild animal. The diamond stack with smoke rolling back over the train, the cab spreading out like crouching shoulders, and the coaches outlined behind had all the appearance of a mad, destructive monster about to leap upon its unsuspecting prey. Then when it seemed as though I would have to jump aside, it would take the curve and assume the outline of a two-car passenger train. The flanges would scream as the train rocked around the sharp curve that ended up against the mainline where connection was made by the old stub switch. With the brake shoes screeching loudly the train would stop to clear the mainline. The switch would be properly lined and the train moved out on the mainline. The switch would then be realigned for the mainline and the train would start backing up on its way to Eureka and Mammoth. After a while it would come back, streaking down the hill on its way to Salt Lake.

I remember a time when that train in its wild descent from Silver City did not stop to have that old stub switch lined. The engineer that day was an extra man who was not familiar with the road. He hit that curve at a pretty fast clip. When he attempted to stop he was already too close to the switch. At the last moment he swung the Johnson bar over into the back of the quadrant and gave her steam, thus reversing the engine. The wheels began to spin backward, and the whistle howled out a long despairing wail. When the train came to a final stop the entire engine was over the stub switch and on the ground.

(After going into engine service myself, I often thought of this. I wondered how that engineer could reverse the engine, give her steam, and hang onto that whistle, all at the same time. Suddenly I remembered: those Short Line engines had a long rod extending the full width against the front of the cab. In the center of this rod another rod connected to it passed through the cab to connect with the whistle. On each end of this cross-rod was a handle positioned so that the whistle could be blown by either the engineer or the fireman.)

After the train came to a stop the whistle let go with four long appealing blasts. This was repeated several times. Pretty soon the mine-run crew came flagging down out of Mammoth. Dad and his gang also put in an appearance.

In order for the mine-run crew to make a pull on the derailed engine they would have to get behind the coaches. In order to get behind the coaches they would have to go around the wye. But that was full of occupied outfit cars, because the bridge and builders gang was building a new water tank at Silver City Junction. So the outfit cars had to be made ready for movement. Then the 518 backed down and coupled onto the coaches. The 518 was a powerful (for the time) mogul. It didn't take long to pull that little eight-wheeler back on the rails. After the section gang made the needed track repairs the passenger train was on its way again.

A big, burly good-natured man named Jim Love was engineer of the 518. Each day this engine and the mine-run crew met the local freight train at Ironton and distributed its consist to the different destinations while the freight crew tied up there for the day. They also made up the train for the local's return to Salt Lake.

My dad had been ordered to build a short derailing spur on the branch that circled up behind Silver City to some new mines that were coming into production. This branch was called the Spy Branch. I do not know why that sinister appellation was applied, but I do remember a comical result of that name. The territory that comprised my dad's section was growing, and Dad was given an assistant foreman. This assistant was of Swedish descent and a very fine appearing man. He was rather quiet, and when he spoke it was with a strong Swedish accent. The name of the branch seemed to intrigue him. When no one was engaging his attention his lips were continually moving as though he was talking to himself. Someone soon found out what he was saying. He was continually spelling S-P-Y—"Spy."

On the day that Dad was to start work on that derailing spur the mine-run crew had orders to move the necessary tools and material to the work place. They spotted a flat car by the tool shed and the gang loaded it up. My brother Pat and I were standing by—wide-eyed and alert. I saw my

Dad talking to Jim Love. Pretty soon he motioned for us to come to him. We did so eagerly, and he picked us up and stood us on the deck of the 518. He climbed up behind us, and we were told to sit on the cab floor just ahead of the fireman's seat box. We were more than glad to comply.

We were sitting there with our backs against the inside of the cab, with our legs straight out in front of us. Our feet did not touch the boiler head. We could not see out the side as our heads did not come up to the cab windows. But since it was a nice warm day, the front cab door was wedged open. We could look to the front along the running board and off the side through that open door. I could, by stretching my neck a little to the side, keep my eyes on the actions of the engineer as he handled the controls, although I could not then identify the Johnson bar from the brake valve or the throttle.

Later I learned the Johnson bar was the lever in the cab that positioned valves which admitted steam to the cylinders. Its primary purpose was to reverse the engine, but it also served to control the consumption and economical use of steam. I discovered engineers and firemen were often at odds over the position of the Johnson bar. If it was positioned to unnecessarily demand steam, it could make the fireman work more than necessary. The engineer could punish the fireman to the point of fatigue or failure by working more steam than was necessary. This was called "rapping" the engine and the engineer given to this practice was called a "rapper."

Subsequently I have spent a little over fifty years in engine service. I have fired and operated many types of engines and received many and various thrills in the process. But there is one event that I would give anything and everything to live over. I would like to sit on that cab floor again and feel the old 518 tremble under me as Jim Love noisily let the Johnson bar slam down into the front corner, to feel that engine take steam as he gently cracked the throttle. I well remember the first time I rode on his engine. It was an exhilarating, nerve tingling, and delightful experience. Oh, the spine tingling thrill as that old diamond stack slowly swooshed clouds of black smoke skyward. Ah, to see again the grin that lighted the face of Jim Love as he noted the effects of the engine's movement on the faces of two small boys across the cab. Entrancing moments! Two small boys transferred into a state of ecstasy as the 518 rumbled slowly over the frogs and switches. (Frogs were forged or fabricated steel assemblies used in switches or turnouts. They permitted one rail to cross another in the same plane.) The feeling that crept into my small body was indescribable. At last I was experiencing the dream of my young life. I was riding in the cab of a smoking monster of the rails. It was truly out of this world!

We raced up through the cedars and rearranged the train at Silver City. Then up and around the mountain to where the work was to be done. The flat car containing the equipment was cut off and tied down. At that point Pat and I had to climb reluctantly down and out of that magic locomotive cab.

As the 518 vanished around a curve and down the grade, I knew positively what I would be when I grew up. I would be an engineer! A locomotive engineer like Jim Love—big, smiling, friendly, and good-natured!

I was to ride in the cab of the 518 a number of times with Jim Love, but the thrill of that first ride will linger till the end of my days. Many times I would draw crude outlines on my slate at school, or on anything else handy, of the 518, and always the figure leaning far out of the cab window would be Jim Love. If I happened to be in Eureka and homeward bound, and if the mine-run crew was going my way, I could always depend on a ride home.

I remember a time when I was on my way to Eureka to buy groceries. The mine-run crew came pounding up the grade. They had cars ahead and behind the engine, heavily loaded, and could not stop on that grade to pick up a little boy. A brakeman was riding on a load of slack coal, the last car in the train. As he saw me trudging slowly alongside the track, he motioned at me to run up to where he was. After a long run I was right behind that car. He jabbed his brake club into the slack coal, then holding onto the brake staff with one hand, he reached down with the other and lifted me onto that car with the other. His name was Jerry O'Neil.

I had an occasion to recall this incident to his mind some years later. I had been firing an engine on the Rio Grande for a short time. We had made a "help" to Soldier Summit and were returning "light" to Helper. The board was out at Kyune, and we stopped for orders. A man climbed on the engine. He had some pipe fitting tools. There was something about him that seemed familiar. After a little while I heard Gibson call him "Jerry." I knew then where I had seen him before.

I said, "Are you Jerry O'Neil?"

He looked me over for a moment, then answered, "Yes."

I pondered for a moment or two on how I could tell him who I was. Then I said, "Were you ever braking behind the 518 on the mine run at Tintic?"

He answered with a grin, "Yes, I worked that job—on the OSL. Why?"

I asked him if he remembered the family that lived in that log section house at Silver City Junction.

He answered, "Yes, very well."

I then told him that I was the oldest of those two boys who occasionally rode in the cab of the 518 between Eureka and Silver City Junction. He seemed surprised that I had grown up. I asked him if he thought he could yank me off the ground and onto a car of coal now. That seemed to refresh his mind, and we laughed long over the incident.

Jerry was then working in the water service on the Rio Grande. He was a boomer. Not surprisingly, I never saw him again.

While at Silver City Junction my mother cooked for and boarded the members of the section gang. They were all single men and were quartered in a demounted box car about a hundred feet from our house. It was customary to feed the boarders first, then the family would eat afterwards. We kids were always hungry.

When the men returned at night they would walk up to the porch and place their dinner buckets there in a row. While they were eating we kids would sneak up to the porch and go through those dinner buckets. Sometimes we were real lucky. Maybe we would find a sandwich, a piece of cake, or maybe a whole egg! Believe me there was very little of an edible nature left in those dinner buckets when they were taken into the house.

As there were always five or six men in that gang, there was a lot of groceries coming into the house. We did most of our buying at the Mammoth Mercantile. It was close, and they had delivery service. At times we would run short, and Mother would send me to Eureka to get what was needed.

One time I was sent to Eureka to get enough meat to feed the gang and the family. It was a three-mile walk from Eureka to Silver City Junction. That package of meat very soon became quite heavy for a small boy. I was loitering along, changing the package from one arm to the other, laying it down while I would throw rocks at a squirrel or some other rodent. All that caused the paper wrapping to come loose and tear and wear out. As the paper became loose I would tear it off and throw it away.

I was nearly home when I heard a rattling behind me. It was the section gang coming home on the push car. They stopped and picked me up. By that time there wasn't a shred of paper left on that package. The meat was hanging over my arm in ribbons. It was sure something for those men who were supposed to eat that meat to see. If the look that Dad gave me could have killed, I would have been dead right there.

Although Mother took pains to tell the gang that she had washed that meat thoroughly, not one bite of it went down their throats. Believe me, I sure got boxed around plenty for that little stunt. However, one good thing came of it. After that, whenever I was sent to the store for groceries of any kind, I always had a small flour sack in which to carry them.

There was an old abandoned pump house across the wye. At one time it had been used to pump water up into Mammoth. Other means of securing water had been found, and so the pump house had been locked and boarded up tight. Through a crack in the boards covering a window I could just make out here and there the glitter from parts of machinery. I was anxious to get inside for a better look.

In prowling around I found a small hole had been knocked in the masonry to permit the entrance of a pipe. I also found that by moving the pipe to one side I could just squeeze my small frame through it. Inside everything was in apple pie order. There was a two-cylinder stationary engine with a long locomotive-type boiler to supply steam to operate it. The engine in turn drove the water pumps. There was a little dust here and there, but not much. Various parts of the machinery of the stationary engine looked bright and shiny. Cans and tools were arranged in good order.

In general the pump looked as though it could be started up on a few moments notice. I swung open the door of the boiler furnace and looked into the firebox. The grates were clean. Not the sign of a clinker anywhere. There were several scoop shovels lined up against a coal bunker that protruded into the building. There also was what must have been a work bench. A vise and several other appliances were attached to it.

It looked as though whoever had left it had expectations of returning soon. There were several drums of oil and oil cans with which to oil the machinery. I think that was the first occasion on which I saw the oil can that gave the fireman his long standing nickname—"Tallow Pot." There were several of those cans.

What drew my attention was the long boiler. It had a fire door just like the one I had seen on the 518. I played with that fire door just as I had seen Jim Love's fireman do on the locomotive. I jerked it open by the chain that was attached to it. I went through the motions of shoveling coal into the firebox. If the coal bunker had been closer I believe I would have filled that firebox with coal. (I think the man who actually fired that boiler wheeled the coal from the bunker in a wheelbarrow that was standing close by.)

I don't know exactly how long I was there that first time, but I do recall I left hurriedly, because I accidentally knocked over a large drum of oil. Since it was too heavy for me to lift back to its original position, I just left it there. The lid came off, and oil slowly oozed out onto that spick and span floor. I simply got out of there as fast as I could.

I didn't go back for a long time. Then, as no one came around to see what I had done, I went back in to play around again. There was oil all over the biggest part of the otherwise clean floor. It had a peculiar smell. I was never to sense that smell again until I went to work for the railroad. It was what they called "valve oil." I have put lots of it into the old-style lubricators we had on the engines in those early days. We had another name for it on the railroad. We called it "master mechanic's blood," because it was so sparingly doled out in very small portions. I knew many engineers who, upon approaching a terminal, would drain any valve oil that was left in the lubricator into a private can of their own. I knew of engineers who had several caches of this oil scattered out in different places along the railroad right of way.

A few years ago an engineer on the Union Pacific and I were reminiscing about the Tintic area. I remarked that I had lived at Silver City Junction when I was a small boy. He knew where the place was because the UP now maintains a small community just a few steps from that original site.

He said to me, "If you lived there perhaps you can tell me something I have wanted to know for a long time. I have asked everyone that I thought might know, but no one has been able to give me an answer."

"What is that?" I asked.

He went on, "A little way off the mainline, and close by to Silver City Junction, there is an old locomotive-type steam boiler almost hidden in the cedars. I have been curious about it for years, but couldn't get any information on it."

I then told him about the old abandoned pump house that used to stand there, and of how I used to play around inside it. I told him how the kids up around Mammoth ran me out of town one winter's day when I had dragged my sled up there to sleigh ride on their hill. They chased me away, hollering, "Go on home, 'Pump House'!"

My dad's section of the railroad was all grade—not a level piece of track on it. It was uphill one way, and downhill the other. Those old hand-pumped section cars were no good in those locations. They were just too hard to pump. The gang used a push car most of the time. If they had a chance they would tie on behind the mine run or even the passenger job to hitch a ride.

They always had a long rope tied on one end of the car. They would slip the free end of this rope through the eye of the drawbar or any other place that would serve the purpose on the engine or freight car. Then they would all get on the push car, and someone would hold onto the end of the rope. When they reached their work site they would just let the rope go, and the push car would come to a stop. When they were ready to quit for the day they would coast down the grade to the section house. Our entire family would ride the push car in this manner when we went to Eureka on Sundays.

One day Dad and his gang were riding into Eureka in this way behind the passenger train. Before reaching the depot there was a short spur that led off the mainline to Adam's Lumber Yard. For a distance of about fifteen or more car lengths the track was almost level. As the engine would be working real hard on the heavy grade, as soon as it hit this level spot the speed would pick up considerably. This morning when the speed attained its highest value the old push car stubbed its toe on the frog of that spur. There was quite a commotion before they could get the car stopped. Those gandy dancers were considerably shook up in the process. Fortunately no one was hurt.

This same place near Adam's Lumber Yard was the scene of a spectacular crash to which I happened to be a witness. The mine-run crew was switching out some cars at that place when a loaded box car got away from the depot area. It was sure rolling when it hit the cars attached to the mine-run engine! I just happened to be looking down that way at the time. When I saw that car clipping down the grade, I knew what was going to happen. The mine-run crew saw it coming and stood still to take the shock. When that loaded car hit, it was just like an explosion. It seemed to bounce into the air about forty feet, then settle down in a cloud of dust. It was a most spectacular sight!

While at Silver City Junction my folks were going deeper and deeper into debt at the Mammoth Mercantile. It took a lot of grub to feed that hungry section gang. Mother set a very good table, and the sixteen dollars a month that we charged each hand for board did not quite meet the bills that were coming in each month.

Mother and Dad wanted to be where we kids could go to school. So my dad was continually heckling the roadmaster for a change of assignment. Finally his efforts brought forth results—we were to be relocated to Cedar Fort.

The roadmaster had painted a glowing picture of how wonderful it was going to be at Cedar Fort—how much better it would be for all of us. He said the town was only a mile or so away from where we were to live; that there were little ranches all along the road to town; that we could always find someone to give us a ride to and from Cedar Fort. Consequently, we had high expectations when we stepped off the train at our new location.

What we saw was a town about two and a half miles away. The road to town was just a cow trail. The nice little ranches he spoke of were just hay and grain fields scattered along the path. We were surely a disappointed family as we looked around at our new surroundings.

At the station there was a water tank, a pump house, and the section house where we were to live. This house stood very close to the track. A short board walk led from our front door to the end of the ties. Our front room also served as a waiting room for passengers expecting to catch the afternoon train for Salt Lake. There was also a tool and car shed and a long passing track.

A man named John Anderson came out from Lehi on the morning passenger train every other day to pump the tank full of water. A young boy rode a horse down from Cedar Fort with the outgoing mail pouch to put on the train and to take the incoming mail up into the town. Those were the two people we saw most often.

While at Silver City Junction we had a dog. We had raised it from a pup. When we moved we left the dog there. After we had been at Cedar Fort a short time, we developed such a longing for our dog that mother wrote a note addressed to one of the section hands at Silver City Junction, asking if he would find our dog and put it on the train and send it to us. We also made arrangements with the baggage man to bring the dog along.

That evening we wishfully watched that train come tearing along the straight piece of track toward our home. We hoped it would stop and let off our dog—no such luck! I believe that train went past us even faster than usual. There was so much dust that it almost obscured the train as it went by. We were downhearted. We weren't going to get our dog! Then, as the dust cleared away, there was our dog standing down the bank a little ways from the track with its tail between its legs. She had apparently been thrown from the train. If you can imagine a dog displaying a bewildered attitude, you have the picture of that dog.

Then we called to her: "Flory! Flory!" At first she just looked at us with that bewildered stare. Then as she recognized us, she started yelping and running toward us as fast as she could cover the ground. That dog displayed all the emotions of which any human is capable. She would jump and run around in circles. She would tear off down the tracks barking and yelping, then she would turn sharply and race back. I never saw any creature display the pleasure that dog did that day. I am sure she was just as glad to see us as we were to see her. Later that baggage man told us that while still at our former home, she would stand beside the track just looking wistfully up at the train each time it passed. So we got our dog!

Every morning that little Tintic passenger train stopped at our water tank to fill her tender. Those little diamond stacked eight-wheelers were sure a beautiful sight to see! The boiler had a shine that would dazzle your eyes.

Spick and span, they glittered from the point of the cowcatcher back to the cab. As they stood there at the water tank with their pumps churning away it was for all the world like a race horse panting for breath after a brisk run.

After the passenger train had departed to the west, it was followed shortly thereafter by the morning freight train. It too would stop for water. After they left the tank westbound the track was straight for about a mile before it circled to the left and then vanished around the foothills on its way to Fairfield.

One morning a double header, a train with two engines, stopped for water and then took off to the west. It hadn't covered more than half the distance to the curve when the head engine let go a series of short sharp blasts of the whistle, after which the train came to a stop. There seemed to be some confusion. Dad just happened to be ready to follow the freight train. Sensing something unusual, I tagged along. The train was still standing when we arrived. When we reached the head end we discovered that they had run into a herd of cows. It developed that they had killed eleven head. Those animals had been cut up pretty badly, and the stench was awfully strong.

I heard Dad remark to the engineer on the head engine that killing eleven head of cattle was quite something. The engineer's answer was, "That's nothing. I killed over seventy head of sheep the other day."

I thought to myself, "Boy, you sure are bloodthirsty!"

(I recently visited an old friend, Barnsey Cook, at Cedar Fort. We drove down to where our house once stood—the "station" as the townspeople used to call it. I looked up along the old grade, now devoid of tracks, and remarked about the time, now sixty years past, when that catastrophe took place. Barnsey remembered it with some bitterness. He has been a cattleman all his life. I was about to tell him of a time when I had killed fourteen head, but I thought better of it. A cattleman can't understand why an engineer kills his stock. He can't recognize the fact that a rolling train cannot stop on a dime.)

One morning while the freight train was standing at the water tank, Father stepped out on the short platform that led away from our front door to the tracks. He looked up toward the top of the train. A man's foot was hanging over the top of a box car. The conductor came walking along the side of the train about that time.

Dad pointed to the foot hanging over the top of the box car and said, "That's a funny way for a hobo to be riding."

The conductor climbed up the ladder to find it was the head brakeman. His head had been smashed, and he was dead.

There was much speculation among the tight little group of men that formed at the foot of the box car ladder. The verdict was that he had been standing up on top of that car when the train had gone under the bridge that spans the Rio Grande tracks between Mesa and Lehi. Not knowing that the train was approaching a low clearance obstacle he had been taken unawares and received the fatal blow to the head from the bridge structure. His foot was caught in the grab iron on top of the car and had held him on the car until the train arrived at Cedar Fort. Maybe the poor fellow had not died instantly and had purposely wedged his foot in that position to hold him on the train.

The conductor asked Dad to ride on top of that car to Fairfield to see that the body did not fall off. There was a company doctor at Fairfield who could attest to the cause of death and do all else necessary to properly report the matter. In those days a conductor had the authority to call upon the section boss for assistance when necessary. Dad did this without any qualms. I guess his army life in India and the fighting at the Khyber Pass had conditioned him for this.

We were at Cedar Fort a little over a year. Dad must have had a little of the boomer blood in his veins, because he wasn't satisfied at Cedar Fort. He kept asking for a change, so the roadmaster finally moved him back to Salt Lake as a section hand. He also worked later for the Rio Grande as a section hand at Salt Lake. A section man in those days got a dollar and a quarter or a dollar and a half for a ten hour work day. A section boss got a flat sixty dollars a month. He was not paid for overtime. That sixty dollars was his salary. If he was unlucky enough to get his hand car smashed by a train, he got nothing for one full month.

Many years ago a similar policy applied to men in engine service. But that was before my time. I would hate to think that I would have had to pay for everything that I had broken or damaged.

I have heard the story of an engineer who bent a main rod on his engine—probably too much water in the cylinders. The company took the price of it out of his pay, then straightened the main rod and put it back in service. The engineer cut his initials in the main rod together with other data pertinent to the incident. After the company had used it for some time, he brought suit against them for using his property. He won a considerable amount of money in settlement, or so the story goes. That lawsuit was credited with having stopped the practice of having railroad employees pay for damaged equipment.

Along about 1914 or 1915 the labor organizations were trying to get a car limit bill through the state legislature. One of the men, an engineer who was lobbying for this bill, told me this story: A train in charge of a conductor named Connely dropped a journal bearing on the axle of a car. A "hot box" is caused when an axle journal bearing is run too long without lubrication. In such a case the journal overheats and breaks off from the remainder of the wheel and axle assembly. The company fired Connely for lack of attention to duty. The lobbyists in a meeting with a group of state senators told them of this incident. A question was asked of the senators; "Do you think the company was justified in firing this man?" One of the legislators answered: "No, I don't think so, not if Connely was willing to pay for the damage." This shows the primitive state of labor relations on the railroads in those days. We have come a long way since, perhaps a way too far.

We returned to Salt Lake and lived in a little three-room adobe affair arranged in a row with other similar houses at South Temple and Fourth West. That area is now all Union Pacific railroad yards. At that time it was a poor residential district. A narrow gauge railroad owned by the Oregon Short Line went by our door. There was a depot at First South and Fourth West. There was also quite a little business community on those four corners.

A narrow gauge passenger train left that depot every morning, returning later in the evening. A freight train also ran each way during the daylight hours. The other end of this little railroad was at Stockton, to the southwest of the Great Salt Lake and about forty-five or fifty miles away.

Their engines were identical with the Oregon Short Line's motive power, only smaller. Their yard extended along Fourth West between First South and South Temple. They also had a lot of storage tracks just south of First South. There was an engine house that would hold about six engines. At one time this railroad had quite a large volume of passenger traffic. They operated a resort comparable to Saltair at Garfield. At the time I write about, the resort had been closed, and all the excursion passenger cars were stored on the storage tracks. There were four or five little narrow gauge engines stored in the engine house.

When the freight train returned at night they did a lot of switching along Fourth West. Pat and I, if we could get out, would jump on the pilot of the backing engine and ride it until it stopped. Then we would get off and walk up to where they started to back up again. We had a lot of fun doing this until one night Dad caught up with us. We were gleefully riding on the pilot of a backing engine when he appeared out of nowhere and jerked us off the footboard. We started running for home. He was right behind us, kicking us ahead of him at every step.

We didn't get a chance to hook a ride again. We were confined to the house whenever the switching operations were in progress.

2

From Newsboy to Roundhouse: Starting to Work

It was during this time that I started selling newspapers. I had heard kids say that they could get two papers for five cents and sell them for a nickel apiece. I couldn't believe this. Why would anyone give five cents for something that cost only half as much? The whole idea of profit didn't make sense to me. When I got a nickel one afternoon I found my way up to the distributing office of the *Deseret Evening News*, right about where the Hotel Utah now stands. I bought two papers with my nickel. I was so surprised that I ran all the way home to show Mother. She asked me what I was going to do with them. That was something I hadn't thought about at all. She thought I should sell them. That seemed to be a pretty good idea. She suggested that a good way to sell them would be to go back up town with them. After thinking it over for a while I agreed.

What a feeling came over me when I realized that I had doubled my money! I now had two nickels where before I had only one. Instead of getting more papers to sell, I again ran home to show Mother what I had done. But I gradually learned that the more papers I sold the more money I made.

There was no newsboys' union when I first began selling papers, and the newsboys weren't out on strike. Yet it was then that I first heard that I was a scab. I didn't know what that epithet meant, but I was soon to understand that in this situation it applied to a beginner—someone who was an outsider cutting in on the trade. So for a few months I was a scab. Gradually that term wore off, and I was accepted as a regular.

If you had a favorable place to sell your papers it was because you fought for it and were thereby able to hold it. If you couldn't lick the guy who wanted your corner, you just moved off and hunted another place. I had very little trouble holding the northwest corner of First South and Main in the evenings, and the southeast corner in the mornings.

As a rule I made very little money in the evenings—maybe twenty or twenty-five cents—unless something of singular interest developed. But in the mornings I very often made as much or sometimes even more than did my dad. There was a reason for this: I would be roused out of bed at 4:30 or 5:00 every morning. Mother would fix me a hot breakfast and send me on my way. In the winter she would bundle me up so that I would not feel the cold.

I would get up town before the streetcars started to run. Both the *Tribune* and the *Herald* had a few bundles of papers to be placed on the first car leaving for Murray. I was the boy who carried the papers from the pressroom and placed them on the streetcars. For this little chore I received most of my papers gratis.

The man in charge at the *Tribune* was not as liberal with me as the one at the *Herald*. He always gave me four papers for my work, while the guy at the *Herald* just reached over and grabbed a handful, maybe fifteen or twenty, and passed them through to me. So on my first round everything I sold was clear profit.

Another reason for the favorable earnings in the mornings was that there were very few newsboys on the street that early in the morning. The market was divided between fewer sellers. I would meet the streetcars as they came out of the car barns and sell most of my papers to the streetcar men. If I had any left after the cars were all out, I would finish up at the corner of First South and Main. Then I would hike home and go to school.

We also made a nickel or two now and then by swiping beer bottles from the freight platform of the OSL Railroad and selling them, three for a nickel, at the back door of the Hurry Back Saloon. The same price was paid for empty whiskey flasks. So you see there were many ways for an active kid to get an occasional nickel or dime.

During the summer months we would find ourselves headed for the Jordan River. It was there in that sluggish stream that I first learned to swim. But in the process of learning I was almost drowned.

A gang of us smaller kids were splashing around near the edge one day. A much bigger boy came along the bank with a ball bat. He threw it out into the middle of the river and said, "Anyone who gets it can have it."

I don't believe any of us could swim, but we all started after that ball bat. I was walking along in the river. The water was up to my armpits. All at once I stepped into a hole, a "chuck off," as we called them, for which the Jordan River was famous. The water came up over my head. I kicked and splashed around frantically and vigorously. I think I swallowed a good portion of the Jordan River. I got a glimpse of the big kid on the bank. He seemed to be getting rid of his clothes in a hurry.

They say that a drowning person sees his past life come up before him. From experience I know that to be a fact. I sure thought I was a goner. I again saw the features of a drowned boy that I had looked upon with awe at Sandy. I didn't give up. I kept going under and kicking my way up again. Finally, with great relief, I felt ground under my feet again, and the boy who had thrown the bat was almost to me. I was glad to take hold of his hand and walk out. I don't know if anyone got the bat, and at the time I didn't much care.

I then made a silent vow that I would stay away from the Jordan River. But you know how kids are. In a few days I was back again. If my folks had known what had happened you can bet that I would not have been there, then or ever.

I had another terrifying experience in that same vicinity. My brother Pat also shared in this one. We were playing with our friends on the bridge that carried the narrow gauge rails over the river. Some of the kids, those who could swim, were diving off the bridge. The rest of us were merely bluffing. All at once a whistle sounded, and the narrow gauge passenger train came puffing up only a short distance away. I was in the middle of the bridge. Pat was closer to the end. There was a great clamoring among those kids when that little engine let go with a series of short, terrifying blasts of the whistle.

Those who could swim hesitated no longer and immediately dove into the river to swim ashore. I remember looking to where I had last seen Pat. He was walking deliberately and calmly toward the end of the bridge; it looked like he could make it in time. I knew that I and several other kids caught in mid-span could never make it to either end.

In playing around the bridge we had often slipped down beneath the ties to climb among the under-timbers. This is what we did now. I heard that engine hit the end of the bridge as I cowered under the ties. There was no other place to go. Above would be death under the wheels of that engine, and below death from drowning in the river.

Although it wasn't evident to my young mind at the time, we were quite safe where we were if we didn't fall into the river. I believe that engineer had his train well under control as he went over that bridge, for it seemed to me a long time that the engine and cars rumbled overhead. At last the ordeal was over, and we poked our heads above the ties to see the rear of that train gathering speed as it vanished into the distance.

Now that the danger was over, it was time for much hysterical laughter again. But believe me, I lived it over again several times during the night. I could still see the front end of that little engine bearing down upon us for a long time to come.

We later organized a newsboys' union in Salt Lake City. I held office in this union under the impressive title of sergeant at arms. I don't know who thought that up, but my duties were to keep order at the meetings.

There were newsboys at those meetings whom we never had seen on the streets with a bundle of papers in their hands. Our meetings, if I remember rightly, were held one night a week in the Federation of Labor Hall on West Temple and Second South.

The president we elected was a boy named Tom Claypool. I think he was elected because he had more gab and was the biggest bully in the union. (Not an uncommon event in anybody's union.) If he was a newsboy it must have been before my time, because I don't ever remember him as a newsboy.

He was very crude and had none of the finesse of one you would expect in that office. I remember one meeting when we had a couple of visiting delegates from one of the building trade unions in attendance to give us talks on unionism. After their delegates had made their speeches and settled back in their chairs, this president of ours suddenly jumped to his feet and exclaimed:

"How many of you G—— d—— kids want me for president?"

I can still see the slightly amused looks on the faces of our visitors as most of the kids screamed out their approval. Some few had nerve enough to object. There was bedlam for a few minutes, but in the final event Tom Claypool was sustained as president.

The *Deseret News* was for a long time the only evening newspaper. Eventually another afternoon paper made its appearance. It was called the *Salt Lake Telegram*. The *Telegram* was a more popular paper for a while than the *Deseret News*. It played up the news in a more vivid, sensational, and scary manner than did the others. But I think it over-spiced the content of the paper, for it soon got the reputation of being unreliable in its presentation of the news.

The *Deseret News* sold for five cents a copy. The *Telegram* sold for three cents a copy. That is, it was supposed to sell for that price. The only trouble was that we newskids always seemed to be out of pennies when it came to making change. Unless a customer presented three pennies in exact change he would usually wind up paying a nickel or going without his paper. It eventually got to the point where we refused to sell the paper for less than a nickel.

The management of the paper soon got wise and started to clamp down on us. They refused to let us have papers unless we could show that we had a handful of pennies with which to make change. I think this rule was what caused us to organize the union. We boycotted the *Telegram*. If any kid showed up on the street with those papers, he had them taken away and torn to pieces by the goon squad. After a few days of this the *Telegram* changed its advertised price to five cents a copy.

Our union did not survive for very long after our victory over the *Telegram*. I think when the novelty started to fade, so did the interest. Before it did, our union arranged for two kids to lead a big yellow dog between two lines of marchers during a Labor Day parade. This dog was carrying a placard on each side which read, "A yellow dog is better than a scab." I don't think we kids knew the full meaning of that term. However, it went over big with the other labor organizations. The morning papers featured it as one of the highlights of the parade.

One morning while riding to get my papers—it must have been about 4:30 or 5:00 in the morning, because it was still dark—the sky seemed to explode into a bright light. Up ahead flames were pouring out of the upper windows of the buildings of the Atlas Block. These buildings were just east of where the Capitol Theater now stands on Second South between Main Street and West Temple. Before I could get to it I could hear the fire bells clanging, and the fire apparatus soon came into view.

I still think that one of the greatest spectacles that anyone could witness would be those three very large and fine-looking horses galloping up those old dirt roads as fast as they could go with that black smoke belching from the stack of the fire engine behind them.

When I was about fourteen, I thought I was getting too big to be a newsboy. One morning as I was walking down Second South after selling all my papers a very nice guy stopped me. He asked me if I would like a job. I told him I would. That same day I started working for the Salt Lake News and Book Store, located at 72 West Second South. My pay was four dollars a week. My job was to work around the store and deliver out-of-town newspapers to regular customers. We sold office supplies, books, stationary, and other such lines.

At first I tried to hold onto my newspaper job as well, but after a few months I gave up as a newsboy. It was too much. My pay of four dollars a week was much less than I could make as a newsboy, but I thought the job was more respectable, so I kept the position at the bookstore.

I worked at that job for a full year. Then one day I landed a job as a janitor and part-time pin setter in a bowling alley at 222 South West Temple. The pay was one dollar a day. That was more like it! But it had one drawback: the job lasted just four days. It was well into the summer and business was not too good. The St. Louis World's Fair was then in progress; the two owners of this place decided to close up for the summer and go back and see the fair. So I was out of a job at the age of fifteen.

My dad was working at the cement works on Fifth West and Eighth South at the time. He talked to the superintendent, and I was hired on as a roustabout. I worked at odd jobs around the mill for ten cents an hour, twelve hours a shift. I tapped clinkers into the conveyor from a storage tank to be sent to the grinding mills. I cleaned up with a wheelbarrow, and I helped the blacksmith, swinging a light sledge hammer. If the work demanded the use of a heavier hammer, a man from the mill took my place. After about six months of this kind of work, I was assigned to the laboratory.

My job then was to gather samples and test them: samples of clinkers as they came from the kilns, samples of crushed and refined rock, and samples of finished cement. My pay was raised to sixty-two dollars on the basis of a thirty-one-day month. I worked thirteen hours a day, usually every day of the week. I did this for about a year on the night shift exclusively. The hours were from six at night to seven in the morning.

The Rio Grande Western passenger depot at that time was at Second South close to Sixth West. All trains passed my west windows. They whistled for that Ninth South Pedro crossing, where the tracks of the San Pedro, Los Angeles, and Salt Lake Railroad crossed those of the Rio Grande, and I got so I could usually tell the engine number before it came in sight by the sound of the whistle—especially if it were one of the little Rome ten-wheelers.

There was an engineer on the Manti passenger "plug run" who had a peculiar way of whistling for the crossing. When I first heard it, I thought he must be blowing that way over the entire length of his run over the road. I afterward learned that he only whistled in that way when approaching town. I also learned that the object of that mode of whistling was to let his wife know he was returning safely. Some of the wags said it was no such thing! It was only to give his wife a chance to get the other guy out of the house. It would be hard to describe that whistle, but I will try: ————— ——, —————————. ———— —, ———— —. The long marks denote long sounds, the shorter ones short blasts.

There were several engineers at different points who had a mode of whistling all their own to notify their wives of their arrival when coming into town. An abuse of this practice at times led to misunderstandings and hard feelings. Some smart alec engineer, thinking he was doing something funny, would imitate a fellow engineer's special whistling style when he knew his friend was still up the hill. The dutiful wife would prepare the dinner only to have her engineer husband fail to show up.

(This also happened on our railroad. Ratliff had the habit of whistling for his dinner when coming down out of the tunnel at Martin. Some wag imitated his whistle. His wife, thinking it was her husband doing the whistling, got dinner ready. Then Ratliff didn't show up for several hours. It seemed Ratliff didn't like his dinner cold and would become quite angry.)

But no matter how they whistled, I always got a thrill out of watching those little Rome ten-wheelers. There were almost always two of them double heading on the through passenger trains.

They would come dashing up to the Pedro crossing where they had to stop. They would shut off about the time they went over the Eighth South crossing. The firemen would have their fireboxes loaded, so when the engines were shut off each fireman would open his firebox door in the hope his engine wouldn't "pop" (safety valves lift). Each fireman would be down on the deck with the door chain in his hand. As soon as the stop was made the head engine would whistle off and the engine stacks would start blasting.

The firemen would then get busy "flashing the door." This was the practice of alternately opening and closing the fire door between each scoop of coal thrown on the grates. The flash from the inferno of the furnace or firebox would light up the back part of the engine and, at night, the entire sky. It was quite a sight!

Those trains going by my window at the cement works were a stimulus to my thoughts of railroading. I was about eighteen when I decided to do something about it.

I was on night shift at the time. I would wake up in the early afternoon and sometimes wander uptown. One afternoon my wanderings took me out to the Oregon Short Line yards and roundhouse. I wanted a job as fireman or any other job that would lead to it. I approached the roundhouse half fearful to seek out the foreman. When I finally found him there were two other guys with him. When he asked what I wanted I was tongue-tied. For a while I couldn't say a word. Finally I blurted out that I wanted to be a fireman.

He answered, "I've got plenty of firemen." I think I detected a note of amusement in his answer. Also something seemed to amuse those other two guys that were with him. After all, I was only eighteen and looked about sixteen. I turned away with a heavy heart.

I broached the subject of getting a job on the Rio Grande Western to my dad. He was night watchman in the Rio Grande yards. He said he would see what he could do. Of course I would have to work in the roundhouse for a while. A few days later Dad told me he had spoken to the night roundhouse foreman. He had agreed to hire me as hostler helper. ("Hostlers" were in charge of servicing and moving engines in the yard and roundhouse.) I was delighted. At last I was on my way to being a fireman. The goal was in sight.

I went around to see the night foreman. He looked me over and I think he regretted his promise. However, he had the clerk make out a note of acceptance. This piece of paper I was to present to the general foreman for his approval in the morning. With high hopes I found that official the next day. It would only be a short time now until I would be a fireman— peaked cap over one eye, red bandanna loosely knotted around my neck, high gauntleted gloves on my hands and a gold watch in my bib pocket. Oh, boy!

I handed the note to the general foreman. He read it and looked me over critically. He slowly shook his head in disapproval.

"How old are you, boy?" he inquired.

I was fearful of this. I answered softly: "Going on for twenty-one."

He smiled and again shook his head slowly. He placed a hand on my shoulder. "Young man, you come back in a couple of years," he said.

He turned away, slowly tearing that note that I had prized so highly into little pieces, little pieces that slowly fluttered in the breeze and out of my life.

I had told my girlfriend just yesterday that I was going to be a fireman soon. She had looked a little sad. I had detected a tear in her eye. Was she crying? What for?

"I would rather see you go to the mines," she faltered. "You'll get killed on the trains."

Well, I still had my job at the cement works. I could tell her now that the firing job was off for awhile. Yes, I still had a job. But as it turned out it was not for long.

In the spring of 1908 the demand for cement took a flop. There had been a depression in the country during the latter part of 1907. The storage bins at the cement works were overflowing, with few buyers in sight. The decision was to close down the plant for awhile. On the last day of the operation a big farewell party was held in the machine shop. The company furnished the refreshment, which included two kegs of beer. The officials told of their hopes that business would shortly pick up, and that soon we would all be back on the job again. We all toasted that. Others got to their feet and told what a swell bunch of guys we were, and of the good fellowship that prevailed. We toasted that also. Then a Scotsman got to his feet and sang "Annie Laurie." We all joined in and then disbanded.

My days at the cement works were over.

That night I walked uptown. I met a man I had formerly known as an electrician at the cement works. I told him I was out of a job. At that time he was chief electrician at the Boston Consolidation Mill at Garfield. He told me that if I would meet the train that left Salt Lake shortly for Garfield he would take me out there and give me a job helping electricians. I rushed home, got some blankets rolled up, and met the train. He was there.

This was a workers' train. It left Salt Lake in time for the men to make the midnight shift. Trains left the OSL depot on regular schedules so that those who worked at Garfield and wanted to live in Salt Lake could do so by riding the workers' trains to and from work.

I was put to work on the switch board at the mill. My job was to record the readings on the different gauges. I was called several times during a shift by telephone and asked to hold a switch in place while some kind of a test was made somewhere out in the mill complex.

After several weeks on the job I was promoted to electrician's helper on the day shift. We bunked in company houses. Four bunks to a tent. We ate at the company boarding house for a dollar a day—three meals. I must say that they fed very well at this boarding house. Good grub and plenty of it. But there are always some who are hard to please. I heard several complaints flung at the attendants that I thought were way out of line. My own opinion was that those meals approached banquet quality, in a rough sort of way.

I worked eight hours on the day shift and rambled over the hills when off duty. In my rambles I discovered a reservoir up in back of the mill. This was great! After getting up a sweat climbing the mountain I would strip off and plunge in the reservoir for a swim. It wasn't too long until others found out what I was doing, and from then on that reservoir was well patronized.

I liked it very well at Garfield, and I liked the work. However, I hadn't given up the idea of becoming a fireman. I was just biding my time until I could land a job on the railroad. That time came sooner than I had expected.

One night there was a big electrical storm. A motor was burned out or shorted. We, the daylight crew, were called out to remove the motor and replace it with a spare. We had removed the damaged motor and had the good one up in the air over the place where it belonged. I was guiding it into position as it was being slowly lowered. I happened to have one finger under the base when it finally settled into place. That motor came down on my finger. I screamed in pain. It seemed like hours that I was in agony before they finally raised the motor sufficiently for me to get my finger out from under it.

There was a man who was acting as foreman to whom I was beginning to take a dislike. He had hired on there after I did. I was assigned to be his helper. He didn't have a dime when he arrived. I fed him on my "pie book" several times. A "pie book" is a small pocket-sized book of coupons for prepaid meals at railroad eating houses or beaneries. When he had worked long enough to get a pie book of his own I thought he would pay me back. But he made no offer to do so.

When they finally released my finger I was in a frenzy with pain. I didn't know exactly what I was doing. I saw the face of this guy before me and I struck out with all I had behind me. I guess I socked him with a pretty hard jolt. I wouldn't have done it if I hadn't been crazy with pain.

Well, that ended my apprenticeship as an electrician. The big boss heard about it and I was on my way home in the morning. I got home and was out of a job again. Dad told me to take it easy for a while.

After three days of loafing I was hired as supply man in the Rio Grande Western roundhouse at Salt Lake. My duties were to supply outgoing engines with tools and oil. The guy that had this job before me was promoted to fire lighter. He was glad to get off the supply job, and I soon found out why.

During the depression of 1907 the Rio Grande had "white-leaded" (laid up) the engines that were not needed because of reduced traffic. They had been stripped of all tools and supplies and had been relegated to the "white-lead line," also called the "dead line."

Now business was getting better, and almost every day engines were being taken off the dead line and placed in service. All their original tools

Gilbert Gould, his daughter, Pauline, and his father, Richard John Gould. Photo from the W. J. G. Gould collection.

and other supplies had been long since used to supply engines in active service. The storehouse had not anticipated this condition and therefore had not prepared for it. The result was that I had to rob engines coming in off the road to supply those going out. I had even gone down to the dump and rescued tomato cans, or anything else that would hold oil, to supply outgoing engines.

This did not make a hit with the engine crews, and I was necessarily the scapegoat. They wouldn't believe me when I protested that there were no supplies to be had. When they complained to the roundhouse foreman, that courageous individual merely sent them back to me. He was just passing the buck. He knew as well as I did that there was nothing I could do but rob incoming engines to supply those called for the road. I did the best I could even though I made a lot of enemies among the engine crews, who would later try to take it out of my hide.

One day a newly promoted engineer came to the supply house where I was supposed to keep all the surplus (that did not exist). He had been promoted off the Bingham Branch and was going back to run an engine out of Welby. He had a brand new tool box with his name painted on it. He came in the door and laid that newly painted tool box on the floor. It was completely empty. He wiped his hand on a piece of waste and extended it toward me.

"Mr. Gould?" he inquired. I acknowledged the identity with some apprehension. He told me his name, and we politely and solemnly shook hands. Then he told me what he wanted. He was going back to the Bingham Branch to work, but while he was here in Salt Lake he thought he would get a full set of tools.

He had made out a complete list of what he needed. Mr. Roberts, that fearless, white-bearded roundhouse foreman, had signed it in approval and sent him to me. He laid that authoritative document on the counter and started to read what the list specified.

One ball-peen hammer and cold chisel.

One twelve-inch stilson wrench.

One twelve-inch monkey wrench.

I was inclined to interrupt and break the bad news, but I didn't have the heart. He seemed so confidently sure of getting what he wanted. The list went on:

One fifteen-inch monkey wrench.

One eighteen-inch monkey wrench.

I wondered what old man Roberts had been thinking when he signed that list in approval and sent him to me. Still the list went on:

One dope cup wrench.

One engineman's torch.

And so on and on he went until he had named a dozen tools that I hadn't seen since I had been on the job. When he got through he looked at me, expecting that I would start handing out those items.

I just looked at him helplessly. "Did Mr. Roberts tell you that you could get those tools here?" I asked.

He didn't know how to answer for a moment. "Why, yes. He told me that you would fix me up. Here, he signed this request."

"Do you see any of those items hanging around here?" I asked.

"Well, where are they?" he inquired in a puzzled manner. "Isn't this the supply house?"

I assured him that it was the supply house all right, but there were no supplies. For a while he couldn't believe that I was serious. After a short time he picked up his newly-painted tool box and reluctantly left the supply house.

I felt bad about this incident, but there was nothing I could do. I would have liked to have had all those tools that he so confidently expected. With that inventory I could have supplied several outgoing engines.

That was what I was up against on my first job as a supply man. But there was one time when I got partial revenge.

I happened to be up at the general storehouse one afternoon, looking for something. I can't remember just what it was at this moment. There were two men employed there, and it seemed to me that each one tried to outdo the other in downright orneriness. One was called "Coal Oil Johnny." He accompanied the pay car on its rounds with the supply car and doled out oil and tools to the section gangs every month. That's how the name Coal Oil Johnny came to be applied. They both acted as though they personally owned everything in the storehouse.

While I was at the storehouse that day Coal Oil Johnny left the sliding door to one of the cabinets open. I looked inside. I couldn't believe my eyes. There were brand new stacks of tools of every description: hammers, torches, monkey wrenches, and many other items of short supply that I had been crying for. I started to reach inside when Johnny approached and kicked the door shut.

I asked him about all those tools, and why had he kept saying there weren't any in stock?

He said, "You didn't see any tools in there. You just think you did."

I beat it back to the roundhouse and told Old Man Roberts what I had seen. He got on the phone and called up Mr. Brown, the general storekeeper, and told him what I had related to him. The general storekeeper had an office upstairs over the storehouse. He told the foreman to send that smart alec kid up to his office. When I arrived he was all worked up into a frenzy.

He yelled at me, "Did you say there were new tools locked away downstairs?"

I told him that I did. He glared at me for a moment.

He said, "We are going down there and see. If you are lying, you and I will tangle." By that time we were out of his office and on the stairs. In a sassy voice I told him that it would be alright with me.

On entering the storeroom he ignored Coal Oil Johnny and said to me, "Alright, now where are they?"

I pointed to the cabinet, a padlock on the door. He said to Coal Oil Johnny, "Open that door."

Johnny's face was a sickly white as he fumbled for the keys. He finally opened the door. There in neat stacks just as I had described were the tools.

Mr Brown turned on Johnny. I don't believe I ever heard a man take such a bawl out as Johnny did without fighting back. Brown wanted to know how long that had been going on. Here the mechanical department had been hollering for tools, and all the time you said we were out of them.

He turned to me. "You make out the necessary requests, and take everything out of the cabinet." I got a wheelbarrow and did just that, and for a while there were new tools in circulation. I thought that Brown was going to fire Johnny, but he didn't. And that guy just got more ornery than ever.

When I wasn't too busy on my job I would be trying to help the fire lighters. They were at that time Johnny McKenna and a little guy named Reese Phillips. Reese was well under five feet tall, but he was quite a man for a little fellow. Sometimes when he was really busy he would step out to the supply house and ask, "Would you like to exercise your muscles?"

I would usually answer yes. He would then tell me what engine to fire up.

The method that prevailed then in building fires in a cold engine was thus: About a ton of coal would be spread over the grates. Then a lot of wood cut up from the tie pile would be laid on top of the coal. A lot of greasy waste would be thrown in on top of the wood. The waste was then lighted. Pretty soon the whole mess would be on fire. If there was any steam in the boiler, the "blower" would be in operation. If not, a live steam line in the round house would be tapped to operate the blower.

The "blower" is a pipe leading from the fountain (a manifolded steam source) on top of the boiler and inside the cab to the smoke box. It ends in a upright nozzle directed at the stack. When steam is turned into this pipe it creates a draft up through the stack. This draft works on the fire to build it up and raise steam pressure. I was always willing to help the fire lighters if I wasn't busy on my own job.

One day I learned that Reese was spreading unfavorable reports about me. A guy told me that Reese had made this remark to a gang in the roundhouse: "You know that kid out in the supply house? Well, he's a real sissy. He says 'gosh dang' instead of 'G—— d——.'"

When I heard this I just laughed. I took it as a compliment, but I noted from subsequent incidents that some of the guys really thought I was a sissy. Then something happened that permanently changed that opinion in a hurry.

It was a morning in the middle of November, and there had been a heavy fall of snow during the night. Early in the day, while I was coming out of the main oil house after filling my supply cans, a machinist came out of the roundhouse. He picked up a handful of snow and playfully threw a snowball at me. I set down my oil cans, and we engaged in a friendly little snowball fight.

We were having a lot of fun, when a switch engine came down the "back lead" with a string of coaches. A switchman was leaning on the handrails of one of the coaches laughing at us. He was a big, burly young fellow. I was making a snowball in my hands when he came on the scene. Instead of throwing it at the machinist with whom I had been snowballing, I playfully threw it at the switchman.

If I had really been trying to hit him I am sure I could never have done it. I just wasn't that good in pitching a ball. But the snowball that I threw in fun went straight to the mark. It hit him right square in the forehead!

He quit laughing and jumped off the steps and started running at me. At first I didn't know what to do. This switchman was a big fellow and here he came straight at me like a charging bull. I thought first of running away into the roundhouse, but on second thought something seemed to say to me: "You're getting too big now to run." So I stayed. I got set and waited. Here he came in a blind rage. As soon as I judged he was close enough I let go with a straight right with everything I had in my 135-pound frame!

The result took me as much by surprise as it did everyone else. I landed right on his left eye. The force of him running at me like that when I was in a set position, and with the timing perfect, all combined to do an effective job of stopping him in his tracks. The big 200-pounder's feet went up in the air, and the back of his head hit the ground. He looked at me from that prone position on the ground for a second or two. There seemed to be a hurt and a surprised look in his eyes.

Meanwhile, I had resumed a fighting stance and was dancing around waiting for him to get up. When he did get to his feet, all the fight was gone from him. He hurried back and climbed on the still slowly moving coaches. I must confess that I was somewhat relieved at the outcome. That guy could have broken me in half if he had gotten hold of me.

I looked around to find that I was not alone. The machinist with whom I had been having the friendly snowball fight was standing still like he was glued to the spot. He hadn't moved. All the windows in the roundhouse were full of heads of the surprised roundhouse staff.

From then on no one thought that I was a sissy.

During my days on that supply job I made several enemies among the enginemen. I was to encounter that enmity later in my career. These included Old Head Conners, Pokey Cowan, Pie Book Anderson, Jack Hardesty, and several others. The trouble was the lack of supplies on hand to fully furnish the needs of each engine called for service. Many engine crews left town with less than a full supply because I just didn't have the required items.

I also made several enemies in the roundhouse. If a machinist left a hammer, a chisel, or monkey wrench lying around without keeping a good watch on it, that tool would very likely find itself leaving town on some outgoing engine. Of course I hotly denied any accusation that I had anything to do with the disappearance of these tools, but somehow I couldn't make those guys believe me. It just goes to show how suspicious some people can be. I didn't realize it at the time, but those whom I had offended could make it quite rough for me when at last I would be going out on the road firing. I was to learn this later.

$\mathcal{F}ireman\ J$

The coal mines of Carbon county had enjoyed a good coal business during the winter. But now with the spring pushing its way into the calendar, coal orders were falling off. The dusty, crashing, loading tipples were slowing down. Mines which had worked five and six days a week were being reduced to a two or three day a week schedule. Miners were being laid off in increasing numbers. Every coal train that slugged its way up the winding canyon picked up these ex-miners. Some had saved their winter earnings and were going home. Others were just reaching out for greener pastures. Over the hill and far away. Most of them would be back in the late summer to again enter the black holes in the mountainside, to bring out the blacker coal.

This old guy that sat in front of me on the little drop seat that hugged the side of the cab was one of them. We had picked him up at Castle Gate. In those days we could always use a third man on the engine to shovel the coal in the tender up to the front where the fireman could reach it handily. This way he paid for his passage over the road. That would be this old fellow's job.

All the way from Castle Gate to the Summit, he had been back in the tank pushing the coal up within my reach. Now as we drifted down the long grade, his work was finished, and he occupied the vacant seat ahead of me.

He seemed lost in retrospection as he sat there in silence. Contemplating the fringe of grayish brown hair that crept out from under the corduroy cap, I tried to visualize what his past may have been. He must have been quite up in years. What had those years meant to him?

Although I judged him to be up in his sixties, he gave me the impression that he was quite capable of taking good care of the future. His rugged, weather-beaten features, the square outline of his head, and the piercing dark eyes seemed to speak of a fearless outlook on life. His manner, I had noticed, seemed to border on the truculent side.

The night was dark and comparatively cold, yet with the smell of spring in the air. Back on the top of the winding train, two lanterns would bob into view at intervals, and were gone again. Those lights indicated the position of the two brakemen. George Westinghouse was not yet the dominant power on those heaving grades. Successful train operation still required the presence of the brakeman with his brake club at the brake wheel to help control the train. I turned to consider the broad back in front of me.

The old guy's posture seemed to indicate complete oblivion to his immediate surroundings. His bodily movements coincided directly to the roll and jerk of the engine. In the slight exchange of words that we had had, I thought I had detected an accent. That accent seemed familiar, yet at the moment it eluded me, and puzzled me also.

As the long tangent spread out in front of us, I strained my mind for an explanation. At last I again turned to the silent form in front of me. I nudged the old fellow almost apologetically with my gloved hand. He seemed slightly annoyed as he started to turn his face to me; then, as though on second thought, he again faced the front as though to ignore my gesture. I nudged him again, harder. Before he could turn away again, I asked:

"Are you English or Irish?"

He turned now to face me directly. His sullen expression of features and those piercing dark eyes seemed to scrutinize me with growing irritation. His entire attitude seemed to declare loudly that I was prying into something that was no concern of mine. I began to feel a little foolish under his sullen stare. Silently we faced each other for what seemed moments. Abruptly, he turned his back to me, at the same time he bit out one word: "Neither."

I was beginning to feel a little irritable myself now. Who was he to hold me in contempt? Who was he to snub me? If it weren't for me, he would probably be seated on top of the train out in the cold, instead of being privileged to ride in the comparatively warm cab. True, he helped in keeping the coal up within reach. But that had been a privilege too. What was biting this old guy anyhow? Didn't he know when he was well off?

I tried to figure him out. All I could make out was that he was a coal miner. My folks had all been coal miners in the old country, in Wales. Welsh coal miners they had been. Yes, Welsh coal miners. Then an enlightening thought streaked through my mind. The accent that had puzzled me told me the old guy was a Welshman.

Again I nudged him, not too gently. He turned those sternly annoyed features toward me. His whole demeanor was one of complete annoyance. He didn't scare me; I was rather amused. I smiled tolerantly; I could be tolerant now.

"I was born in Merthyr Tydfill," I remarked casually.

I watched the old guy's countenance change from one of deep annoyance to one of sudden friendliness, and I thought of how similar the experience was to one of having been out in a cold drizzling rain and then seeing the sun suddenly rip the clouds apart and blaze down to warm up the world. An incredulous smile split the old guy's features. His hand reached out to grasp mine.

"You was?" he asked. "Well, so was I."

Gone were all the signs of animosity now. We were friends. We were pals.

Although at least forty years had separated the events, we had both been born in the same town, now we met thousands of miles away, behind the boiler head of a locomotive.

The author, *left*, as a fireman, Salt Lake City, ca. 1909. Photo from the W. J. G. Gould collection.

Learning to Fire

I t seemed that every day business was getting to be a little better. Engines were being pulled off the dead line and readied for service. New names were appearing on the fireman's "extra board," where they waited to be assigned jobs in order of seniority. Every day that I thought Old Man Roberts was in good humor I would remind him of my desire to go out firing.

One day I was going through the roundhouse on my rounds of duties. I saw Mr. Roberts talking with another man whom I afterward learned was Jack Snyder, the traveling engineer. When I got close the foreman called to me. I approached wonderingly. He said, "This is the traveling engineer. Tell him what you've been telling me."

This man Snyder was not a very big man, but there was something about him that commanded respect. He had black piercing eyes that seemed to look right through you. He could ask questions with those eyes! I didn't know at first what Mr. Roberts was referring to. Then he said to Snyder, "He wants to go out firing."

Mr. Snyder was grinding a chew of tobacco in his teeth. He turned aside to spit. Then: "Is that so?" he asked.

I assured him that indeed I would like to go firing. His black eyes bored through me. "How old are you, boy?" he asked.

I unhesitatingly answered: "Twenty-one." I would win or lose right now, I thought. Those black eyes still looked inside me. I was not really close to twenty-one, and I now believe that Jack Snyder knew it.

"What do you weigh?" was the next question.

"One hundred and fifty-five," I answered. Well, I did weigh close to that with the heavy overcoat that I sometimes wore. One hundred and fifty-five was the required weight to pass the physical examination for fireman.

His black eyes never wavered. "You go in there," he said as his eyes turned toward the call room, "And tell Mickey to fix you up," he said. "Tell him I sent you."

Mickey was Mickey Fitzpatrick, his chief clerk.

I had a case of the jitters as I approached that office. This had been too easy. It just couldn't be happening, after all this waiting and longing, all those hopes and fears. It didn't seem that it could all be settled so off-handedly, with so few words. Something was sure to interfere.

I went in and told Mickey what the traveling engineer had said. Mickey and I had kidded each other about going firing several times. When I told him the news he had to have one last shot at me. He said "You—go firing! Why the exhaust will drag you into the firebox!"

Mickey made out a request for a physical examination. "You go up and see Doc Benjamin," he said, "And when you get back I will have something else for you."

"So far, so good," I thought. But now, "passing the doctor" appeared to assume the form of an ordeal. I had passed the doctor before getting the supply job. But engine service was a more important job, so the examination would surely be more exacting. Several times in my young life I had been given to understand that my eyes were not what they should be. In fact, at one time it was feared that I was going blind. All of this now preyed upon my mind as I contemplated the examination.

I really dreaded having to go before the doctor. I had heard of cases where others had substituted at physical examinations. However, I couldn't think of anyone I could get to substitute for me. I went home and changed clothes. I wondered if there was any way I could influence the doctor to my advantage. At last I hit upon a plan.

It was mid-morning. If I could enter the doctor's office when he was getting ready to leave for lunch, maybe he would pass me over lightly, if he was really hungry, and I hoped he was. But I still had to kill almost two hours before putting in an appearance if I was going to follow this plan.

By now I was passing the old sanatorium. The doctor's office was only a half-bock away. He couldn't be very hungry yet. So, I went into the sanatorium and had a good swim. I was watching the time pretty closely. When I judged it was about time I dressed and headed for the doctor's office. I had timed it just right! As I entered the office he was just getting into his overcoat. As he read the order I presented, he seemed to be just a little bit irritated. That was just how I wanted it.

He took off his overcoat and started the examination. Everything was going along lovely. In fact, he had his overcoat half on again while I was going though the eye test. He hurriedly validated my order and almost beat me out of the office. I clattered down those stairs with a much lighter heart. I couldn't wait for the elevator!

When I got back and presented the doctor's okay, Mickey made out an order for me addressed to all freight engine crews. It read something like this:

"You will allow Mr. W. G. Gould to ride your engine for the purpose of learning the art of firing a locomotive. Anything in the line of help that you can give him toward this end will be greatly appreciated. Please make note, in space provided, whether in your opinion, he will make a satisfactory fireman."

I was also given a book of rules to study.

I now went home and gathered up what I thought I would need on the student trips I would have to make. What I took with me was plenty. Anyone would have thought I was going to China. Among other things, Mother had made a large chocolate layer cake. I stowed that in a large grip along with the rest of the lunch.

I found out that there was an extra east called for somewhere around 6:00 P.M. The engineer on this train was to be a man named Johnson. Being a Swede it is not surprising that his nickname was Olie. I couldn't think of any time in the past that I had offended him so I decided that I would start my student trips with him.

His fireman was a man named Alma Ostler. This fireman gained a lot of fame later on when he was in a head-on collision at the Lehi Sugar Works. On that occasion he sustained the loss of both legs. His one leg was completely cut off in the accident. The other one was broken and mostly severed. He was pinned in the wreck by that remaining leg. He deliberately took out his pocket knife, and with the live steam leaking and surging all around he actually cut off the remainder of the pinioned leg and dragged himself into the clear.

I put my belongings away with those of the rest of the crew and handed Olie Johnson the letter authorizing me to ride his engine. He had seen many letters just like it. He merely filed it away with his time book for future notes.

I helped Alma get the engine ready, and listened lightly to his advice. There came a time when I wished that I had listened a little more attentively.

At the time it seemed to me that I was going on a joyride. I didn't take the serious interest in the duties of a fireman that I should have taken.

We left Salt Lake light—what was known in the vernacular as "caboose bounce." This meant that we had only an engine and caboose—no cars—from Salt Lake to Provo. We picked up cars at Provo, and again at Springville, to make up a train.

Between Salt Lake and Provo the fireman had allowed me to put in a fire, which meant shovel a little coal in the firebox now and then. But he kept a strict watch on me so that I would not spoil his fire. I wondered why he didn't let me do all the firing. I was to learn the reason later.

After we left Springville, on the rising grade into the mountains to the east he would only allow me to sporadically shovel in a few scoops of coal. Most of the time I was back in the tank shoveling the coal up to where he could reach it.

At Thistle we had lunch and after taking coal and water, chores which Alma let me perform, we left town. We had about forty empty cars and a large consolidation type engine on the rear. We met several westbound trains between Thistle and Tucker. At each meet one or the other of us threaded in and out of the passing track.

While on the move I could look back and see the bright flare in the sky toward the rear of the train. This I was told came about when the helper fireman opened the fire door to feed coal into the firebox—flashing the door. I kept wondering when that engine would cut off and go back. I thought a helper was just to help a train get started. But that engine was going right on with us. That seemed most strange to me at the time.

At Mill Fork we made a stop. The fireman handed me the lantern and motioned to the top of the tender. "Take water," he said. I scrambled up over the coal pile, lifted the manhole cover, pulled down and placed the spout. I pulled the rope to open the tank valve. The water was suddenly released into the spout and almost raised it out from under me. I almost ended up down in the tank compartment of the tender.

I learned something there: Always be careful when pulling on the tank rope that you don't have the spout jerked out from under you. Some of those water tanks let the water out with such force that the spout was hard to hold in place. I have been drenched with water in this way many times.

At Tucker I was again ordered to take water. It was getting to be daylight by that time. I also was instructed on how to take coal. This was a haphazard undertaking. Those aprons on the coal chute were all marked as "four tons," "six tons," "eight tons," and so on. You might think you needed about four tons to fill up the bunker in the tender. So you pulled down one marked "four tons." Maybe you would actually get four tons, but there was an even chance you could get eight tons. Then you were there for some time shoveling.

As we left Tucker I could see that we had two more engines on the rear of the train. I asked Alma why we had so many engines and why we were going so slowly. He told me that we were on a very steep grade—between four or five percent.

I remember I answered: "Oh, boy, I'll bet we can go fast when we come down."

All night I had been disappointed at the speed we were making. When I made that remark about speed coming down the hill, it made quite a hit with the crew. In amusement they told me we surely could go fast coming down, but it would not be advisable.

The sun was up over the mountain when we at last arrived at Soldier Summit. While we were cutting off the helper engines and getting air brake inspection, I got out my chocolate cake and shared it with the crew. It was very well received.

When we left Soldier Summit, the crew had only a little over an hour to work, so at Colton the order was out to set out the train and tie up for eight hours' rest. Of course that order didn't affect me. I was not drawing pay for those hours.

The engineer, Olie Johnson, signed my letter stating that in his opinion I would make a very good fireman. How he arrived at that conclusion I can't figure out. I hadn't been allowed to do any firing to amount to anything. My only contribution to the work had been taking water and coal.

How I got to Helper after the crew tied up at Colton I can not now recall, but I do remember coming out of the Beanery, all washed and evidently well fed. I do know I had a toothpick in my mouth.

There was a passenger train standing in front of the Beanery headed west. I walked up to the engine. The engineer was John Hardesty. I had not had too much trouble with him (or so I thought), so I climbed on the engine. He wanted to know what I was doing down here at Helper. I showed him my letter. I asked if I could ride with him. He was undecided at first. Finally he said, "Yes."

I can't remember much about firing that little ten-wheeler up the grade, but I do know I had her "howling"—popping her safety valve—most of the way down the grade. Every time the engineer or fireman glanced in my direction I would start to shovel in some coal. They finally had to take the shovel away from me.

When we stopped at Springville there was a freight train headed west. I thought I had had enough passenger experience for the time being so I got off. John Hardesty told me to have that freight engineer sign my letter as having rode with him right out of Helper. This was because my letter was addressed to freight crews only.

When that passenger train left town, I walked over and climbed on the freight engine. I looked up to see if I recognized the engineer. My heart sank! I surely did recognize him. It was Old Head Conners. I could not have drawn a worse choice! Old Head and I had had several run-ins while I was on the supply job. Our trouble had been over the amount of valve oil issued.

I had a printed schedule in the supply house governing the amount of oil to be placed on the various engines in different service. I had several arguments with a number of the engineers over the small amount of oil allowed. If I remember rightly an engine such as the eleven hundreds was allowed one and one-half pints of valve oil—master mechanic's blood—for one trip from Salt Lake to Helper. I lived up to that schedule and thereby made enemies doing so. Old Head was one of them.

When I climbed on his engine there at Springville he looked down at me, and I thought for a moment that he was going to throw me off. However, I hastily produced the letter and handed it to him. At first he didn't want to look at it. He kept barking at me, "What is it? What is it?"

He knew very well what it was. He had seen many of them in his time as an engineer. I was frightened, but I managed at last to make him understand it was a letter authorizing me to ride that engine. He wouldn't take the letter, but turned his back on me and proceeded to get the train in motion to follow that passenger train out of town.

The fireman sympathized with me and told me to stay on. I put in a few fires between Springville and Provo without any notice from Conners. Leaving Provo, Old Head called the regular fireman over to his side for instructions. He told him, "You put in a fire, and then let the kid put in one. Just put in every other fire." So that's the way things stood leaving Provo.

I think we were getting along too well with this arrangement to suit Old Head. After stopping and restarting at the Pedro crossing west of the Provo River, he told the regular fireman to "let the kid take her alone, now."

It was general practice for all westbound freight trains, after making the Pedro crossing stop, to make all speed possible for the run up the American Fork hill. They would go down through the Geneva sag just as fast as they could turn a wheel, with the Johnson bar hooked up as close to center as possible. It was here that those freight engines took an awful beating, and they had to be hot all the way to get that train up into American Fork without "doubling the hill," without having to make two trips to haul the train up the hill.

There I was, just a punk kid at the "rat hole," with no more concept of what I was up against than a baby. I kept bailing coal into that roaring firebox. The engine rattled along ever faster on the slight dip down through Geneva. I knew I was shoveling enough coal, but was I getting it in the right place? As the speed increased it was hard for me, a greenhorn on the rolling deck, to keep my feet and to stay right side up. However, I managed to keep on shoveling and swinging the door. If I straightened up to get a breath of air the Old Head would scream, "What are you going to do, kid, let her die?" And I would start shoveling again.

I was blinded from the glare of the firebox. The glove on my left hand was actually smoking. I straightened up to shake the glove to cool it. The Old Head screamed, "Put in some coal kid, you know that ain't valve oil, put in some coal." And I would put in more coal. At last as we approached the grade the speed slackened, and I was able to keep my feet a little better. The firebox was full of blazing embers. It got so full that when I opened the door hot coals would roll out on the deck. Still the Old Head hollered for more coal.

We topped the American Fork hill and started to zoom down past the Lehi sugar works. We picked up speed again. I thought that old eleven hundred would tear herself to pieces the way Old Head Conners was hammering her. I straightened up to get the kink out of my back. The left leg of my overalls seemed to scorch my flesh when it pressed against me. I was weary, not from the physical efforts, but from the unaccustomed heat of the open firebox door.

Old Head started to holler for more coal, but was interrupted by the angry fireman. "Ah, for C——t sake, run your damned engine, and leave the kid alone, you old so and so."

He took the scoop out of my hands and guided me over to the left seat box. I was blinded by the hot glaring firebox. I had to feel my way. The fireman slapped the blade of the shovel down on the fire ring and took a long look at the fire. He closed the door and stabbed the scoop into the coal pile. I felt him climb onto the seat behind me. He was a big man; as big as Old Head Conners. I never saw him again after that trip. He must have been a boomer.

The Old Head seemed to settle down after this rebuke. He ran that engine the way it should be run. He didn't say a word to either of us from there to Midvale.

At Midvale the "sixteen-hour law" caught up with that crew. This law was known, in the slang of our railroad, as the "pure food law." Elsewhere, and quite generally on other railroads, it drew the name of the "hog law." It was intended to mean the same all over the country, and that was that after sixteen hours on duty a train crew was required to cease work and have eight to ten hours' rest. I was to see this law violated many times.

The crew headed into the passing track and prepared to leave the engine. Soon another westbound train stopped at the water tank. The crew of the train I had been riding all climbed aboard the second train, leaving their own standing in the passing track while they proceeded on into Salt Lake. Not knowing what else to do I stayed with the tied-up train.

In a short time no. 62, an eastbound hot shot freight, rolled into town and stopped for water. A relief crew unloaded from the train and came to take over the westbound freight I was on.

The engineer on this relief crew was a man named Fisher. He was quite a sport. He played the races and considered himself to be quite the ladies' man. I know, because I fired for him quite a bit later on in my career. He signed my letter without any argument. That raised my hopes a little. I was beginning to feel a little discouraged. I had ridden with five engineers and only two had signed my letter.

After we arrived in Salt Lake I went around to the roundhouse to get the lay of the land. I intended to make more student trips, but the engine dispatcher offered to mark me up on the board if I would go over to a class for new firemen in the classroom over the freight depot. The class was just getting started. There were in the class several newly hired experienced men and some students, about six of us in all. We took the questions in rotation. I don't believe I answered more than five or six correctly. However, the examiner passed us all. They needed men badly. It was getting late in the evening when I returned to the engine dispatcher's office.

He marked me up on the extra fireman's board without any fuss. I was a fireman now! Or was I? Anyway, my name was on the board—last out.

My first call was as a "dog catcher." This meant that I would deadhead out and relieve a fireman who happened to be tied up some place on the sixteen-hour law. The place I was to deadhead on this occasion happened to be Riverton, about seventeen miles out from Salt Lake. Being all down grade into the home yards, I didn't profit much in the way of experience on this trip.

It was close to Christmas in 1908. In fact it was Christmas Eve, I believe, when I received my next call. The girl who was afterwards to be my wife had paid me a visit at my home. I walked her back to her home. On the way a fireman named Roach, who afterwards fired for me, passed us on the way. He cautioned me: "You better get on home," he said, "You're first out now."

All afternoon I had watched my name move up on the board. I wondered what the assignment would be. I also wondered who the engineer would be. I hoped it wouldn't be Old Head Conners, Pokey Cowan, or some other engineer that I'd had trouble with on the supply job.

I had just entered the house when a loud knocking sounded on the door. When I opened it a little fearfully, there stood the caller with the call book in his hand.

"Gould ...?" he leered, or so it seemed to me. "Called for 62—Engine 201—for 12:30 A.M." I waited for the rest of it, the name of the engineer.

"Who's the hogger?" I boldly inquired—although down deep I believe I intuitively knew.

The caller seemed to be enjoying himself. His grin grew wider. "Pokey Cowan," he answered and handed me the call book to sign.

My heart sank in my shoes. What worse fate could be mine at this hour? With a trembling hand I scribbled my name in the call book. I believed the caller enjoyed my discomfort.

Gone now were all my plans! Gone out of my mind was that pretty little speech I had rehearsed: "Mr. Cowan ..." Only I had hoped it would not be Cowan. "I don't know much about firing an engine...." He would now find that out soon enough. "But I'm willing to learn...." Who would be my teacher? Certainly not this man. "If there is anything you could show me, I would be grateful...." I surely would! But I didn't think Pokey would be willing to show me anything that would be to my advantage. Not him!

If I wasn't a fireman I had at least dressed the part. My new cap was peaked down over one eye. That large red bandanna completely circled my neck. Those large gauntlet gloves came halfway to my elbow, and that gold chain anchored in the bib of my overalls was fastened to a large new gold watch on the other end. That's the way I looked when I presented myself to Pokey Cowan on the deck of that little high wheeled mogul that Christmas Eve.

Pokey took a long look at me and then turned away with an anticipated leer distorting his severe countenance. "You'd better get them lamps filled and the lubricator working," he admonished, as he slid down the gangway steps with that long oiler in his hand.

I filled the headlight reservoir in the old box-like oil headlight with coal oil and lighted it, filled and lighted the gauge lights, and swept up the deck while Pokey oiled the running gear. I inspected the tank for water. I put in a few scoops of coal. I thought I was doing all right. By the time Pokey came back up into the cab, I thought I was ready.

He took one look around, and then without a single comment, he seated himself on the right seat box and tooted the whistle inquiringly. He must have received a confirming signal out in front from the brakeman, for he immediately sounded two more decisive blasts. He then tipped the Johnson bar with his foot. It slid noisily down into the front end of the quadrant. The port in the brake valve sighed softly as he released the brake. He tugged at the throttle, and the little 201 tremblingly moved ahead.

We moved out into the "dick lead," the track from the roundhouse to the yards, and backed down onto a string of merchandise cars. Someone came up alongside the engine under Pokey's window. There was a sharp exchange of words between Pokey and someone on the ground.

Then Pokey turned angrily to me. "Your headlight is all smoked up," he announced. "Get out there and clean that chimney, and don't turn it up so high when you light it."

Something would have to go wrong, I thought as I made my way out along the running board to the head end. When I opened the door to the headlight cage all I could see was a dark smoking smudge where the headlight chimney should be. I had sense enough to turn the wick down and blow out the flame. I reached in with my gloved hand to get the chimney out for cleaning. The hot glass shriveled the fingers on my glove, and set up a suffocating stench.

I finally got the glass cooled sufficiently to clean it. I wiped the smoked-up headlight glass and reflector. I trimmed and relighted the wick. I was unaware that Pokey was standing on the ground taking in my every move. If he was going to turn me in, why didn't he do it now, I thought.

As I slid the headlight base back into place and closed the cage door his voice rang out sharply. "Turn that wick down a little," he ordered. I turned it down to where I thought it would lose it's flame, before I received his approval. I had not known that when that headlight got warmed up the flame would rise. If too high to begin with the whole thing would smoke up. That's what had happened to cause it to black out before.

I now hoped that everything else would be okay and returned to the cab. There was, to me, a meaningless exchange of signals, shouts, and whistle blasts, all having to do with the air brake inspection. The conductor climbed into the cab with a handful of orders. He and Pokey read and commented on them. Then Pokey stuffed them into his pocket.

He turned to me. "Have you got a load in her?" he inquired. I justly interpreted that to mean did I have coal in the firebox. I told him that I did. He seemed highly amused at something.

He blasted twice with the whistle and reached for the throttle. The head brakeman crouched down on his little seat between the boiler head and the cab. The conductor took his place—on my seat box. The only place left for me as the 201 ambled ahead was down on the deck. We pulled slowly out of the yard.

I started to shovel in the coal. I thought that was what I was there for. Pokey hollered at me, "Wait till we get out of this yard. You'll have plenty of time to wear out that scoop when we get going."

After a time we seemed to leave the yard and pick up speed. I tentatively picked up the scoop, expecting Pokey to correct me if I was doing wrong. As he made no effort to stop me I thought I was doing the right thing. I started shoveling coal.

As the fire blazed and crackled the light became blinding to my eyes, as they were unaccustomed to the glare. The heat scorched the left leg of my overalls. Everything inside the cab was blacked out. I could not see the water glass reading. The water glass was a half-inch, foot long cylinder which indicated the water level in the boiler. I could not see the steam gauge. I was completely blinded by the intense white heat waves coming from the firebox. When I closed the firedoor everything was in darkness. I had not yet learned to look at the fire with the scoop held as a shield. But we kept going. And I continued to throw coal at that blinding glare coming from the firebox.

Ten miles of this and, as Pokey seemed to ease off, the speed grew less. We were approaching Midvale where we would stop for water. I continued to shovel coal until Pokey commanded me to quit. He finally shut off, and I swear that the pop on the 201 let go on the night air with a bang. The conductor prepared to get off when the stop was made. He tapped me on the shoulder as he stepped down onto the deck.

"She's a good one, ain't she, Kid?" he said.

"I don't know," I answered. "Where is it?"

"Right up there on the mark," he announced.

The head brakeman cut off the engine, and we moved down to the water tank. I had pulled the tank spout down, and was hanging onto the valve rope. I could see down into the cab. I saw Pokey looking at the fire over the overturned scoop shovel. About thirty-five years later as I was a guest on his engine pulling no. 1 between Colton and Soldier Summit I was to see him repeat that scene when another young fireman let the steam pressure lag.

When I came back into the cab Pokey roughly inquired: "What's the matter Kid, are you weak in the poop? Can't you get it up there?" From this I inferred that I was not shoveling enough coal. I could remedy that if indeed that was my trouble. I was young and husky and in good shape physically. That little mogul couldn't burn coal faster than I could shovel it to her. The idea! I would show him!

As I analyzed the situation later I came to the conclusion that I played right into Pokey's plans. I was doing too good a job to please him. That engine had blown it's top when he shut off coming into Midvale. The conductor had commented "She's a good one. Right up on the mark!" Pokey wanted me to overload that fire so that he could turn me in for non-performance. He didn't want me to make good.

Well, that's just what I did. Leaving Midvale I shoveled coal faster than that engine could burn it. The result was that the fire clinkered over. We lost steam. When we stopped before the Pedro crossing approaching Provo we didn't have enough steam to start the train.

After several half-hearted efforts Pokey contentedly hoisted his feet up on the boiler head. "Put on your blower, Kid," he said. I did, and after about ten minutes he tried again. This time he had little difficulty starting that train. We rambled down into Provo, but were late on our schedule.

Pokey stopped at the water tank. While I was up taking water I saw him making his way back to the telegraph office. The significance of that did not dawn upon me until later. Before I was through taking water he was back on the engine. All the while we were standing there the blower had been roaring into the night. By the time I got through taking water the steam pressure was up. We left town.

Somewhere up around Mapleton we again stopped to "blow up"— to raise the steam pressure. We were way off schedule now. The firebox was clinkered over and filled to overflowing. Every time I opened the fire door to put in a scoop of coal it seemed to me that two scoopfuls would roll out onto the iron deck.

We finally dragged wearily into Thistle. We stopped to clear the eastbound siding, cut off the engine, and moved ahead. I thought we were going for water. I started to climb onto the back of the tank. Pokey stopped me.

"Get your stuff together, Kid, and get off the engine," he announced. "You are through!"

I couldn't quite understand for a moment. A couple of men in greasy overalls climbed on the engine. They had clinker hooks and shaker bars.

One opened the fire door and looked into the furnace. He turned to me in a contemptuous attitude.

"You sure got her loaded," he snarled.

They proceeded to clean that fire, entirely ignoring me. Pokey had left the engine. Another fireman made his appearance before the fire cleaners had finished. In a sympathizing manner he enlightened me. Pokey had turned me in by wire from Provo. This man had been called to take my place and to fire that engine for the rest of the trip.

After awhile I began to understand. It was as Pokey had said: I was through! My career as a fireman was over, almost before it had begun. I got off the engine. Carrying my effects I walked back slowly, sadly, and puzzled. I walked by the big lighted bay window of the depot. A man with a green shade over his eyes looked out at me. I fancied that look contained amused contempt. I proceeded a little farther down the platform to a baggage truck. I managed to climb on it and sit down.

Pokey and the head brakeman came out of the lunch counter. They walked by, completely ignoring me in my misery. I saw them climb on the engine. Soon they backed down onto the train. A large consolidation engine coupled onto the sharp end. They whistled off, and the train moved ahead. With my heart down in my shoes, I painfully and sorrowfully watched the marker lamps of that caboose shake and shiver as the train faded away around the curve out of Thistle.

What thoughts went through my mind as I sat on that baggage truck in lonely darkness! I was cold, hungry, but most of all dejected. My days as a fireman had been short indeed. What would I tell my folks, especially my mother, who had contracted for that gold watch? I thought of leaving for other more distant parts. I would get away from it all. Many years later I would come back when I was immensely rich. I would seek revenge against Pokey. Certainly I couldn't go back home. What would I tell that girl to whom I had bragged about one day being an engineer? No, I couldn't go back and face all my friends. It would just be too humiliating.

I slid down off the truck. I walked past that big lighted window again. The man behind that green eyeshade looked up with a smile. That smile turned into a leer, or so it seemed. I didn't go by that window again. I sat, a lonely and dejected shivering figure on that cold baggage truck. Even now, after all these years, I still think the loneliest place in the world is a depot platform in the dark small hours of early morning.

How long I sat there in brooding silence I do not know. The darkness was beginning to pale. The rays of the sun were beginning to peek over the high mountain. I was starting to nod sleepily. Suddenly a voice sounded in front of me.

"You Gould?"

I stirred into wakefulness. What now? The well-clothed figure of a man stood before me. As my eyes began to focus, he again asked that question: "You Gould?"

"Yes," I answered dejectedly, "I'm Gould."

He spoke like one with authority. "Number 61 will be coming into town in a little while. You get on that engine and relieve the fireman. The crew is short of time. You will work the run into Salt Lake." He turned and walked away. I saw him enter the telegraph office. I pondered over his words. "You get on that engine and relieve that fireman!" Then I was still on the pay roll! I was still a fireman!

My throat tightened up. A relieved sob shook me into full wakefulness. I was going to have another chance. I wondered what Pokey would think of that.

How bright and warm the sun looked now as it fully tipped the mountain top. How crystal-like the glazed snow-covered ground appeared. How loudly and sweetly chirped the winter birds overhead. Gone now was that dreadful feeling of utter despair, that feeling of melancholy and of loneliness. How lovely it was to be alive and still a fireman on this beautiful morning.

Soon another figure appeared beside me. Dressed in overalls with that telltale time book and schedule showing from his back pocket. He couldn't be anything but an engineer.

Again that question was asked: "You Gould?" This time I answered eagerly, "Yes, my name is Gould."

He asked me a few questions about my being at Thistle. I told him I was a new man, and that I had been unable to make good with Pokey Cowan.

He commented, "You're not the first who didn't make good with Pokey." He added, "You ought to do all right from here to Salt Lake. It's mostly downhill."

I learned his name was Brown. He made his home at Springville. He was called Springville Brown to distinguish him from several other Browns on the road.

When no. 61 dropped down the hill and came to a stop we both climbed on and relieved the tired crew. I can't remember the number of the engine, but I think it, too, was a mogul. How good it felt to be on an engine again! We had no trouble bringing no. 61 into Salt Lake. Engineer

Above: A "hog," a 2–8–0 consolidation engine of the C-41 class. Manufacturer's photo from the W. J. G. Gould collection. *Below:* An eight-wheeler "mogul"; this engine was later renumbered as the Denver & Rio Grande 943. Manufacturer's photo from the W. J. G. Gould collection.

Brown was then released to deadhead back to Thistle, and I again saw my name adorning the fireman's extra board.

This was a very busy single track railroad, and the winter coal rush was well underway. I know I was fortunate to draw several dog catching trips in a row. This permitted me to learn more about the job of firing without being under the gun as much as I had been on those first few trips. I was determined to make every trip add to my total experience and skill.

One morning I was called to fire a little "hog" on the Park City helper ("hogs" were small consolidation engines of the C-41 class). The engineer was a man by the name of Curley Dyet. His hair may have been curly at one time, but at the time of which I write he had none. Curley had been an engineer on the Park City Branch when it had been an independent railroad. He now worked on the mainline most of the time, but every winter when business was good he was able to go back to his branch again. Every morning in the winter there were two ice trains besides the local freight and the passenger jobs. These runs combined required in the neighborhood of about ten little hogs a day. I was fortunate enough to hold that job with Curley for about a week before a regular man decided he wanted it. Jobs like those on the Park City Branch were much in favor due to the fact that they were all daylight hours, and every night was spent at home in the hay.

Curley was the first engineer to show any interest in me. I learned afterward that both Pokey Cowan and Old Head Conners had tried to get him to turn me in, but he refused.

Every morning we would help the first ice train out of Salt Lake to Altus. Then we would cut off and follow down to Gorgoza where the ice ponds were located. There we would linger around for several hours while the train was being loaded with ice. We would then couple in behind the caboose and help back to Altus. There we would cut off and drift down behind them into Salt Lake. On these jobs Curley had plenty of time to coach me along, which he did to good effect.

One afternoon, as we were coming down behind the ice train, I received the first real scare in my railroading career. We were drifting along on this little hog engine. I had a good fire in her, and had climbed up onto my seat. I had the front and back doors of the cab latched. Those little hogs had a boiler that extended clear through the cab and ended with its back head flush with the back of the cab. They had no deck on the engine proper—only an apron between the engine and the shovel plate of the tender. The only way an engineer could get to the fireman's side was to come out the right back door, walk over to the left side by way of the shovel plate, and enter from the left back cab door.

This afternoon we were drifting comfortably along. Everything was in proper order. As I said, I was on the seat with the windows and doors latched against the winter cold. All of a sudden there occurred what to me seemed to be an explosion. There was a loud blast, and the cab filled with steam. I didn't know which way to turn or what to do. Curley was hollering at me over the top of the boiler, but I couldn't make out what he was saying. He finally came around to my side and started pounding on the back door. At last he made me understand that he wanted in. I unlatched the door and he came into my side. In a very short time the raging noise gradually subsided. The cab soon cleared of steam.

I asked Curley what had happened. He said the water glass had blown out. When he couldn't make me understand he came over to my side and shut off both the top and bottom valves of the glass. The water glass was on the left side of the engine. A blown out water glass never scared me again.

Old Curley Dyet was quite a character. He was my friend for as long as I was on the Rio Grande. Later on after the Park City experience I fired engines 61 and 62 for him as a regular job out of Ogden. He snored more loudly when asleep than any man I every knew. At the YMCA at Helper they had a special room that they put him in which was away from all other sleepers. Even at that you could hear him snore from anywhere on that floor.

On that 61 and 62 job the crew was usually made up of men living in Salt Lake. We rode back and forth between Salt Lake and Ogden on anything on which we could catch a ride. Going to Ogden was an evening trip, since 62 was scheduled out of Ogden at 9 P.M. Sixty-one was scheduled as an early morning arrival in Ogden, which meant finding a ride back to Salt Lake mid-morning.

The best connection we could make would be on the Bamberger Railway, the electric interurban. We all had a letter given us by the superintendent. When we presented this letter at the Bamberger ticket office they would sell us a ticket for thirty-five cents—one cent a mile. We only took advantage of this arrangement if there was no other means of travel, such as a Rio Grande train going our direction.

One morning we were going into Ogden a little late. We were figuring on riding no. 6 back to Salt Lake if we got into Ogden in time to catch it. Time was getting short. The last six or seven miles into the Ogden yards were downgrade, and we were bowling along right smart. That little 955 could sure turn a nasty wheel!

All at once I felt a little jerk on the engine. I looked back in time to see that train piling up. About halfway back to the caboose a car had derailed, and the rest of the train behind it seemed determined to pile up on top of the hapless car. I had a grandstand view. It was just like a football game. When that car left the rails every other car behind seemed determined to jump on top, and that's just what they did.

With the Rio Grande mainline so completely tied up by the wreck, no. 6 left Ogden over the Oregon Short Line tracks that morning. We made it in plenty of time.

That turn on 61 and 62 was a good one. It paid a fireman on the average of one hundred and fifty-two dollars a month. That was pretty good money then. We left Ogden about 9 P.M. We were at Helper about 9 or

10 A.M. the next morning. We would then leave Helper about 6:00 or 7:00 that night and be in Ogden about 6:00 or 7:00 the following morning. Then we would be off the rest of that day and the next day until about 9 P.M. There was only one drawback. It was all night work.

But those little nine-fifties were nice comfortable engines to fire, and they usually steamed very well. I was firing 952 one afternoon. It was a hot summer day. The engineer was a man named Bert Kestler. We called him "Blue Beard," on account of the color of his chin just after shaving. The 952 was just out of the back shop. She was in perfect condition. When working there wasn't a click or a pound in her anywhere, but she did burn too much coal at the time.

I was down on the deck shoveling coal. The sweat was running out from under my cap and dripping off my chin. We were just going under the overhead bridge in the mouth of the Spanish Fork Canyon. Bert looked down on me and said: "You know, Gouldie, a man working on a nice engine like this on a regular job shouldn't expect any pay. When payday comes along he should just sign his check and turn it back to the company, and thank them for the privilege."

I replied, "Alright Bert, you give 'em back your check but I'll keep mine, because I earn it!" I wiped the perspiration from my dripping forehead and waited for an answer. None was forthcoming.

After I got bumped off that ice train helper job with Curley Dyet, I was sent to Helper to take the place of a fireman who had gone to Salt Lake to the take the examination for engineer. The job was mostly firing helper engines on the east side of the Soldier Summit grade. The man whose place I took fell down on the exam, and I thought he would come back and relieve me. I was getting quite homesick, and I couldn't see how I was going to get off that helper job and get back to Salt Lake.

The man I was relieving finally did come back after several weeks. But instead of letting me go back they held me at Helper on the extra board. I was getting desperate. I hadn't seen my gal for over a month. Payday came along, and I bribed the callboy. His name was Tommy Haycock.

I told Tommy that if he would call me for the head end of some train going to Salt Lake I would give him five dollars. A day or two later he called me for the sharp end of no. 61. I give him the five dollars. The sad part was that I got to Salt Lake to find myself still on the extra board there. The very next call I got was to deadhead to Helper for the Helper extra board.

4

Life along the Rails

By now I was getting to be quite a fireman. For some months I had been working as a fireman, marked up on the board out of Salt Lake.

One day I was called for an extra west, going to Ogden. The master mechanic was a man named Powell. He was just about as ornery as any man I ever met. He and Jack Snyder, the traveling engineer, came alongside the engine when we were getting ready to leave for Ogden. He looked up in the cab and saw me, red bandanna, gauntleted gloves, cap, watch, chain, and all. He stopped and said something to the traveling engineer. Jack Snyder came up into the cab. He wanted to know who I was and what I was doing on that engine. I told him my name and said that I was firing the engine.

He wanted to know who had hired me and how long I had been firing. I told him that he had hired me, and that I had been firing for some ten months by that time. He climbed off the engine and I saw he and the master mechanic arguing as they walked away.

I made that trip and was back in Salt Lake expecting the next call. The telephone rang. I answered, and it was the engine dispatcher. He started to give me a call, then interrupted the conversation, and told me to wait a minute. I heard him talking to someone in the office. Then he came back on the phone and said to me, "Cancel the call—you are out of service."

I asked him why I was out of service, and he answered that he didn't know. I went immediately to the call room to see what I could find out. I couldn't think of any rule I had broken.

The engine dispatcher told me that Jack Snyder had told him to take me out of service. He didn't know why. In the meantime Jack Snyder had left town. It was two or three days before he returned and I could see him.

When I did get to see him, he told me that Old Man Powell had ordered him to take me out of service on account of my age. I went up to see Powell. He wasn't in his office. I wandered around the shops looking for him. I came upon him walking through the blacksmith shop. I walked up to him and said, "Mr. Powell, can I speak to you for a minute?"

He gave me a mean look and said, "Talk fast!"

I told him who I was and that I had been taken out of service. He didn't lose a step in his stride.

"Yeah," he said. The tobacco juice was running out of both sides of his mouth. "You're not of age. I don't know how you ever got into the engine service."

I was on the spot. I wasn't yet twenty-one. I didn't have an argument to put up. I said, "Mr. Powell, don't I look to be twenty-one?" That was the first time he stopped walking.

He turned on me and told me most emphatically that I didn't look to be even twenty, and I couldn't convince him that I was unless I produced a birth certificate to that effect.

I tried to tell him that I could fire an engine as well as any fireman on the board. I offered to get enginemen to prove it. I was thinking of Curley Dyet. He started walking away from me. I started to follow, but I could see that it was of no use. He had quite forgotten me.

The next morning I tried to talk to him again. He didn't have time to listen. He later told my dad that I was just a sassy kid. I didn't know the basis for that remark and couldn't think of any time I had sassed him. I hadn't had the chance.

I belonged to the Brotherhood of Locomotive Firemen (the union) at the time, but I didn't think they would take my case if they found out I really wasn't of the required age.

I thought I would try just once more. I dressed in my best clothes. I had on a white shirt and collar. I went looking for him and again met him out in the shops. I got into step and tried to talk to him. No matter what I said he wouldn't answer. Finally he stopped, and his wrath poured out in torrents. He spit tobacco juice all over my white shirt. He slobbered all over himself. I know I hadn't mentioned the firemen's organization, but he said "I'll cut your gallasses for you! I don't care how many organizations you

The author at age twenty-one. Photo from the W. J. G. Gould collection.

belong to. I'll stop you!" He raved like that for several minutes. If it had been anything but my job at stake, I believe I would have clobbered him. He started to walk away, then seemed to cool off a little. He turned back to me.

"I'll tell you what I'll do, Kid. I'll put you back to work! I'll put you on a switch engine, and you stay there until I tell you to get off!"

He walked away. That afternoon the engine dispatcher had orders to put me on a switch engine.

Well, I thought, firing a switch engine was still firing. I concluded that at least it saved my job for the moment.

I was on that switch engine for about a year. I was a few months over twenty-one when I finally got back on the main stem again. By that time Old Man Powell had left the Rio Grande and was master mechanic for the Western Pacific. The man who took his place was an Englishman by the name of Bennett.

I went up to his office to see if it was all right for me to go back to the mainline. They hunted up the records on me but could find nothing amiss. Old Man Powell had evidently made my case a personal matter. But at any rate I was back on the mainline again.

Those switch crews worked ten-hours shifts. The fireman's pay was two dollars and seventy cents a shift. At that, we had the edge on the switch firemen on the OSL. They worked ten hours for two dollars and sixty cents.

I was very lucky in being assigned to what was called the "horn" job. We went to work at eight in the morning and quit at six at night. The new Rio Grande passenger depot was in the process of being built but had not yet been completed. We hauled material for that job. The horn was the name given to that part of the track on Eighth South where the direction was reversed in the process of getting over to Fourth West. Some wag probably thought it was similar to going around Cape Horn. There were a lot of industries along Fourth West that we served, such as a coal yard, a bottling works, and scrap yards.

Every morning we assembled our cars in the regular yard. We had the air hoses coupled up and the brakes tested. Then we proceeded around the horn to make deliveries. It was the same routine in the afternoon. Twice a day we traversed the same tracks, serving all those industries.

At times we also went to the cattle pens at Woods Cross to deliver or receive car loads of animals. Then we would sometimes go down along the Western Pacific tracks to serve the Fisher Brewery, or up past Sugarhouse to serve the cement rock quarry. It was just like a local peddler freight job.

There was, along Fourth West, the Temps Bottling Works, a branch of the Temps St. Louis beer brewing operation. There was also a bottling works for Anhauser Busch Beer. We would deliver beer in bulk to these places—but never more than one car at a time. This was because every time we set out a car of beer at one of these places each member of the crew received a quart bottle of beer. So if we had two cars to deliver in one day one car was always delivered in the morning and the other car in the afternoon.

I think that little old engine I fired must have started life as a narrow gauge mogul. I know from looking at the nameplate on the smokebox that it was built by Baldwin in 1883. That would have been before the Rio Grande or any part of it was changed to standard gauge. She was undoubtedly what we called a "set out." That is, the wheels were set out to standard gauge.

The engineer I fired for was a man by the name of John Cobbly. He was a booze hound. While we were getting our air brake test and before proceeding around the horn, he would go about a block away and get another kid to fire the engine. Sometimes we would be alone all day long on that engine. Just two kids. I have often wondered since how he got away with it. Besides distributing cars around the horn we would sometimes have to go out of town. For this we required train orders. I am free to confess that at that time I knew very little about the rules governing train orders. I wonder how I got by!

On one occasion we were at the Woods Cross stock yards delivering a carload of bulls. It was getting pretty close to eastbound no. 2's time. A cattleman got on the engine at the stock yards to ride into Salt Lake. I was thinking of waiting out there for no. 2. This cattleman wanted to get to Salt Lake to catch no. 2 at the station. If we let no. 2 by at Woods Cross he would not make the connection. He spoke to our crew foreman who told me how it stood. He wanted to know if I thought that low wheeled mogul could go into Salt Lake ahead of no. 2. There was a pleading look in that cattleman's eye.

I wasn't sure, but I was willing to try. The crew foreman looked back to see if he could see a headlight. I turned to one of the switchmen and said, "Open the gate."

He did, and we took off. "Where ignorance is bliss 'tis folly to be otherwise!" Or was it just the foolhardy nerve of a young punk?

I hooked the Johnson bar up as high as I dared, and that little mogul kicked back the miles in great shape. I believe no. 2 must have been running a little late. In any event she never got close to us. The cattleman made his connection, as far as I know, and each member of the crew got a high-priced cigar.

I never saw the day, after I got to be an engineer, that I would place that much confidence in my fireman—to leave him alone all day on my engine. But John Cobbly didn't seem to worry. We would go up to Sugarhouse, out to Fireclay near Murray, and down to Fisher's Brewery over the Western Pacific. If anything should have happened to us, it would have been the loss of jobs for the entire crew, switchmen included.

Bad luck finally overtook John Cobbly. I wasn't firing for him at the time. I had gone back to the mainline. One evening he came staggering down through the yards about time to tie up with the switch crew for the day. A hostler was backing down an engine and ran over him. They picked him up in a blanket.

I think all that experience I gained when I was left alone in charge of that little 828 helped me later in my career. It caused me to become what we call "engine-minded." This is the feeling of being at home on an engine, much as an airplane pilot becomes "air-minded" and is at home in the air.

On this switching job, as we went around the horn, I got in the habit of kicking off a few chunks of coal to a couple of little girls who were always at a certain place with a gunny-sack. After I had done this a few times they handed me a paper sack one morning. On opening this sack I found it to be half full of candy in the form of candy bars. It was very good candy. Candy was just starting to come out with fancy names like Opera Bar. There was also a note in this sack evidently written by a woman. She mentioned that they were very glad to get the coal, and that her husband was watchman at the J. G. McDonald candy factory. She stated further that if I would visit him sometime around 10 p.m. at the factory I would be able to carry away all the candy I wanted. Of course this was to be in exchange for the coal favors.

I fully intended to keep this appointment, and I paved the way for it by continuing to throw off all lumps of coal in the tender large enough to make it worthwhile. But my efforts proved to be too popular. The more coal I threw off the more people there were to pick it up. It got so that the whole neighborhood, men, women and kids, would be waiting for us to put in an appearance each morning. There were several near fights over that coal among those good neighbors. So I quit throwing off coal.

I did not pay the visit to the candy factory, but one evening as I was walking home I met the fireman who had taken my place on the switch engine after I had gone back to the mainline. His name was Shorty Lyons. He had his pockets bulging with candy bars. He told me he had just been visiting the night watchman at the McDonald candy factory. I had to laugh. I told him what had taken place when I was on that job. He told me that he was also kicking coal off the tender to the little girls and had received a similar written invitation to visit the factory around ten o'clock.

I asked him if the entire neighborhood shared in his generosity. He said that they were beginning to be more numerous every morning. I told him of my experiences, and that I had been afraid of the consequences if I continued the practice. I never knew what he did about it, but I am sure I had him thinking about the problem when we parted.

It was a night in wintertime, after a heavy fall of snow. I was firing for Jim Daily. About two o'clock in the morning we were slowly hammering up the grade out of Helper on the sharp end of a train of coal. It had quit snowing after leaving about a foot of the white stuff on the level. The night was calm and still. A big, bright, silver moon came out, and with the help of all that snow it made the night almost as bright as high noon. We were dragging along very slowly and Jim Daily was sound asleep with his feet propped up against the Johnson bar of that old eleven hundred engine. I was standing in the left gangway after putting in a fire.

Shortly after leaving the snow-covered rock walls of Castle Gate, I happened to be idly sizing up the snow between the paralleling eastbound rails. I saw footprints in the deep snow pointed up the canyon. There seemed to be two sets of prints.

After putting in a fire I came back to look again. Those footprints still disturbed the deep, soft snow. I knew they couldn't have been there very long because it had been snowing heavily. Always, between fires, I watched those tracks in the snow.

We slowly passed the Hanging Rock and made the next curve to the left. Jim Daily still reposed peacefully in that awkward position, and that big moon gave added brightness to the snow. We started to curve to the right. I hurriedly put in a fire so that I could glance ahead as we came out on that half-mile tangent. There, about halfway up the straight track, I could see two bulky dark figures plodding along between the eastbound rails. They hesitated as our headlight brought them into focus. As we drew nigh they edged over closer to the westbound rails. Then, as we drew closer, I could see they were women—two women trudging along up that snow-filled canyon in the dead of a winter night miles from any habitation.

We were about to pass them when one grabbed the hand rail and slowly drew herself up on the slow-moving step. I reached down and took hold of her hand and helped her up into the cab. Jim Daily slumbered on. I glanced back from the left gangway. The second woman was clinging desperately to the hand rail on the back of the tank and slowly pulling herself up onto the tank step. I climbed the coal gate, slid down the hand rail on the back of the tank, and guided her over to the tank ladder. We went over the coal and down into the cab. Jim Daily hadn't moved. I motioned to our guests to seat themselves on my seat box. I opened the fire door to put in a fire.

To start a conversation, I asked what they were doing way up here on such a night. Without hesitation they told me of a big celebration in Castle Gate. The party had gotten rough, and several fights broke out. These gals became afraid for their lives, so they took off. They didn't know quite where they were going, but they just wanted to get out of Castle Gate.

I looked at Jim. He still reposed peacefully. The girls were sitting on my seat box with their backs to the closed window, gazing into the center of the cab. I cracked the firedoor till the glare held them in a spot light. I took the coal pick and edged over to the right side behind the back of the cab. I then brought that coal pick down in a sharp blow on the apron between the engine and the tank with all my might.

Old Jim Daily almost fell down onto the deck. He tried to stand but couldn't get his feet under him. Before he could get them untangled he glanced across the cab. Those two girls were just as frightened as he was. The light from the fire door shown on their faces. Their mouths were half-open, and blinded as they were by the firebox glare, their eyes were bulging in their fright.

That's what Jim Daily saw across the cab when his eyes finally focused. I was standing behind the cab on the right side where he couldn't see me, but I could see him. He would take a look at the girls and shake his head. He looked around the cab for me. Then he would look at the girls again. Jim and they were speechless. Then, when it looked like Jim was reaching to shut off his throttle, I put in my appearance.

I kicked the firedoor shut. Jim took another look across the cab. Those girls were still there. Jim finally found his voice. "What the hell's carrying on here?" The words came out haltingly.

"Unh-unh, Jim. There are ladies present. We've got company," I admonished.

It was some time before Jim understood the situation. Those girls were much relieved, I'm sure, when he took it good-naturedly. Between there and Colton, Jim and the girls became quite friendly. They told him more of their plight than they had told me.

When I got up on the tank to take water at Colton, Jim took our visitors over to Cad Thomas's hotel. Cad herself was sleeping on a cot behind the door leading upstairs. Jim told her he had a couple of friends whom he would like her to put up for the night. Cad woke up just enough to tell him what room they could have before going back to sleep. Jim came back to the engine and we left town.

The next morning Cad Thomas was surprised to see those two friends of Jim Daily come down the stairs. It wasn't long before the whole railroad knew that Jim Daily had lady friends. I never found out what became of those girls, but I was awfully glad that Cad Thomas had no way of connecting Jim Daily's fireman up with them.

I fired all makes and types of engines for eight years on the Rio Grande before promotion. I had many experiences, some serious and some comical. In the busy season Colton was about as far as a freight train crew could expect to get on the sixteen hours of allocated duty. If you were, in those rare cases, able to make it through to Helper, you patted yourself on the back and went around bragging about it.

On the westbound runs crews would tie up anywhere between Provo and Midvale. I have even tied up at Springville. During the busy seasons the company could not afford to leave its engines and other equipment standing idle on some sidetrack while the crew was taking rest. So every passenger train that left Salt Lake would have as high as a half a dozen deadhead crews going out to bring in some tied up crew. However, in the less busy seasons, if the power was not needed, the train could stand while the crew was resting.

Sometimes it would be hard to find a place to eat or sleep. Although our agreements with the company plainly stated that crews would not be tied up where there were no eating or sleeping accommodations, the company paid little attention to that requirement. It contended that if there was one private house or even a section house at any point, that meant eating and sleeping accommodations were available.

Another way the railroad company would interpret the sixteen-hour law, and for which they paid dearly later on, was as follows:

There was a clause in the law that stated that if a crew had worked sixteen hours and were held up through no fault of their own but through what was called an act of God, they could be worked in excess of sixteen hours. This so-called act of God was intended to cover cases of emergency, created by an unexpected washout, wreck, or such similar condition. Even in those circumstances it was only intended to allow additional time to get the train and crew off the mainline and into the nearest sidetrack.

But the interpretations of this clause were bizarre, to say the least. They were created to keep the trains moving and the crews working beyond the provisions of the law. A crew getting close to sixteen hours on the road could expect the dispatcher to put out a message such as the following at the next open telegraph office.

"Add three hours account of bad steaming engine."

"Add three hours account of poor coal."

"Add three hours account of pulling out draw-bar."

Anything a dispatcher could think up he would use to keep that train and crew moving. It didn't matter whether the condition he chose actually happened or not. It could be a complete fabrication or fiction. Likewise, it didn't matter whether or not the chosen condition had any effect on that particular crew. He would use anything and everything in any way he chose to keep the crews working long hours.

This practice finally came to the attention of the framers of the law and the Interstate Commerce Commission, charged with its enforcement. The Rio Grande was found in violation in over three hundred counts by this commission. Thereafter they were very careful not to allow any violation of the sixteen-hour law. Those "add three hours" messages became things of the past. But in the interim flagrant abuses continued.

I was once on a crew that was close to thirty-two hours getting from Salt Lake to Tucker. We had used up numerous add messages to keep going. We all decided that on reaching Tucker we would not accept any more add messages but would insist on ten hours of rest.

Sure enough, at Tucker we received another three-hour extension. The conductor notified the dispatcher that we were not going to accept any more time; that we intended to get some sleep. The dispatcher stepped across the hall to the superintendent's office and notified him of our decision. The superintendent sent a message over his own signature:

"You are going to Helper if it takes a week. Do as instructed!"

We did. We went to Helper in a little less than a week.

One night we had tied up at Tucker. It was several years after the above incident took place, and conditions had improved relative to the observance of the sixteen-hour law. I was firing for good old Toby Sheldahl. We were eastbound and they tied us up at Tucker for eight hours rest. There were no sleeping accommodations open in town. Toby, who had previously worked out of Tucker, met a friend who took him to a bed in his home.

There being no bed for me, I rolled up my overalls, and using them for a pillow, I stretched out under the table in the call room. Sometime in the night the trainmaster, a Mr. Slattery, came along and pulled me out from under the table. He wanted to know what I was doing under there. I told him I was getting my rest as there were no open places in town. He promptly fired me because I couldn't find a bed.

Johnny McKenna, who was working out of Tucker at the time, showed up on the scene. He was called for a trip with a hill crew. He took me back to the shanty in which he was staying and gave me his bed. In the meantime, I guess the trainmaster thought better of his action and reinstated me, because when my crew's rest was up I was called along with the rest of them.

This trainmaster was once an engineman on the Colorado end of the system. He had been promoted to air-brake instructor on the west end. From there he went to trainmaster and finally to superintendent at Salt Lake.

They tell lots of tales on Slattery after he acquired a little authority. He would fire a man without any consideration of his case. Then later on after considering the case and before it could come to a formal investigation, he would reinstate the offender and write him out a personal check for the time he had lost. He made the remark that he was learning the employees' work rules and schedules the hard way, but that he would learn them if it took his whole bank roll.

Very early in my career as a fireman, I saw the sun rise three times going from Salt Lake to Soldier Summit. Then when we finally tipped over the Summit we were on duty only a little over an hour before we were tied up at Helper. It happened this way:

There were a lot of small engines out of service and stored on the dead line in Salt Lake. They had been there for some time. The management decided that they would send some of them to Burnham for overhauling.

Burnham was where the general shops of the Denver and Rio Grande (D & RG) were located, a short distance out of Denver.

They lined up three of those small engines and coupled them together. The idea was to run them light over the road. I was called to fire one of them. We were all lined up in a row ready to leave town. I was on the rear engine. It was a little ten-wheeler, a little larger than a Rome.

When we were about ready to go the engineers proceeded to the telegraph office to get their running orders and instructions. When they applied to the dispatcher, he was very much put out that the mechanical department was intending to run engines over the road light when the transportation department was begging for motive power to move trains.

He brought in the superintendent and told him of the situation. He in turn called up the master mechanic and wanted to know what was the big idea, running power over the road without tonnage. He told him that when he had engines to run or move to a new location to notify the dispatcher and let him arrange the movement.

The result was that we had to wait while they called a train crew and built up a train of empties for us. That was our first delay. But we finally left town with those three little engines triple-heading a string of about sixty-five empties. I think we made Provo the first night. Something was found to be wrong with one of those engines, the one I was firing, and a machinist and his helper came down from Thistle to look into it. They tied us up while this was in progress.

Those engines had been standing on the dead line for months. The one I was on wouldn't make enough steam to pull herself. It later developed that the nozzle tip had been removed from inside the the smokebox. It had probably been cannibalized to replace one in an engine of the same class. The result was she just would not "cut her fire." We could raise the steam pressure when we were standing around or when shut off, but as soon as we tried to work the engine the steam gauge pointer would start for the lowest reading on the dial.

When we arrived at Thistle it was decided that since we had no more than tonnage for three engines of that class we would go as we looked— that is, without a helper. The engineer that I was with complained that the engine would not make a pound of steam while working. We took her to the enginehouse, and a boiler maker climbed in the front end to try to adjust the draft appliances. It was there they discovered that the nozzle tip was missing.

There was no replacement at Thistle. They decided that something must be done to make that engine cut her fire. They finally hit upon a plan.

They got a long bar. It was what was known as a regulation pinch bar used to inch railroad cars a short way forward or back when no locomotive was around. They stuck this bar down the center of the stack with the end just inside the nozzle aperture. They used many strands of bailing wire to hold it there. We started again. Everybody seemed quite optimistic that we would have no trouble generating steam.

The three engines whistled off in rotation, and we started the train. The engine stayed hot. At a point about a half mile out of town my engineer got a little more confidence. He opened the throttle a little wider. Nothing adverse happened, so he gave her another few niches. The result was astounding: there was a loud swooshing explosion. That pinch bar broke loose from its wire tethering and went straight into the air about thirty feet.

The pointer on the steam gauge immediately started to relax and lay down. Soon it was at essentially zero pressure. The engineer—we were on the engine next to the train—whistled a long stop signal. He acquainted the others with what had happened. When the conductor arrived at the head end it was decided to return to Thistle.

This we did, and it was the opinion of those in authority to provide us with a helper engine. But all the helper engines were busy on other assignments. So after waiting around Thistle all the rest of the day and part of the night we finally were provided with a large consolidation engine to help us to Soldier Summit. At Tucker we were again subjected to hours of delay on account of no helpers available or those that were being needed to help more important trains.

So, as we finally tipped over the grade at Soldier Summit on the third morning out from Salt Lake the sun was just coming up over the mountain peaks to greet us for the third time. We were then only about an hour and a half from a tie up at Helper. Leaving Summit we dropped down the Price River Canyon like a stone falling down a well. Quite a contrast to our ascent on the other side of the mountain.

Yes, truly railroading has changed since I was a boy!

We were standing in the side track at American Fork headed west one afternoon. We had been there for several hours. I was quite famished. I should have had my feet under the table at home but this layover in the passing track at American Fork seemed as though it would never end.

We were waiting for two eastbound trains. I was sitting on the pilot just to clear the road crossing. It was a hot afternoon. As I sat there a couple of old men came down the road. They seemed to be in no hurry. They stopped to say a few words to me. Our conversation was general. They remarked about our long train of coal. Who would use all that coal in this kind of weather? We talked about storing coal for use when the cold weather came. They said their coal bins were getting empty.

I thought this would be a good time to say what was on my mind. I told how long it had been since the engineer and I had eaten. I said I would help them replenish their coal bins in exchange for a sandwich or two. We made a deal right away. I would unload a pile of coal while they went to their homes and brought back some sandwiches. They lived in the first house down the highway, about five hundred feet away.

They started for home, and I threw off all the lumps I could get to in the tender. Then as neither of those old fellows returned, I climbed up on the first car and unloaded a lot more. Pretty soon one of those old men came back up the road. He had a large paper sack in his hand. I had already thrown off better than a ton of coal, so I got down off the car when I saw him coming.

I roused the engineer and told him we were going to have something to eat now. We grew hungrier with anticipation. When the old fellow got within talking distance, he started to grin.

"You know," he said. "My wife says she hasn't got a thing in the house to make a sandwich." "But," he added, "You know what I got in this sack?"

He reached into the sack mysteriously and brought up a quart fruit jar filled with a reddish-colored liquid. He held it out to me. "I'll bet you will say that's the best homemade raspberry wine you ever smacked your lips over!"

Raspberry wine! And I was faint with hunger! If it hadn't been too much of a job I believe I would have reloaded all of that coal back on the car and tender.

I remember another time when we were going east. We were parked in that same passing track eastbound. The head brakeman was a few car lengths back, close to the depot. I could see he was engaged in conversation with a farmer. Pretty soon he came up to the engine and called me down on the ground. He asked if I was hungry. Was I hungry? Was there ever a time when a healthy young punk firing one of those engines over the road with a scoop shovel wasn't hungry?

The guy he had been talking to said if we would throw him off some coal he would fix us up a lunch. I agreed to throw off the coal. The brakeman accompanied the farmer to his home which was up the street a little ways. I threw off about five hundred pounds of coal into the weeds on the opposite side of the engine from the depot.

The westbound man with whom we had the meet came pounding up into town. I looked up the street. The brakeman was running toward the engine with a paper sack in his arms. He climbed on the engine just as we started to leave. He tried to talk several times but he was too much out of breath. I was busy building up steam pressure for the run down through the Geneva sag.

Finally, after he had calmed down, he asked, "Did you throw off any coal?"

I told him I had thrown off about a quarter of a ton. He started to cuss.

He said, "I wish you hadn't." He showed me what was inside the sack—four little lady club sandwiches made of cheese!

He said, "That old S.O.B. charged me four bits for that!"

Aw, well! That was American Fork!

But I can also paint you a brighter picture where food is concerned. I lived at Salt Lake while I was firing no. 4 and no. 5 out of Ogden for Art Campbell. I would leave home about two-thirty in the afternoon and ride up to Ogden on the Bamberger Electric Railway. I would eat dinner at home about one or one-thirty. We would come out of Ogden at 5:10 P.M. So in the late evening, by the time we were in the Spanish Fork Canyon, I was starting to feel the pangs of hunger.

There was an engineer at Tucker named Lindsdy, a friend of Art Campbell's. We called him "the Moose." Moose Lindsdy started a restaurant close to the depot at Tucker. Every night when we would drive up to the water tank at Tucker, the Moose would be there to hand Art a paper sack. In that paper sack would be a large wedge of pie and a big sandwich. The sandwich would be made of large, thick slices of homemade bread and a huge slab of dripping hot roast beef.

As we slowly hammered up that four percent grade, Art would almost always eat the pie. Then he would turn and hand me the sack containing the warm, luscious, and generous sandwich. There was nothing ladylike or dainty about that sandwich, and after having eaten at about 1 P.M. and shoveled about sixteen or eighteen tons of coal into the old 768, to say that I relished and enjoyed it would be an understatement. In those strenuous and hectic days of hard work and long hours, I believe I was always overfed or famished.

There was quite a large railroad restaurant in Helper when I first started firing an engine. If you were there at the proper time, you could get a good full course dinner in the dining room for twenty-five cents. However, it was only open for an hour or two around the time of normal meal hours. At other times all meals were served at the lunch counter. The waitresses in the dining room were always just a step or two above those at the short order counters. At least they tried hard to give that impression. It seems they were chosen for their good looks. They were all boomers, and each one claimed to be a former Harvey Girl.

The Harvey Houses along the Santa Fe Railroad were supposed to be famous for, among other attributes, having the best looking and best trained waitresses in the world. If a girl could claim to be a Harvey Girl you could bet she tried to live up to those claims. They were quiet, considerate, well-mannered and agreeable. They did not associate with the girls of lesser charms at the short order counters. And they carried this out in their contacts with the male customers. A rough looking ordinary rail got no special attention. They tolerated him and that was all. But if a member of the town's aristocracy sought their service, he got it.

In those days a young fireman, firing an engine with a scoop shovel, spending hours before the open door of an engine's firebox, could put away a lot of grub at mealtime. I can remember eating steak and egg dinners at Thistle for twenty-five cents. There was at Thistle, just across the tracks from the depot, a large green frame building that housed Ma Henderson's boarding and lodging house. I have often eaten dinner there.

Ma Henderson was a widow. She was well up in years in my time around there. She was regarded with tender affection by all the old rails. I have heard it said that she was wonderfully beautiful as a young girl. In the early days of the railroad at Thistle she had fallen in love with a handsome boomer engineer. They were married, but after the first month or so this boomer, his name was Henderson, disappeared, never to return.

The young wife, after a spell of grieving, started the Henderson boarding house. In due time she gave birth to a baby girl, who grew up around Thistle. She was also a very beautiful girl. She married an engineer named Cramer, but she must have inherited the boomer traits of her father. She left Bert Cramer and started to roam. This happened to several husbands in several successive marriages. Whenever she tired of one husband, she would leave him and after a while return with a new one.

Ma Henderson served a wonderful dinner at her place. I am not sure now, but I think the price was thirty-five cents. Everything was served family style. There would be large platters of meat, potatoes, pies, cakes, and everything that went to make up a fine meal. I never saw bread on the table, but there were always fresh biscuits, hot from the oven. A meal such as Ma Henderson put out could not be duplicated in my opinion for less than three dollars years later.

There was another place, at Manti on the Marysvale branch, that served a specialty. It was located right near the depot. Dinner was always served upon the arrival of the passenger train out of Salt Lake. In those days those passenger trains carried many passengers. It seemed that they would all make it a point to eat at Manti. I was never fortunate enough to fire that job, but I have heard others exclaim loudly on those bounteous banquets. The menu was always chicken—fried chicken, mashed potatoes, cream gravy, and hot biscuits. And a large piece of cream-covered lemon pie!

In 1911, just before I was married, I worked out of Welby. Welby is, or perhaps I should use the past tense since it is no more, about five miles above Midvale on the Bingham Branch. Those were the days before the Bingham and Garfield Railroad had been built, and the Rio Grande handled all the traffic between Bingham and Garfield. Welby was a terminal of sorts where all the crews working in the area were based. There were the usual accommodations for the crews. We would work both ways out of Welby. If we went to Garfield we took all the accumulated tonnage in the yards at Welby across those rolling flatlands to Garfield.

About halfway between those two points was a large farmhouse about half a mile up the slant and off to the side of the tracks. I don't believe a crew went by that place in the daylight that didn't find a large lemon pie and a jug of milk alongside the track. And you can bet your life that this treat was never passed up. As the speed across those flats was slow, it was no trick to gather in the pie and milk on the fly.

I have counted as many as four young ladies standing up the slope at a distance. I was never able to recognize one of them if we ever met, and I don't recall hearing of any of the other crews who did. None ever got that close to them. But they were always there, just out of speaking distance. But I am certain that never before or since did I taste such wonderful lemon pie!

In return for our favor, every engine crew that left Welby or Garfield saved all the lumps of coal that they could get hold of to kick off the engine at "Lemon Pie Slope."

There was another fireman on the road for awhile who was much like me in the quality of his hunger. I truly believe that all he lived for was eating. He was a young fellow about my age. He was from the deep south, and he was a boomer. Already he had seen service on a dozen railroads. His name was Virgil Green. I can't begin to describe the way he pronounced that name with his deep southern accent. While he worked on the Rio Grande that "Casey Jones" song was becoming very popular. There was one verse of that song that he changed to suit his version. The way he would sing it sounded something like this to me.

> *All the hashus knew by the engines scweem,*
> *That the man at the scoop was Vegul Gween!*

There was a tantalizing melody in every word he uttered with that southern accent.

He would say to me, "Next payday let's you and me go up to the Chesapeake or some other place and order the best meal they put out."

I really enjoyed listening to this guy talk as he drawled out that accent. He only stayed on the Rio Grande a few months, then he was off looking for greener pastures. He wanted me to go with him. I have often wondered what my life would have been if I had left the Rio Grande then and went booming along with him. I wonder sometimes what ever became of him.

The present depot in Provo was built late in 1910 or early 1911. Before that the depot was at University (then Academy) Avenue, facing south to the tracks. It was a big lumber structure, a barn-like affair that looked like anything but a railroad depot. There was no part of the yard extending west beyond University Avenue except a few spurs leading off to some local industry. There was a water tank about ten or twelve car lengths east of the avenue.

Over between the legs of the wye was a large ice house. Ice was stored there in the winter to ice the few cars of fruit that originated at Provo during the summer. There was no Utah Railway yard nor the many buildings of the Union Pacific and the Utah that are there now.

The UP maintained a switch engine at Provo during the busy months. But there was no roundhouse to shelter it. During the hours when it wasn't working, this switch engine reposed on a spur leading off the UP mainline about twenty car lengths east of University Avenue. They maintained an engine watchman to coal it from a car load of coal on an adjacent track. He had to clean the fire as well.

The UP ran a little two-car passenger train out of Salt Lake through Provo. Each morning it went down to Nephi or Lyndal. It returned through Provo in the late afternoon. The engine on this job was a little 4–4–0 eight-wheeler with a diamond stack.

I don't think they had a regular carded freight train, although they did run freight through there because every once in a while on the Rio Grande we would race one to the crossing at Lakota. They would usually beat us in this race because they would not have a full tonnage train. They very seldom pulled full tonnage trains until the Utah started turning over trains of coal to the Pedro at Provo. Until that time Provo was just a sleepy little country village.

In the evening when the passenger trains would be due to go through town (both local and through trains) the townspeople would stroll down to the depot just to see them arrive and depart. It was almost the only entertainment in town.

One day a circus was to play at Provo on the vacant spaces south of the tracks. I came out of Salt Lake on a little hog engine early in the morning with four or five coaches. I was firing for Toddy Magee. We went up the Heber branch and picked up passengers for the Provo circus.

We started down the canyon back toward Provo. Every so often we would pick up more passengers; we stopped every time a few people grouped together alongside the tracks. We ran very slowly in order to give the conductor time to collect as many fares as he could. At that I don't believe he got anywhere near all of them. Long before we got to Provo we had passengers crowding into the cab and tender. They were even standing on the running boards.

After unloading our passengers we received orders to take our train and go out on the Springville Branch as far as Goshen and return. We were standing on the lead that ran behind the depot waiting for no. 409, the Tintic passenger train, to come in.

Our conductor, a man named Sealy, was standing on the ground under our cab, flipping silver dollars first to Toddy and then to me.

Number 409 came in, stuck her nose over University Avenue, and stopped. I have often regretted that I had no way of getting a picture of some event in my life, but no more so than of that passenger train.

When that little ten-wheeler came to a stop, passengers climbed down from every conceivable place that they had found room to sit or stand. There were women and children standing out on the running board holding onto the handrail. That would sure have been a picture to show now in this age of automobile and air travel.

In those days, a circus was something to travel far to see. And the main mode of travel was the railroad. There were very few automobiles then or roads on which to run them. When one went by everyone ran out to get a good look.

It was a Fourth of July about 1910 and the Saltair Railroad was faced with handling the holiday traffic. They only had two engines, both little 4–4–0s, eight-wheelers. And they were the neatest little machines you would want to look at, elaborate in color and in tip-top shape.

I don't think those engine crews ever worked anywhere but on that thirteen-mile stretch between Salt Lake and Saltair. What they did in the winter months when the resort was shut down, I have no idea. They did haul a little salt into town from the salt works near the lake, but that wouldn't keep them all in work.

When business on this railroad became heavy on a big holiday, such as the Fourth of July, it would have to borrow power and crews from the Oregon Short Line or the Rio Grande. This day in 1910 it was the Rio Grande. They borrowed a little Rome passenger engine, and I went with it as a fireman.

The engineer was a man named O. S. Dean. He afterward was fired by the Rio Grande for getting out on the mainline in front of no. 61 with a little shay engine. This incident caused a wreck between Murray and Salt Lake that pinned down and killed Vern Wilson under a little hog engine.

This Fourth of July, when we reported for work on that little Rome, a Saltair road employee was there to conduct us to his properties and instruct us in procedures. There was one thing he neglected to tell us that was to give us a very bad scare. I will tell of it later.

When it came our turn to perform we coupled onto the sharp end of ten of those open air cars used during the summer months on the Saltair and Lagoon trains. Those coaches were loaded! Young bucks and even gals were idly walking along the running boards that ran the length of each coach. We left Salt Lake with quite a gang of holiday passengers.

That little Rome was a much bigger and heavier engine than either of the little eight-wheelers. We had orders not to exceed twenty miles an hour.

Halfway between Salt Lake and Saltair was a passing track. On a busy day such as this the westbound and the eastbound trains would meet at that point. We always had to wait for the other train. Our little Rome handled those coaches without effort on that level track.

Just before reaching Saltair there was a wye on which to turn the engines. This wye had a new-fangled switch at the west end. I have never seen anything like it either before or since. I think it was an experiment, although why they should experiment with trainloads of passengers is something I could never figure out. The diagram below illustrates this situation.

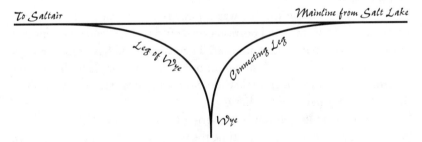

When coming into Saltair this switch looked like the old-fashioned stub switch. It seemed to be lined incorrectly for the oncoming train—as if to lead the train off the end of the track.

O. S. Dean closed the throttle. He was about to big hole a train solidly loaded with passengers. He called to me. I jumped across the cab. I saw a guy standing beside the switch. When he heard O. S. shut off he began to wave us ahead frantically. This was very puzzling, to say the least. That switch was clearly lined to drop us off the right of way, and this guy standing there was signaling us on.

My engineer made a heavy reduction of the pressure in the train line anyway. This, of course, produced a heavy application of the brakes. I was down on the step ready to unload. The guy at the switch with his hat in his hand was still vigorously waving us on. It was a strange situation.

All of a sudden the switch took on a different aspect: It shifted to line up in our favor! We rolled safely over it and continued on to Saltair.

It was supposed to act that way. At a distance of a few feet the oncoming train actuated a device to operate the switch and cause it to line automatically in favor of the oncoming traffic. What benefits were supposed to derive from all of this I never knew. I do know that it gave us an awful scare for a few moments.

The new grade down the western slope off Soldier Summit had only been in operation a few months. When we began handling trains down this new grade we had quite a problem for a while. On the old grade thirteen or fourteen cars of coal were a train. On the new grade we were handling sixty-five loads in a train.

If you held the brakes too long on those long trains you were in danger of stalling. If you didn't keep your brake valve in full release long enough between applications you could break the train in two or three pieces. In the case where the break was so far back that you couldn't back the head end portion up to a re-coupling (in the event it was only a broken knuckle), you would usually wait for a light engine to come down the hill and shove you together.

Of course, if the trouble was a pulled-out or broken drawbar you would have to take the head portion down onto the flat somewhere and set out the car with the broken drawbar. Then you would have to return, get the rest of your train, take it down onto the flat, and couple both portions together. This sometimes took the better part of a day to accomplish, depending on where the break was.

On the day in question I was firing for Needham. Although it was getting quite close to Christmas time the weather was still quite warm. We were in the habit of cutting ourselves a Christmas tree from the hillsides of the canyon. There was an abundance of trees on the hills in those days. At this time I had not yet had the chance to get a tree.

Needham came down into Gilluly with sixty loads. On the big curve above town it happened. Needham broke his train in three pieces. The breaks were too far back to shove them together, but luckily those breaks were both knuckles. After putting in new knuckles there was only one thing to do—wait for a helper engine to come down the hill and shove us together.

I thought this would be a good time to get that Christmas tree while we were waiting. There was nothing on the engine with which I could cut down a tree except a hammer and a cold chisel. I had seen several nice trees on the other side of the canyon.

I took the hammer and chisel and told Needham what I intended doing. He gave his permission. I went to the slope on the other side of the canyon where I had seen what I wanted. It was really a nice tree, although on close inspection it was really bigger than I wanted. I thought it would do.

I started pecking away with the hammer and chisel. As I said, it was quite warm, and I had been walking rather fast in order to get that tree back to the engine before that helper came down the hill to push us together. The sweat was pouring out of me and I was not making much headway with the hammer and chisel. I was getting desperate. I got up off my knees and wiped away the sweat.

I looked upward and said, "Oh, God, give me an axe!"

Now I would not blame you too much if you doubt me, but there, not ten feet away from where I stood, what looked like an axe handle was sticking out from under the brush. I took hold of it and pulled out a lumberman's double-bladed axe! Believe it or not!

With that axe in my hands I soon had my tree. I also had an axe. It was in perfect shape except for a little rust. I think I can explain the presence of that axe. At the time that they were building the new grade down Soldier Summit there were construction camps all over that mountain. When we went up the old grade at night while this was going on the whole mountain would be lighted with flares. If you didn't know where you were and what was going on you might think you had taken the wrong course and entered Satan's territory.

After the grade was completed all these contractors folded their tents and fled into the night. Lots of tools were undoubtedly lost and left behind in the moving. That is probably how that axe came to be there.

There is one little thing that has puzzled me all down through the years. Why didn't I see that handle sticking out before I uttered that makeshift prayer? Do you doubt that someone up there must like me, too? I all but tripped on that axe handle before my supplication. Yet I didn't see it until I made my request.

One cold winter night we were dragging up the Price River canyon. There were lots of trees along the right of way at that time. It was dead of night, and we were slowly dragging up the hill. We had reached the last hard pull just before the let-up where we entered the Kyune tunnel. We were going so slow that I thought I would be able to get a tree, throw it on the train, and catch the helper engine into Kyune.

I told the engineer what I wanted to do. He told me to go ahead and that he would slow down some more. As usual, all I had to cut down a tree was the old reliable hammer and chisel. With these in my hand I dropped off and crossed the frozen Price River to the edge of the mountain on the other side.

There were lots of nice trees there. I had little trouble getting one. I looked at the caboose coming slowly along quite a ways back. I decided I had time to get another one for the engineer, so I went to work.

By the time I got the two trees cut that caboose had moved up toward me. I stuffed the hammer and chisel in my back pocket, grabbed a tree in each hand, and started back across the river. Everything was going along fine. I began to think I would make it with time to spare.

I had reached the middle of the river when the ice broke under me, and I went down in that ice-cold water clear up to the trees. I believe the fact that I was carrying a tree in each hand was all that kept me from going under. After those first few breath-taking chills I managed to climb up on the ice again.

I had lost time and the caboose was moving closer. I decided I would not be able to make it up the bank with both trees, so I left the smallest one on the ice and started to scramble up with the other. I was not having much success. That bank was steep and slippery. My clothes were starting to freeze, and that caboose was coming right along. I saw I wasn't going to make it even with that one tree, so regretfully I let it roll down the bank.

My clothes were ice-encrusted, and it was hard to move. I was beginning to wonder if I would be able to climb on those steps of the engine. The mallet helper was just coming by, and I decided to try for it first. If I missed the engine I would have another chance at the caboose. I don't know how I was able to do it, clothed as I was in those icy clothes, but I did.

I climbed into the cab of the mallet. I reached out for the chain and swung the firedoor open. I stood in that hot glare of the firebox in my icy clothes.

Dave Gibson was the engineer on the mallet. When I opened that door both he and the fireman turned to see what was carrying on. What they saw was the ice-encased, dejected figure of a young male human. The hot glare was turning the ice into steam, and the vapor streamed into the firebox, drawn in by the suction of the exhaust. It was several seconds before they were able to identify what that object was.

Believe me, when I got back to my engine I let the blaze from the firebox play long on my wet clothing. I think, taking everything into consideration, that guy up there was favoring me, even though I didn't get the tree.

My Mentor on the Road

An engineer whom I respected was Toby Sheldahl. I came in off the Bingham Branch, where I had been working for a while, when I got married. Business was booming, and I landed in the mainline pool. This "pool board" consisted of mainline freight crews, working first in, first out. All the engines—mostly eleven hundreds—were pooled as well. No one in the pool had a regular engine.

Lots of new men were hired—students as well as experienced men. It seemed that Toby had been plagued with students. On my first trip with him he learned that I was studying air brakes. He told me that if I would stay on the job as his regular fireman he would teach me to handle trains on the Soldier Summit grade. That was great for me.

After the train had been made ready at Soldier Summit on our second trip westbound, Toby whistled off and then called to me. He had a high, shrill, squeaky voice, and when he was angry, it got higher and squeakier. On account of the pitch of his voice, some of the men called him by the nickname of Squeakie. He said, "All right, Gilbert, come on over and take 'em."

I was not really prepared to take on that responsibility yet. I had already been on a runaway off that summit, and I was still a little bit fearful. I said, "Well, Toby, don't you want to see how they're holding? Don't you want to make the first application?"

"What's the difference whether I make it or you make it?" He squeaked.

He tugged on the throttle and the train started to move into the tunnel. He then stepped down onto the deck and said, "Go on, Gilbert, take 'em."

My feet dragged me very reluctantly over to the right side. When we emerged out the west end of the tunnel I don't believe I ever saw such a dark night. That old oil headlight cast its feeble glow a few feet ahead of the engine. I looked across at Toby. He was sitting on my seat box perfectly contented. How I wished then that I was over there and he was where I was.

Of course I wanted to be able to handle trains on that grade. I would have to if I were going to progress in engine service. And there was no better way for me to learn than under the watchful eye of an artist like Toby. Still, I couldn't help but be a little fearful. I could still feel that little old 951 bouncing along under me, as it had the night I ran away with old Bill Boucher.

When the train edged over onto the grade, I tried to remember all the ways of the different engineers I had watched. I shut off and opened the cylinder cocks. I gradually eased the Johnson bar over into the back motion. As she started to move freely I opened the valve in the water brake line. Saturated steam began swishing from the cylinder cocks. Then the swinging movement of the engine indicated she was pushing back against the train.

I made an application of the brakes. In a short time they responded. When the train was slowed down to a walk I released the brakes. I didn't stop at running position; I pushed the brake valve clear back to release position and left it there. After a short time the train started to pick up speed. I set the brakes again. Then, at a walk, I released. That faintly uncomfortable feeling in my stomach seemed to be easing a little. I was beginning to feel somewhat better. All the way down the canyon I didn't let the speed vary more than a few miles per hour. I was beginning to wonder how I would do when we reached Media. I knew I would have to bring that train to a full stop there or follow the 951 up the side of the mountain.

I looked across at Toby. He seemed to be relaxed—much more than I was. I thought, he sure has got a lot of confidence in a punk like me.

In years afterward I handled lots of trains down that grade for different engineers. But I don't believe I ever did a better job than I did that first time—notwithstanding that my heart was in my throat, so to speak.

At Media, the stop was made with no trouble. Four blasts of the whistle brought one of the lady switch tenders out to line the switch. While we were stopped there, two Tucker engineers with their wives climbed on the engine to ride down to Tucker with us. They had been visiting at Media. Those engineers looked at me rather fearfully, I thought, when they saw who it was that was handling the train. However, I gave them no cause to worry.

I did a very good job going the rest of the way down the hill and into Tucker. I even stopped behind a hill crew caboose at upper Tucker. Our passengers left us there, after those engineers had told me I had done a good job. I knew I had, but if I had had to walk around that engine at that moment I couldn't have done it. I was too weak! My legs had turned to water. I had no feeling there.

When I was firing for Toby I not only handled trains on that grade, I handled trains for him all over the road. I truly believe that I spent almost as much time on the right hand side of the cab when I was working for him as I did on the left. Toby must have been in his late thirties at that time, and he could still do a good job of firing. He had fired regularly for the Casey Jones of the Rio Grande, Tom Loftis. And he did his job as he had learned it from his hero.

He told me that no matter how others ran their engines, when I was running his engine I would have to run it as he did or not at all. I will tell of a little incident in this connection.

At Media the stop board was up out of sight of the derail switch. If you stopped at the board you could not see the switch from the engineer's side of the cab. You would have to depend on the fireman to see the signal. But if you went by the board about ten or twelve car lengths you would be on straight track where the switch could be seen from both sides of the engine. Toby always went by the board before stopping so he could see the switch, and he expected me to do the same.

I always tried to do this, although I would get a little fearful when I got close to the board. One day I was handling our train down that grade. The train was not holding quite as good as it should. When I got down pretty close to the board I set the brakes a little harder. Before I could let go of them again the train came to a stop. I could reach out the cab window and touch the stop board.

Toby didn't say anything just then. He got down and slowly slammed a few scoops of coal into the firebox. Then he looked over at me.

"Gilbert," he said, "how many times have you seen me stop way up here? How many times have you seen me go down onto the straight track?" I believe that was the first time I had displeased him.

I started to say something about stopping at the stop board. He didn't hear me through.

"If you're going to run my engine, you're going to have to run it the way I do. You run it the way I do, and I'll be responsible."

Well, we both became angry, and I gave him his train back right there. I've done a lot of ungrateful stunts in my life, but that was about as silly as any one of them. Toby took a great interest in me, and it was not unreasonable for him to expect me to pattern after him. I could surely do no better. I guess I was always just a punk! I can tell of another incident to illustrate that.

We had been coming up the hill out of Helper on the head end of a drag. As usual, when stopped at the water tank at Colton the water would show at its lowest point in the water glass. I got up on the tender to take water. I thought Toby would keep his injector on until the water level in the boiler rose a little. We had a hard steaming engine and had to take advantage of this stop to gain a little water. Instead, Toby had discovered that he had a hot box on the right side of the tender. He had shut off his injector as soon as we stopped and was down on the ground doctoring this hot box.

When I came down into the cab after taking water I found that we hadn't gained on the water level in the boiler. I started to put on my injector when Toby hollered at me to bring him some waste. I started to grumble, and he heard me. He wanted to know what I was mad about. I told him how low the water in the boiler was, and all the while we had been standing there with no injector on.

He told me that he knew where the water was, but that this hot box was more important right now. We argued back and forth until we were both angry. After leaving Colton neither of us spoke again.

When ready to leave Soldier Summit, Toby said, "Do you want to take 'em down the hill, Gilbert?"

I told him no, and to take 'em down himself—which he did. When we stopped at Tucker, it developed that the trainmaster had been riding in the caboose. He walked up to the engine and congratulated Toby on the fine handling of the train down the mountain. He said, "You could have stopped anywhere on a dime."

Toby answered and said, "Yes, and my fireman can do just as good a job as I did."

If that wasn't heaping coals of fire on my head I don't know what would be.

Toby once pulled a little stunt that I thought was pretty good. About five miles west of Provo the Union Pacific and the Rio Grande mainlines cross each other on a conventional diamond crossover. At that time all trains on each road had to stop before going into this crossover. The UP trains were very light compared to those of the Rio Grande. If UP and Rio Grande trains approached this crossing at nearly the same time it was always the UP train that was able to stop and start the quickest.

One morning we were going west with a heavy coal train. A light UP train was dogging along on the paralleling track. We could tell that he was in no hurry. With that light train he knew he could get stopped and started again before we could with that heavy coal drag (a slow, heavy coal train). But Toby fooled him!

Instead of driving right up to the usual stopping place, Toby stopped almost a half a mile back. He hurriedly whistled the required two blasts and started up again, moving slowly and laboriously. By the time the UP man, who had gone on to his usual stopping place, was stopped we were underway again. and with increasing speed we were approaching that crossover.

Having made the stop and whistled off, under the rules we had the right of way. That UP man didn't dare try to beat us to the crossing! I can still visualize the foolish look of chagrin on his face as we passed him by.

In the early days of railroading, before the introduction of automatic lubricators, it was quite a problem to keep the valves in the steam chest oiled. All engines had a suction cup, or relief valve, on top of the steam chest. If a person poured oil in this suction cup while the engine was drifting with the throttle shut off, the oil would be sucked into the steam chest. That was the only way to oil those valves before the advent of the lubricator.

For this purpose all engines were originally supplied with a tallow pot full of mutton tallow to be poured into those relief valves. That's where those cans got the name of tallow pots. The fireman was also called a "tallow pot," because it was he who had to grab that can whenever the engineer shut off and started to drift. He would run out on the running board, jump down on the steam chest, and pour mutton tallow into those relief valves.

Those valves were still maintained on all engines long after I quit firing. If Toby and I were called for an engine that had been standing around for any length of time, Toby would run the engine down the track and shut off. I would be out on the steam chest with the tallow pot containing valve oil. The moment he shut off I would start dribbling valve oil into the relief valves. In this way our valves were always well oiled before the lubricator started working.

One day I was out on the right steam chest waiting for Toby to shut off and drift. I had a tallow pot in my hand. As soon as he shut off I started pouring oil into the relief valve. I noticed that the valves seemed to give out a little more smoke than usual. All at once I heard the high piping voice of Toby:

"Gilbert! Gilbert! What the h—— are you doing!"

Then after a few oaths he yelled, "Come in here!"

Still I didn't know what I had done wrong. When I got back in the cab Toby had his cap off and was mopping his forehead with a chunk of waste. He looked at me with a very disgusted look on that Swedish countenance of his.

"Gilbert, what kind of oil do we use in those valve chambers?"

"Why, valve oil, of course," I answered.

"All right, get the tallow pot with the valve oil and go back out there, and let's try it again," he said disgustedly.

It was then that I tumbled. In my hurry to get out on the steam chest I had grabbed the can containing engine oil. Engine oil is no good on a hot valve. It just burns up and emits a stenchful smoke. Toby recognized my error before I did. As the years go by my memories of Toby grow fonder and fonder. How grand he really was!

One morning we were called to help no. 5 from Helper to Soldier Summit. We were a mainline pooled crew at the time, so we had a caboose between our engine and the road engine. At Colton we spotted the road engine for water. At Soldier Summit we cut off, together with that caboose and deadhead train crew. We received orders to make up a train at Soldier Summit and proceed westbound.

We had quite a job getting that train together. At last, when we were ready to leave, I began to experience trouble getting my injector to pick up the water. Just before leaving town I scrambled back over the coal in the tank to take a look at the water level. I raised the manhole cover and looked down into the tank. There wasn't enough water in that tank to wet the soles of your shoes! I began to wonder what we would do. There was no water tank at Soldier Summit at that time. Toby had already started the train.

"Toby!" I yelled, "we're out of water!"

A slightly impatient, worried look crossed his face for an instant. He looked out the cab window for a second. We were just entering the snowshed.

"Don't put any more coal in her, Gilbert," he said.

He continued on through the snowshed. On emerging from the west end of that shed the grade dropped sharply to a steady four percent. This was the old grade. As soon as the train started to roll Toby shut off. I was in a sort of a quandary.

He turned to me and in a matter-of-fact tone said, "Kill her, Gilbert."

I wondered if I had heard right, although I knew it was the only safe thing to do. But what were we going to do then? We were just tipping over onto a four percent grade with a train of coal and would have a dead engine on the point.

"What did you say, Toby?" I queried. I knew what he said the first time, but I couldn't believe it.

"I said, 'Kill her, Gilbert, kill her!'" he replied.

I knew there was nothing else to do. I grabbed the long shaker bar and proceeded to shake the fire into the ash pans. Already what water remained in the boiler had rolled down into the slanting front end. I knew the "crown sheet" must be bare. The "crown sheet" is that part of the boiler on top of the firebox which must be kept covered with water or it could cause an explosion. It was up to me to get that fire out from under that crown sheet fast, and that didn't take long.

I climbed up on my seat box. This was a new one on me. Here we were rolling down that four percent grade with a full train of coal shoving us on down with a dead engine. The nearest water was forty-five minutes away at Tucker.

After thinking our situation over for a few minutes I gradually came to the realization of what Toby was intent on doing. He was going to get that train down to the water tank at Tucker before what steam was left in the boiler was all exhausted. As long as that steam was enough to run the pump we were safe. It was a case of taking the train with us on our run for water. I had never heard of this before, and I was worried.

Once in a while, as we descended that treacherous grade, Toby would slant an encouraging glance in my direction. I thought, well, if he wasn't afraid, why should I be?

We made the stop at and left Medea okay. We still had quite a bit of steam. I began to think we would make it to Tucker and the water spout before that steam ran out on us. This was one time I was glad that Toby was handling that train and not I.

It was a little better than forty minutes since I had killed the fire in that engine when Toby finally spotted her under the spout at Tucker. As I rode that spout to let water into the tank I could see Toby throwing pieces of wood up into the gangway.

Between the two of us we soon had a wood fire roaring under that dead engine's crown sheet. We lost a little time at Tucker getting that old eleven hundred back to life before proceeding on our way. It was just one more lesson I learned at the hands of the old Swedish master. But this was not all. On two occasions afterward I saw Toby pull that same stunt.

I had heard a tale about Toby that went the rounds before I became acquainted with him. At the time I heard it I had laughed somewhat in disbelief.

It seems that Toby was working on a hill crew out of Tucker. One warm afternoon they were coming down the old Soldier Summit grade. Toby, it seems, was having a little difficulty keeping his train under control.

The brakemen were lolling about out on top of the cars where they belonged on that mountain.

Still having difficulty, Toby finally grabbed the whistle cord and sent a long call out for brakes. The head brakeman was riding about three cars behind the engine. When Toby sent out that call for brakes, instead of going after those brake wheels with his brake club he strolled leisurely over to the engine. He climbed down into the cab and glanced up at the air gauge and remarked, "Oh, you got lots of air."

Toby got angry. His high, piping voice really squeaked as he said, "I didn't call for an argument; I called for brakes! Now get back out on top and tie 'em down."

That brakeman got back out on the car tops of that train and tied 'em down. It suddenly dawned on him that if Toby had reported his actions he would be joining the boomers. What he had done was a dischargeable offence. When an engineer called for brakes on that grade, that call had to be taken seriously.

After I go to know Toby, I brought this legendary incident to his attention one day when we were in a genial mood. I asked Toby if the way I heard it was right. He said it was accurately told.

He added with some indignation, "The idea of a brakeman coming over to the cab to tell an engineer that he has plenty of air after he has called for brakes!"

He was right! After all, who is better qualified to know what was needed than the engineer who was handling the train?

I have known several brakemen and conductors who were fairly well up on air brake operation. But the majority of them knew little more about it than the average layman. The brakeman in this case thought that as long as the air gauge showed a supply of air, that was all that was needed. I have seen many trains where the condition of the brakes and not the air supply made the difference in braking operations.

There were a lot of the old engineers who were not up on the latest practice in air brakes. This was especially true of those older men who had taken the examination in the early days of air brakes.

I was firing for old Art Campbell one day. We were coming west on no. 5 with engine 768. On approaching Midvale the train seemed to drag. In fact, after passing the water tank, Art started to work steam. He called to me. He knew that I had made quite a study of air brakes.

I glanced up at his air gauge. Both hands were together and far lower than they should be. Art looked at me inquiringly. I thought a moment.

At that time the SF4 pump governor had two heads with three pipe connections. The SF4 was a particular speed control applied to the air pumps or compressors on locomotives. I thought I knew what the trouble was. By now those brakes had almost dragged us down to a stop. I grabbed a monkey wrench and a hammer. The pump and governor were on my side of the engine. As I hurriedly pushed the door open and stepped out on the running board I knew my diagnosis was right. I could hear the air squirting from the top pipe to the excess pressure head of the governor, which was broken.

I held the monkey wrench under the lower, or main, reservoir connection to that head and brought the hammer down sharply on the pipe. The connections were of copper and about the thickness of your little finger. When I brought the hammer down on that pipe it put a kink in it, closing the flow of air to the underside of the governor. This cut the excess head out of service, allowing the pump to start again, which it did merrily. We were still pulling against stuck brakes, but I knew that would be only momentary until the pump built up the train line pressure and backed off the brakes.

I went back into the cab and told Art, "It will be all right in a minute."

Sure enough, when the pressure in the train line built up sufficiently, the brakes released and we began to pick up speed.

"What did you do, Eddie?" Art asked. (Somewhere in the dim past, Art had had a fireman named Eddie something-or-other. He must have thought a lot of this fireman because everyone who fired for him thereafter was Eddie to him.)

I told him that the top pipe to the excess pressure head was broken at the point of connection with the governor, and that I had plugged the bottom pipe by putting a kink in it. I said that when we stopped at Salt Lake I intended to plug the top pipe the same way. Thereafter and until we reached Ogden the high pressure head would stop the pump at 130 pounds, but he could control the train line pressure with the feed valve. At Ogden he could report the governor system as in bad order and in need of repair.

We did this and had no further trouble. That little repair job that I had done saved a delay to no. 5 that day. Not only that, but it was recounted among those old heads all over the road. I was then known as an air-brake crazy fireman.

An International Correspondence School air brake car stopped at Salt Lake for several weeks. I visited it several times and became well acquainted with the instructor. When he found out that I was a pupil of ICS he arranged for me to conduct a class. Of course it was a boost for his school to have a student so well advanced in the subject conducting a class.

I also conducted an air brake class at the railroad YMCA at Helper. This class consisted of firemen who had received instruction to report for the examination as engineers. They were all east-end men.

The way I got into this was as follows. There were some large air brake charts on the wall in the reading room of the YMCA. An engineer running a switch engine in the Helper yard had been injured some time before. He was off duty and moving about on crutches. Several of the firemen who had been notified of the coming examinations had persuaded him to instruct them with these charts. He was sitting in front of those charts with a long pointer in his hand. The would-be engineers were gathered around him as he explained their workings. I wandered over to see what was carrying on. When I found out it was air brakes I became interested right away. Whenever there was an air brake discussion I tried to be in on it, so I joined the gang. I didn't know any of those east-end men, nor did they know me except by sight.

I listened to the guy with the pointer for a while. Soon I detected a mistake in his instructions. I called him on it. We had a short argument; then after I explained, he admitted that I was right. He didn't like it though. To get even he asked me a question about an incident that had recently happened in the Helper yard. I had heard of this before and had already formed my opinion. I gave him my answer. He conceded that I was right.

About that time the fire whistle at the roundhouse let go, and we all ran out to see where the fire was. It proved to be a minor blaze near the coal chute. When things settled down again, those east-end men came to me in a body. They told me they were trying to wise up on air brakes, as they had all been called up for promotion. If I didn't have anything pressing, they wanted me to go back to the YMCA and talk air brakes with them. I was always ready to talk air brakes at that time, so that's what I did.

At one time I had quite a collection of charts on air brakes and Mitchell models to go with them. These models were made of heavy cardboard. They had movable parts, so you could move them to the different service positions and note the different connections and ports.

I remember the last time I saw Toby. Business had fallen off a bit, and Toby had gone to Helper to take a helper turn. He had obligated himself for some acreage out at Orem on the Provo Bench, so he needed a job that paid more than the Salt Lake pool. I was firing fast freight out of Ogden. One morning we were going down the Price River Canyon on no. 62. At Nolon a westbound drag was pounding up the hill with a mallet helper on the rear end.

As we came even with this helper and were about to pass I could see the engineer standing in the left-hand gangway. He waved a friendly greeting to me and then crossed back to the right side. It was Toby Sheldahl!

That night when they woke me up at the YMCA to call me to return on no. 61, the callboy told me the news: Toby Sheldahl had been killed in a rear end collision on the curve just east of Colton! To say I was shocked would be putting it mildly. I was grief stricken.

I don't remember much of our westbound trip. It was usual for a death to have a sad effect on all members of the crew, to cast a pall of melancholy over the entire railroad for that matter. But with me this was something beyond that. I just couldn't get used to the thought that Toby— good old Toby—was gone. I remembered the many times he had favored me, and the many times I had shown little gratitude. Why, I was even called Toby myself by some of the railroaders who knew us and knew that we worked together. It was not uncommon to nickname a fireman after his regular engineer. So it was with us.

Many a time on the road I would have gone hungry if it hadn't been for Toby's interest and generosity. He treated me like a son, not like the ungrateful pup that I was.

I do know that all the way home I had a hard time. It was all there in my throat, and I managed to keep it there. But when I arrived home I couldn't hold back any longer. I went into the bathroom, closed the door, and gave way to my feelings. I sobbed like a baby. Mom pounded on the door and wanted to know what the trouble was. I told her Toby had been killed. Then I really let go.

It isn't the usual thing for an engineer to cross the deck to wave a greeting at a crew going in the opposite direction. I wonder what prompted him to do it on that last trip.

Toby had made his help to Soldier Summit and was returning to Helper. On the east end of the big curve just out of Colton he had been stopped by a work train. This work train had held him there until his time was up. They decided to couple into his engine and back him up into Colton to await the dogcatcher crew. They were outside of yard limits and should have had a flag out.

An eleven hundred-class engine had made a help to the Summit and was coming down the eastbound mainline. The engineer was a man named Joe Newman. He stopped and took a little water at Colton, then started again. Rounding the curve below Colton he saw the work train backing the mallet. It was too late to stop.

He hit the mallet that Toby was riding pretty hard. It seemed that Toby must have had some warning of the impending collision, and must have been trying to get out of his seat, because when the impact came it smashed the tender up against the brake valve stand, pinning Toby between them.

It developed that Newman with that eleven hundred hit Toby's engine just eleven minutes after leaving Summit. When you consider that he stopped to take a little water at Colton, he must have been travelling pretty fast—too fast.

They got Toby out and put him in a caboose and started to make a dash for Salt Lake for medical attention. He was still alive at the time. They notified his wife at Orem, and she got to the depot at Provo just as the engine and caboose with Toby came into town. She went aboard the caboose and took Toby's head in her lap.

"What happened, Daddy?" she asked.

Toby started to say, "Aw, that crazy Joe Newman ..."

She interrupted him, "No, No, Daddy. It was an accident."

Toby said, "Yes Dear, it was an accident." Then he died with his head in her lap.

The conductor on that work train was a man by the name of Richardson. He left the Rio Grande and went to the Utah Railway when I did. I worked with him quite a bit before he became incapacitated. I never looked at him without thinking:

"If you had used a little horse sense maybe Toby would be alive today."

Of course, this was before the advent of block signals. If block signals had existed they would have prevented this occurrence.

I have been around a lot of accidents. I have lost a number of acquaintances whom I considered good friends. I have seen men stretched out in death to whom I had been talking a few moments earlier. But the death of Toby hit me harder than anything that had happened to me previously. I didn't get over that for a long time. I just couldn't forget how ungrateful I had acted to his favors and his interest in me.

ℱireman JJ

The wind blustered against the back curtain, and it sneaked with stinging fury in under it where its length was just short of reaching the deck. The old fellow stood facing the open fire door, his back against the flapping curtain. His hands were sunk deep in the side pockets of a dilapidated old overcoat that he huddled in to keep out the weather. At best it only partially protected him from the cold. He was almost hidden in its many folds. Being much too large it reached almost to the shoddy footwear that encased his feet.

He was quite old. The dull glow from the open fire door flickeringly revealed the lines of many years on his shadowy features. His faded blue eyes swimming in water, his feeble shuffling and his asthmatic cough attested to his misery.

Fall weather had come and gone, and now we were deep in the clutch of a brutal winter. Most of that traveling fraternity that habitually rode the freight trains had long ago journeyed to the warmer climes, but occasionally a late straggler could be seen shivering with the cold on top of a boxcar. Rather than witness their agonies, we the crew members would get them up in the comfortable warmth of the engine cab.

In those long gone days of steam we could usually use an extra hand on the engine. We always had an extra shovel. When the coal in the tender got too far back for the fireman to reach it without taking additional steps, that third man could exercise that extra scoop to keep it up within his reach. In this manner he earned his passage and frequently a hot meal at some beanery along the way.

This old fellow had fulfilled the duties of a coal passer, and now as we waited in the passing track for an eastbound hot shot to roll, he shivered there on the deck trying to soak up a little of the heat that radiated out from the open firebox door.

What a study in the scale of humanity he made as he stood with his back against the storm curtain, his features outlined in the flickering glow from the firebox: his watery pale blue eyes, the white stubble of beard, and the dirty grey hair that peeped out from beneath the rim of a ragged cap.

"Where was he going?" The engineer asked that often-asked question. He received that many-timed answer.

He didn't know—just on the go—or maybe to that mythical temporary job somewhere further on. Maybe he was going to meet a friend—or a long neglected relative. Anyway the grass must be greener on the other side of the mountain!

A few ragged shreds on the bottom of the overcoat swept back and forth over the deck as the wind shrieked in. The old man shivered miserably.

The engineer casually remarked. "You're pretty old to be looking for a job. What could you do?"

There was no definite answer, just an evasive muttering.

"You would have to have other clothes," the engineer persisted unfeelingly. "No one would hire you in those rags. What have you worked at?"

Receiving no answer the engineer, with a smirk, turned away.

Except for the moaning of the dying wind, and the doleful whine of the engine dynamo, there was only silence in the engine cab—that cold, lonely, silence that comes in the sleepy hours of the night. The old fellow kept his bleary eyes focused on the lazy flames in the firebox.

The engineer stamped his feet on the floor boards and started to sing in undertone to keep away the approach of sleep. His efforts ceased, and he turned abruptly to the old man. The slight grimace of a smile played around his mouth.

"Can you sing, Dad?" he asked of the old fellow.

"I could sing ... and I have sung a lot ... when I was younger. I can't sing now... but," and his eyes glittered in the fire's glow, "I can recite poetry."

The engineer smiled across the cab at me. "Well, let's have something," he commanded.

The old fellow stepped a little closer to the open fire door. He glanced down at the snow filming in over the deck—the curtain rattled behind him. He produced a rag from somewhere in the folds of the long overcoat and asthmatically blew his nose. Then after coughing a time or two, he started.

Have you ever heard or read that poetical gem that was written by that Hoosier poet, James Whitcomb Riley, and labeled "That Old Sweetheart of Mine"?

If you have, I wonder if you heard it under more incongruous conditions and surroundings than I was privileged to hear it from the faltering lips of that wreck of a man as he shivered there on the cold deck of our locomotive. At times his voice sank almost to inaudibility. Again it rose to an emotional pitch that seemed incredible from such an unbelievable source!

After he had started, he had, except for the wind and the mournful whine of the dynamo, a completely silent audience.

> *An old sweetheart of mine,*
> *Is this her presence here with me?*
> *Or but the vain creation*
> *Of a lover's memory?*
> *A fair elusive vision*
> *That would vanish into air.*
> *Dared I even touch the silence,*
> *With the whisper of a prayer?*

I must say I learned to love that piece of poetry after hearing it recited by that shambling shivering wreck of humanity, there on the cold deck of a locomotive. I have read it over countless times since.

> *As one who comes of evening*
> *Or'e an album all alone,*
> *And muses on the faces*
> *Of the friends that he has known.*
> *So I turn the leaves of fancy*
> *'Til in shadowy design,*
> *I find the smiling features*
> *Of an old sweetheart of mine.*

Could this old fellow at one time in the distant past have called someone "Sweetheart"? If so, where and what had come of it? With eyes that appeared tear-washed and in a voice that sometimes seemed choked down, he struggled on!

> *Tho' I hear beneath my study*
> *Like a fluttering of wings,*
> *The voices of my children*
> *And their mother as she sings.*
> *I feel no twinge of conscience*
> *To deny me any theme,*
> *When care has cast her anchor,*
> *In the harbor of a dream.*

I am here quoting only a few lines of that beautiful poem:

> *In fact to speak in earnest,*
> *I believe it adds a charm,*
> *To spice the good a trifle,*

With a little dust of harm.
For I find an extra flavor
In memory's mellow wine,
To make me drink the deeper
To that old sweetheart of mine.

Yes, I concluded that even he must have had a sweetheart at one time or he couldn't put so much passion in his reciting. And the tears were starting to stream down his seamy cheeks.

With eyes half closed in clouds
That ooze from lips that taste as well,
The peppermint and cinnamon,
I hear the old school bell.
And from Recess I romp in again
From Blackman's broken line,
To smile behind my lesson,
At that old sweetheart of mine.

Along about here the old fellow hesitated momentarily, and I wondered if that could be the finish. It didn't seem right that it should end that way. The engineer turned to look at him, too, but there was no ridicule in his glance, only respect.

A face of lily beauty
With a form of airy grace,
Floats out of my tobacco,
As the Genie from the vase.
And I thrill beneath the glances
Of a pair of azure eyes,
As glowing as the summer
And as tender as the skies.

To continue this narrative would only be to quote the poem to the end as it was recited by our guest:

I can see the pink sunbonnet,
The brightly checkered dress;
She wore when first I kissed her
And she answered the caress;
With a written declaration that
As surely as the vine
Grew 'round the stump she loved me,
That old sweetheart of mine!

Again I found myself wondering if anyone such as he could have had a sweetheart. Did this beautiful classic have special significance for him?

Did it bring back fond memories of a distant past when he as a young gallant courted a maid such as he was describing? I vainly tried to picture him as a young man.

Although the tears streamed down his cheeks, and although the shrieks of the wind and the whine of the dynamo tried to drown out his efforts, he continued to the end:

> But Ah! My dream is broken
> By a step upon the stair,
> And the door is softly opened
> And my wife is standing there.
> Yet with eagerness and rapture
> All my visions I resign,
> To greet the living presence,
> Of that old sweetheart of mine!

Surely he must have had a sweetheart at one time. But what had happened to put him in the condition and circumstance he now found himself? We can only guess.

All this happened when I was a very young man. So whatever it was that separated them, by now they must be together again. He must be with his old sweetheart now.

At the Rat Hole
Flashing the Door

*T*he town of Tucker imprinted itself deeply in my memory, although I only actually worked out of there not more than one week. It was a station on the pioneer Utah and Pleasant Valley narrow gauge railroad that ran from Provo to the coal fields in and around what later came to be known as Scofield. At Tucker the primitive tracks followed the South Fork of the canyon and through a series of switchbacks crossed the spine of the Wasatch somewhat south of Soldier Summit.

When the Rio Grande came through in the eighties they purchased this early railroad and incorporated the trackage from Tucker to Provo. That part of the line that went up the South Fork was abandoned and a new line built up the North Fork to cross the range at what is now Soldier Summit. This put Tucker at the foot of a seven mile stretch of line that was something just over four percent in grade. This presented a very difficult operating problem.

To get trains over this grade required many of the little engines of that day. It was at Tucker that several helpers, in addition to the one usually picked up at Thistle, were coupled on to the passenger trains and some "hot shot freights" for the last assault on the treacherous grade. It was also here that the slower "drag freights" were broken into more manageable shorter segments.

The mainline crews with helpers pushing and pulling would take the first cut of cars on up the hill. The remaining segments were worked up the grade by what came to be called hill crews working out of Tucker. At Summit these segments were reassembled into normal length trains to be taken by the mainline crews on down the Price River canyon to Helper. The hill crews would then return to Tucker to repeat the process.

These hill crews were a society unto themselves. They lived and worked at Tucker, making many trips just up that seven mile stretch of heavy grade. They contented themselves with the lonely and somewhat primitive living conditions of their town, which had some of the atmosphere of the Old West. The hillsides of the several canyon spurs extending out from the center of railroad operations at Tucker were lined with shanties haphazardly built. Some were no more than dugouts in the sides of the mountain. The amenities of life were few.

It was there, early in my railroad career, that I first witnessed violent action. I was making one of my first trips as a fireman. I don't remember who the engineer was, but the conductor of our train was a man named Tom Gleason. We had arrived at Tucker and were on the eastbound track spotted at the coal chute taking on coal. Number 3, for some reason that I can't now recall, came down into town over the eastbound track.

Taking coal in those days was not the simple operation it developed into later. It was cumbersome and time consuming. On this occasion we were clearly in no. 3's path, and we were holding them up—"laying them out," in the parlance of the railroad.

Our conductor, Tom Gleason, was doing all he could to hurry the operation up after no. 3, contrary to the usual practice, came down the eastbound mainline. The conductor of no. 3, Mr. Moss, came down resplendent in his passenger conductor's uniform. He was a large man, really too big for his own good. Our conductor, Gleason, was just of ordinary size and stature.

Moss came forward from the coaches to see what was holding up his train. He promptly became abusive and got into an argument with Gleason. Tom told him that we were getting out of the way as quickly as we could. That didn't satisfy Moss. He continued to heap loud verbal abuse on our conductor. He started to say, "you sons of ———," but got no further. Gleason flashed out a straight left that landed directly on the chin of Conductor Moss. He went down like a bull hit in the head with a spike maul. I later learned that Conductor Gleason was a part-time professional wrestler.

Conductor Gleason was a little fearful of being fired for this stunt. We tied up at Colton on this trip. He learned that I had just lifted the coal apron into place and from my ringside seat was looking directly at them when the action had taken place. He wanted me to testify in his favor at the investigation if there was one. Of course his only defense was the abusive language of Conductor Moss.

I assured him that I had heard and seen all that went on and would testify to it at the investigation. Curiously, there was never an investigation called, and I never worked on the same crew with Gleason again. He took a hill crew job, and I worked on the mainline.

Sometimes unusual incidents will have a strange aftermath. It was about a year after the above incident took place that I was boxing a preliminary to one of the professional fights being held in Salt Lake. After the fight a well-dressed man stepped up to me and said:

"Gould. You are Gould, aren't you?"

There was reason to question my identity, since I boxed under the name of Johnny Gilbert. I said, yes, my real name was Gould.

He said, "Well, I just wanted to ask you a question. Did you copy that straight left you used tonight from the one you saw me land on Moss that night at Tucker?"

To my surprise it was Conductor Gleason. I had not seen him in street clothes before. That was why I had failed to recognize him. We laughed heartily over a fervent handshake.

Very early in my railroad career I was working out of Tucker with a bridge and building gang. We had a little Rome engine, the 37, afterwards renumbered as the 544. We had a pile driver in the outfit and were replacing old piles in the bridges between Thistle and Tucker. Every night we tied up at Tucker. I think we had worked about five days on this job.

Those little Rome engines were ten-wheelers. They were the second series of ten-wheelers built for the Rio Grande Western after the line was converted to standard gauge. Their driving wheels were a scant 57 to 60 inches, depending on the thickness of the tires. They had a long narrow firebox set on the frame between the driving wheels. They had been built for mainline passenger service in the nineties. With the coming of the T-29 class ten-wheelers in 1909 they were downgraded to other duties. This is why we had one at Tucker on the bridge and building work train.

One night while we were asleep there came a call boy into the room who rudely awakened us. It developed that a few minutes earlier the hostler, in backing an engine out of the roundhouse, had run over a young fireman named Russell and a hostler helper. The fireman's legs were cut off just

A Rome ten-wheeler. This Rio Grande Western 54 became the Denver & Rio Grande 506. Photo from the W. J. G. Gould collection, photographer unknown.

above the knee. The hostler helper was somewhat luckier. His right leg was cut off between the ankle and the knee.

They hurriedly loaded these two injured men into a little four-wheeled caboose normally used by one of the hill crews and called us to take them to the hospital at Salt Lake.

The engineer I was working with was a man by the name of Delany. He was a new man, a boomer, and had not been employed by the railroad as long as I had. Consequently he didn't know the road. Our conductor was an old head, but had always worked on the hill crews, and he was likewise unfamiliar with the mainline east of Summit or west of Tucker. I recall he had a large black handlebar moustache and looked fierce like an old time pirate. But his looks belied him. He was a very fine man. I had occasion to work with him quite a bit in after years. However, at that moment of excitement and fear I didn't know which presented the rougher picture, the conductor or the boomer engineer.

We left Tucker with rights over all trains from Tucker to Thistle. I knew the stations in succeeding order, and that was about all. Delany depended on me to keep him informed as to our whereabouts. When we passed a station I would tell him what it was. If I happened to be down on the deck he would call out, and I would tell him what station it was.

At Thistle the "stop board" was out, and we stopped for orders. Our conductor came over and advised the engineer to go faster. We dropped down to Provo pretty fast and spotted for water. A doctor with a nurse climbed into that four-wheeled caboose. Again the conductor told the engineer he wasn't going fast enough. This seemed to make Delany angry. He told me to watch the stations and always tell him where we were.

We left Provo and Delany hooked that rattling Johnson bar very close to center. He gave her plenty of throttle, and we bounced along right smart. Those little Romes could sure kick back the miles when they had a train they could handle. That one little four-wheeled caboose was just like we were running light engine. After leaving town I had my work to do. Not a little of it was trying to stand up on that bouncing quarter deck.

From Tucker to Provo, being all down grade, I had very little to do in the way of stoking the fire. But after we left Provo I had to keep up the steam pressure. This kept me down on the deck most of the time. When we went by a station Delany would yell and I would call back the name. I had plenty of trouble trying to keep my feet and shovel coal into that roaring firebox. I think about half of the coal I aimed at the fire door went in. The other half spewed all over the deck. I was wading in coal ankle deep when the conductor pulled the air and stopped us at Murray. It seemed like we had just left Provo. After he stopped us the conductor called Delany down to the ground. They walked slowly around the engine conversing.

The conductor told Delany that there was no rush now. The fireman had just died. The nurse was in tears. The doctor was down on his knees praying. All on account of the high speed. The conductor's words didn't seem to pacify Delany. When he climbed back on the engine he told me to watch out, and not let him run by that Pedro crossing at Ninth South.

It seemed to me that we had no more than got nicely underway again, and I was bouncing around on the deck like a rubber ball trying to get a little coal in the firebox, when he yelled, "What's this light we're coming to?"

I was thinking of the distant signal light for the Pedro crossing. I said to myself, you're not there yet.

But I dropped the scoop and straightened up to see. Delany was just going under that distant signal! I could hardly believe it! I told him he'd better shut off and start getting under control. About that time we caught the home signal, and it showed green. We zoomed over Ninth South without hesitation. We then drifted through the yards under control to the depot at Second South between Fifth and Sixth West.

When we had stopped Delany looked at his watch. It had been just forty-two minutes since we had left Provo. That included the several minutes that we were stopped at Murray. Now how is that for fast running with those comparatively low driving wheels on that little old Rome? They don't do any better than that today with all the fancy power they have in the newer engines!

In the spring of 1911 business took a nose dive. I couldn't hold a job on the mainline, so another fireman named Bill Fullmer and I gathered a roll of bedding and went to Welby. Welby was a terminal on the Bingham Branch five miles west up the grade from Midvale.

Welby was quite a place before the Bingham and Garfield Railroad was built. There was a twelve stall roundhouse and a large coal chute. There was a large hotel, an eating house, a pool hall, a general store, and about twenty-five or thirty dwellings. There were also a dozen or more shacks built by and batched in by employees who lived at Midvale and worked out of Welby.

All the small mallets worked out of Welby, besides a few eleven hundreds and a couple of little hogs that handled the "ping pong" jobs. "Ping pong" was the name given the short trains that plied the track between Midvale and Welby. They worked night and day, moving loads or empties up and down, to and from Midvale. Anyone working for the railroad could ride these trains without a pass. In addition to other traffic there was a commuter's special to accommodate employees who lived at Midvale and worked at Welby.

While I worked at Welby a new general superintendent was installed at Salt Lake. None of us had seen him up to that point. I was quite a fancy dresser in those days. I had on a nice brown suit and a grey vest, with a watch chain strung across the front, hooked to a watch on each end. Sometimes I also wore a lady's little gold watch in my upper left coat pocket. I had what seemed to be about a yard of thin gold chain threaded through the hole in my coat lapel to secure that watch. It wasn't everyone who wore low cut dress shoes at that time, but I did.

One night I came out of Salt Lake on the street car. The ping pong was standing by the depot at Midvale ready to take off for Welby. The engineer was leaning out of the cab window, half asleep. I walked by the cab without saying a word. I climbed on the caboose, and as I was about to enter the door I heard the hoghead say to someone below the cab on the ground:

"Was that the new superintendent?"

My fancy clothes got me in bad at another time. I was firing out of Welby when an engineer named Jappy Bar turned an eleven-hundred class engine over at the switch at Ritter. Ritter was about nine or ten miles from Welby on the way to Garfield. That wreck tied up the railroad for a while.

The wrecker came out from Salt Lake on its way to Ritter. We all knew it was coming. I got all dressed up in my best and had a Kodak hanging on a strap from my shoulder. When the wrecker arrived I climbed on to ride out to the wreck—Kodak and all.

When we got out there, the old 1192 was lying peacefully on her side. I approached the wreck and started to unlimber my Kodak. The branch superintendent came up and said in what I thought was quite a friendly manner, "Hello there!" I returned the salutation.

He then said, "What are your intentions?"

I said, "I'm going to get a picture."

He said rather nonchalantly, "Oh, what are you going to get a picture of?"

"I'm going to get a picture of that engine," I replied. His cordial manner changed instantly.

"No you're not!" He said rather belligerently. "If you want a nice picture you can take one of that old jackass standing over there on the other side of the fence. You fold up that thing and get the h—— off the right of way."

I folded up my camera and beat it back to Welby on foot. I hadn't learned at that time that railroad companies are rather touchy about having pictures taken of accidents on their properties.

A few days later I went into the telegraph office to see if there was any mail for me. Alongside the wall were pigeon holes in alphabetical order for the placing of mail. There was a door leading into the superintendent's office from the hallway. The door was wide open. Leaning back against the wall, relaxing in a chair, was the superintendent. He eyed me up and down closely. I had just got off the engine and was in my greasy overalls. I was about to walk out, when he called to me.

"Come in here a minute," he said.

I walked into his office, wondering, what now?

He said, "Stand over there."

I did while he looked me over. Finally he said, "The next time you doll up out here kid, I'm going to give you twenty 'brownies.' Out there at the wreck the other day I thought that you were some d—— smart alec reporter. Why didn't you speak up? If I had known who you were you could have had your picture." Brownies were demerit marks.

While I was working at Welby, I was firing an eleven hundred engine one day for an engineer named Ben Bailey. We had made a help to Cuprum. That was just over Bingham on the left mountain. At Cuprum there was quite a lot of yard tracks. After leaving the yard going down the grade there was a short tunnel. Coming out of the tunnel on the downhill side there was a derail.

This day we were following a train of loads down the mountain. Ben came out of the telegraph office with his orders just as the loads were leaving. I heard him yell at the conductor to let the derail go. He meant to leave the derail off the rail because we were following him closely and would replace the derail after we got over it.

Instead of following him right away, Ben got his oil can and proceeded to oil around. By the time we got out of the tunnel the loads were out of sight. That derail was on a curve on my side.

Ben hollered, "How's the derail?"

The target was staring me in the face as plain as day. It was in the derailing position. But I hollered back, "Okay."

I was confused after hearing Ben tell that conductor to let the derail go. I likened it to leaving the switch lined for the passing track as we did under similar conditions on the mainline. Too late I realized that this was different.

I screamed out, "It's wrong! It's wrong!"

But Ben had let go his brakes, and we were beginning to roll. He did everything he could to get stopped, but it was too late. We stopped with all four drivers over the derail and on the ground. I never felt chagrin so much in my life. It was my fault entirely. Old Ben was pretty mad.

We had a meet with a train of empties at a station called Midas, two miles down the grade. Ben and I decided that I should run down and get that train to come back up and help us get back on the rail. My roommate, Bill Fullmer, was firing the 1057, a mallet, and after about two hours of sweating and swearing we pulled the eleven hundred engine over the last rerailing frog and were back on the rails. We backed up to Cuprum and the 1057 followed us in.

We then proceeded down again. I didn't let that derail fool me again. Not much I didn't!

Came the winter of 1916–1917. I was by that time promoted and running out of the Salt Lake pool. It was a bad winter—lots of snow. Every morning for a week or so a train was called out of Salt Lake to go to Cuprum. This train consisted of about four coaches of snow shovelers. They would shovel snow all day at Cuprum and return to Salt Lake at night. One morning I was called as the "hoghead" for this special.

I got those snow shovelers up to Cuprum all right. The train and engine crews then loafed around all day. Toward night we got ready to return to Salt Lake. On the way up that morning I had missed seeing the derail below the tunnel. I afterward found out they had moved it and placed it in the lead connecting the yard to the mainline.

When we were ready to leave we headed down through a clear track in the yard. Bill Fullmer, my old room mate, had also been promoted and was running the Cuprum switch engine. As I started to leave he hollered at me.

"You know there is a derail down there!"

I thought he was kidding me about the time I had put Ben Bailey on the ground.

I hollered back at him, "I know all about that derail!"

But I didn't! I went down through that yard track, out on the lead, and too late I saw the derail! I frantically tried to stop, but I managed to go over the derail. When that little monkey (ten-wheeler locomotives of the T-29 class, called "monkeys" because of the "monkey motion" valve gear), the 783, finally stopped, I had the "pony truck" and the "first driver" parts of my engine on the ground. Was my face red!

We had to get Bill and his switch engine to pull us back on the rail. You can bet I took a lot of kidding over that performance.

In the first instance, when I left Welby to go back to the mainline I took with me on my record the twenty brownies given me by Joe Stevenson, the traveling engineer, for my responsibility in putting Ben Bailey over that derail. Six years later when I put myself over a derail, it went by unnoticed by officialdom. It was wartime and too much was happening to worry about anything so trivial as a derail.

It would be hard to name an eleven hundred class engine that I preferred over others. Those eleven hundred engines out of Salt Lake were in pooled service as long as I was on the Rio Grande. No one had a regular eleven hundred except at a few outside points. The first engine of this class that I regularly fired was in my early days as a fireman, for an engineer named Dave Gibson in helping service out of Helper. This was during the machinist and boilermaker's strike that started in 1908 and dragged along for a good many months. All the engines at the time were in poor condition due to this strike.

Toby Sheldahl had the 1160 in hill service at Tucker. He was forever telling me what a wonderful engine the 1160 was. I afterward fired this engine regularly for an engineer named Olaf Johnson on the Midvale-Scofield tramp job. Even then it was a mighty good engine—a testimonial to the wonderful care of Toby Sheldahl.

The Rio Grande 2–10–2s came to the Rio Grande about 1916. I didn't see one on the west end until about 1920. They were a little heavier

The Denver & Rio Grande 1151 at Provo. Photo by William R. Gould.

than our 2–10–2s, but not nearly as nice an engine to handle as ours were. They were not as comfortable in the cab.

When I started firing in 1908 all the eleven hundreds had Stevenson link valve gear and used saturated steam; that is, all except the 1151. The 1151 used saturated steam but had Walschaerts valve gear. It was used in passenger helping service out of Tucker.

The 1142 was the first engine to be superheated and equipped with Walschaerts gear in the Salt Lake shops, and I was called to fire her on her test run. My engineer was a young runner named Palmer DeLong. He was only a few years older than I was. We had been schoolmates a few years previously at Eureka.

We had most of the motive power officials in, on, and around that 1142 when we left Salt Lake. We went caboose bounce to Springville. At Springville we turned the engine and picked up loads of ore. We went west to Provo and filled out to twenty-six or twenty-seven hundred tons.

Before superheating, those eleven hundreds were rated not over twenty-two hundred and fifty tons west of Provo. When we received orders to fill to twenty-six hundred tons, no one on the crew figured we would get them out of the yard. How wrong we were! We had a little difficulty starting, but after we got them rolling that old 1142 handled them like an ordinary passenger train. She seemed to pick up speed at every turn of the wheels.

After stopping at the UP crossing just west of Lakota, it was the usual thing to start making the run for the American Fork hill. This was necessary if you had a full tonnage train with one of those "soaks," as we called the

The Denver & Rio Grande 1193 at Vivian Park on the Provo Canyon Branch. Photo from the W. J. G. Gould collection, photographer unknown.

eleven hundreds before they were superheated. If you didn't take every advantage to get your train rolling as fast as you could turn a wheel down through the sag at Geneva you were in danger of stalling and then having to double the hill into American Fork.

DeLong ran his engine as though he was afraid of doubling the hill. As soon as he got them rolling he began hooking that Johnson bar up toward center, one nick at a time, with the throttle wide open—pointing back toward the tank.

Very soon we were really moving. Long before we hit the bottom of the sag Palmer had eased off considerably on the throttle. Still our speed increased. I had never before ridden a freight train so fast down through Geneva, and that old 1142 steamed like a house afire, as we used to say.

My one worry was not whether we would double into American Fork; it was whether or not the 1142 would hold the rail around the curve at the lower, or west end, of Geneva. We were certainly stepping along. We sailed up into American Fork seemingly with hardly any effort.

The officials were all happy with the test. They finally raised the tonnage west of Provo to thirty-three hundred tons on those superheated eleven hundreds. As fast as they could be put through the shops those engines were all superheated and equipped with either Walschaerts or Baker valve gear. Everyone seemed happy with the result, except the engine and train men. They could see less work as the result of the increased pulling capacity of those engines.

In the spring of 1911 when Bill Fullmer and I rolled our bedding and landed at Welby, we little knew that we were invading enemy territory. But that turned out to be the case. Those train and engine crews at that point of time had all been recruited from Midvale and the surrounding towns. They were in a class and a society somewhat apart from the rest of the railroad. Most of them had never been over the mainline at all, and they looked upon us as interlopers. We had come out to take the bread and butter out of the mouths of the rightful owners of those jobs, as they thought of themselves.

As far as my situation was concerned I was all right. I landed on a job with an engineer who had worked at different points on the railroad before settling down at Welby. He understood the rules regarding seniority. The engineer that I landed with was named Bill Parker. He was a man who had done all of his firing on the mainline. He had bumped onto jobs and had in turn been bumped off of jobs.

With my pardner, Bill Fullmer, it was different. He landed on a job with a man named Billy Maycroft. Maycroft had done all his work right there on the Bingham Branch, and would remain there until it began to fade. Only then would he come to Salt Lake to work on the mainline. Meanwhile that branch was private territory to him and to others like him.

He was reported to have made the remark that they would make those mainline men wish they were back on the mainline. And, according to Fullmer, he tried to make that threat a reality. He would do everything he could to make it disagreeable for Bill.

The favorite way that any engineer had of discouraging a fireman was to rap an engine unnecessarily. By this is meant to work an engine at a longer stroke of the valve with the Johnson bar, or reverse lever, too far down on the quadrant. "Working it in the corner," it was called. In this way of operation, more steam was admitted to the cylinder than was necessary (the valve stroke being longer) and therefore the engine burned more coal than was needed. That kept the fireman down on the deck shoveling coal. "Down at the rat hole," as the saying goes.

An engineman who worked an engine in this manner was known as a "rapper." There were lots of rappers on the road in those days of hand-tamped engines, but most of them only practiced this when they wanted to make it miserable for the fireman. Some of those, like Old Head Conners and several more I could mention, could sure make a poor fireman wish he had never been born.

Old Art Campbell was in this class, but I don't think he did it with malice. I think he did it sort of unintentionally and unknowingly. That little old 768 that I fired for him could sure burn plenty of coal, and it always did with him at the throttle.

One night the traveling fireman rode with us, and there was all the difference in the world in the way he handled that engine. She didn't burn nearly the coal she was used to burning because Art paid close attention to where she was working and had the Johnson bar hooked up several notches higher than usual. I could "blow the dome off" of her, to use a popular expression of the day—meaning to raise the pop valves.

Another time we had a trainmaster riding with us. On those eastbound passenger trains, after leaving Springville, the coal would be so far back in the tank that the fireman was kept very busy. Between fires, when he was not shoveling coal into the firebox and when he should be resting, he would be back in the tank shoveling the coal up ahead where he could reach it.

This night that the trainmaster was on the engine I was very much surprised to see Art scurry back into the tank and go through the motions of shovelling coal ahead into my reach. I almost felt like telling him to get back up on his seat box and tend to running the engine.

But to get back to Bill Fullmer and the 1057: Bill said that Maycroft really rapped that engine. Of course on that little mallet he couldn't hurt a young buck like Bill on a slow job like those runs on the Bingham Branch. But, according to Fullmer, he sure tried.

One day after arriving at Cuprum, Maycroft got down to oil around while waiting for the conductor to appear with the orders. Fullmer got a piece of wood, took out his pocket knife and sharpened it on the end. He watched for Maycroft's appearance in the cab. When that happened Bill was down on his knees with the sharp pointed stick of wood cleaning the grease and dirt out of the notches in the front of the Johnson bar quadrant.

Maycroft wanted to know what he was doing down there. Old Bill was a slow, droll talker. He spoke very distinctly as he answered.

"Why ... I'm ... just ... trying ... to ... clean ... out ... the ... notches ... in ... front ... here ... so ... that ... you ... can ... work ... her ... a ... little."

Bill said that Maycroft had no comment to make on that one, but that from then on things began to get better.

When business started to pick up on the mainline early in July we both left Welby and went back to the Salt Lake pool. On the eleventh of July I went back out to Welby to get my paycheck. (I know it was the eleventh of July because I had just been married the day before, the tenth of July, 1911. A memorable day!)

While I was there getting my check, Billy Maycroft came into town on his 1057. He saw me come out of the office, and hollered at me.

"Hey, where's that pardner of yours?" he shouted. "Where's Fullmer?"

I hollered back, "He's working on the mainline."

"Tell him to come back here," he said, "I want him to fire this engine."

So you see he wasn't all bad.

A few months later I again couldn't hold a job out of Salt Lake. Bill Fullmer was up at Ogden firing on the extra passenger board. I was a few nicks older in seniority than Bill and could hold a couple of regular passenger jobs. I went up to Ogden and bumped a man named Charlie Bible. He was firing no. 6 and no. 3 for old Ben Rugg. Ben liked Charlie as a fireman, whereas he had never seen me before. He was running a little Brooks ten-wheeler—the 726. Every trip we would double head over the road and back again. The man on the head engine would always be Dick Carter. I knew from later developments that they had it rigged up between them to get rid of me.

Every day old Ben would rap that little Brooks a little harder while Dick Carter on the head engine would barely raise the smoke out of the cab. This went on for about two weeks. One morning coming south out of Ogden on no. 6 I had a tank of almost pure slack. I couldn't see a lump of coal as big as a walnut anywhere in the pile. Out of Ogden the grade rises sharply for six or seven miles. Old Ben was rapping her on the back as usual. The steam pressure began to lag. Old Ben began to take notice. He gave me several looks of contempt. Finally I blew my top.

I pointed to the coal, and pointedly asked how he expected me to keep her hot with that dust the way he was rapping her, while Dick Carter was almost shut off. He didn't answer me. He didn't have to. He was the engineer. I was only the fireman. But after we tipped over the Layton hill Ben seemed to ease up a little, and the 714 on the head end took up a little of the slack. He did better all the way to Helper that trip.

When we called to come back on no. 3 that night we learned that something had happened to the 726. There was only one engine available for the return trip. That engine was the 714 that had double headed us out of Ogden on no. 6. Dick Carter and his fireman, a man named Harry Clark, were extra men. Ben Rugg and I were the regular crew on the job. So we got the 714 to handle no. 3 while Dick and Harry were to deadhead back to Ogden.

While we were standing at Helper waiting for our train to come into town from the east, Carter and Clark came up to the engine to sympathize with us—mainly me, I believe. They harped on what a poor steamer the 714 was. According to them she wouldn't make a pound of steam. When our train came into town they got off the engine and started back to board a coach. Before he stepped out of the gangway old Dick Carter put his hand on my shoulder and said, "You've got my sympathy, Kid."

They gave us a big mallet to help us to Soldier Summit. Number 3 consisted of fourteen cars that night. That was an unusually heavy train for that run. The 714 was a ten-wheeler, not quite as big as the 726. She had a long, narrow firebox. I had previous experience with this type of engine. I now called upon that experience, and formed my plan of battle.

I had a good load in the firebox before we started, and it was all burning freely. With the mallet on the head end, there was no need for me to be up on the seatbox looking ahead. I stayed down on the deck. I started flashing the door, swinging it shut after every scoop of coal.

I didn't try to place each scoopful in a specific spot on the grates as was customary. Instead, I opened the door, bounced the scoop on the fire ring, and shut the door. Each scoop of coal bounced just barely inside the door. I heard Ben put on his "gun" (injector) supplying cold feed water to the boiler. I thought, now we will see. I watched that steam gauge needle. It was on the two hundred pound mark—right where it should be. I continued bouncing the scoop of coal on the fire ring, letting it fall just inside the firebox. and relying on the draft of the working engine to drag it forward. I heard Ben increase the flow of water through the gun. I looked at the needle—still on the two hundred mark. I began to hope.

I continued my carefully formulated plans. All at once that pop valve let go with a shattering roar. For a moment I disdained to look at Ben. When I did he was sizing up the water glass, squeezing the gauge cocks, and looking at the steam gauge. He acted as though he couldn't believe what he could see and hear. He dropped the Johnson bar down a nick. Still that needle hugged the two hundred pound mark as though it was welded there. I felt good. I remember having a thought: did old Ben think Charley Bible could do as well as that?

It was that way during the entire trip into Ogden. I kept bouncing that coal just inside the door, and the draft carried it to where it was needed. From that time forward on future trips Dick Carter did his laps on the head end and old Ben favored me.

I had another experience with that type of firing. While working out of Ogden on no. 61 and no. 62, I was living at Salt Lake. Due to the long layover at Ogden I would get on the Bamberger, or anything else that I could ride, to go back and forth between home and Ogden.

Late one afternoon I was on my way to the Bamberger depot to get a ride up to Ogden. In going through the Rio Grande yards I saw a freight train ready to leave town for Ogden. It had one of the nine-forties—a consolidation—on the head end. I could ride this train to Ogden and save thirty-five cents fare.

I climbed on the engine as they took off. The fireman was named Sprattling. He later served two terms as mayor of Helper. The engineer was Clarence Rawlins. I had fired for him in the pool. He afterward became general air brake instructor. He was the man who later examined and promoted me.

Right from the start Sprattling lost his steam. We barely made it to the water tank at Farmington. When he got up to take water I stripped off all my excess clothing and placed it in the seat box. The blower was on full, rumbling into the night. I got down on the deck and looked at the fire over the back of the scoop. I started to build it up just inside the door. Those nine-forties had long narrow fireboxes.

After Sprattling had taken water and we had blown up a full head of steam, Clarence got the train in motion. From the looks he gave me I knew he would like me to do the firing. I started firing that nine-forty just the way I had the 714.

That pointer on the gauge hung up on one hundred and eighty-five—which was the pressure they carried—as if it was glued on the mark. The harder Clarence worked her the better she steamed. Going up under the highway bridge over the tracks on the long Layton grade the pop let go with a roar.

I saw Clarence turn a grinning face toward the window. The only comment was made by Sprattling, the fireman. He said, "You can't keep a good man down!"

I think Clarence must have broadcast it around for I heard about it later from several engineers.

In the summer of 1911 I was a newlywed, and like all young fellows with a lovely wife at home I wanted to be there as much as possible. Those mainline trips were just plain voyages. When leaving Salt Lake in the pool, a man never knew when he headed east out of Salt Lake whether he would be gone ten hours or ten days.

How would you like it if you had been away from home a few days, then on the way back you were stopped within ten or fifteen miles of your goal and given orders to turn around and go back down the line again? I don't think the average rail nowadays could take it.

So I marked up for the little Tintic passenger job. It consisted of a little Rome engine, a combination smoking and baggage car, and two day coaches. We would leave Salt Lake about 4:30 P.M. and arrive at Silver City about 9:30 P.M. We would tie up there until the next morning, when we would depart at 6:30 A.M. arriving at Salt Lake about 10:30 A.M.

Those little Romes were wonderful steamers if you fired them right. If you kept a level fire all over the grates, not more than five or six inches in depth, they would steam well. But if you loaded them a little heavier they would die quickly.

Many times I would get scared upon looking into the firebox of a little Rome and seeing that fire bouncing around like popcorn in a popper. You'd swear that your fire would all go out the flues before you could get any coal in there. But that's just the way they liked it, and they steamed freely on that kind of a fire. I have fired those Romes in freight service during busy seasons and four scoops of coal to one firing was sufficient.

At Silver City there was an engine watchman to take over when we arrived. While we were sleeping he would clean the fire, fill the tank with coal and water, and get the engine ready to return in the morning.

The man I fired for was named Bartlett. He stood about six feet tall and carried no excess weight whatever. He was of fine stature and walked straight as an arrow, although at that time he was well into his seventies. He was an old Civil War veteran, and had fought on the Union side. He told me of being with Sherman on that famous march from Atlanta to the sea.

I have forgotten the name of the conductor. He was also a veteran of the Civil War, on the Confederate side, in the transportation department. At the time I write of trains were getting longer. The railroads were going tonnage crazy.

I remember this conductor remarking that the trains weren't heavy compared to some that he had handled. I recall him saying that during the war he had come into some town in Georgia with a hundred and twenty freight cars in a single train. I thought to myself, there couldn't have been any grade, and those cars must have been very light, and without air brakes. I still had some trouble believing it.

When we tied up at Silver City for the night we would stay in the baggage car. Those two old fellows would make a pot of coffee or tea. They had a portable table and two chairs. They would spread their lunch, and as they ate they would fight the Civil War all over again. This was one of the highlights of the trip for me. There were several bedrolls in the baggage car. I would hurry and eat my lunch and roll up in the bedding and listen to those two old fellows refight the Civil War. It was very interesting to a young fellow like me.

From where we crossed the prairie I could look down and see where we had lived at Silver City Junction. I could locate the spot where our old log section house once stood. It was now gone, and so was that old pumphouse and the wye. The mainline of the Oregon Short Line that once continued on down for about a mile and a half before turning toward Salt Lake now turned directly behind where we used to live.

That change was brought about when the San Pedro, Los Angeles, and Salt Lake (called the Pedro) took over and ran their mainline to Los Angeles through that country. They took over all the properties of the Oregon Short Line. They later shortened their name to the Los Angeles and Salt Lake Railroad. It is now all part of the Union Pacific.

Bartlett said that many years before, when he was a fireman, the engines were crude affairs compared to what we then had. He told of the old feedwater pump connected to the crosshead of the main engine. An engine had to be in motion in order to pump water into the boiler. An alternate solution while waiting in a passing track would be to oil the rail under their engines' driving wheels. Then steam would be applied to the cylinders to spin the wheels in order to operate the pump. Another option was to uncouple the engine and run up and down the track to accomplish the same purpose.

He told of the old safety valves located in the cabs to relieve excess boiler pressure. These valves were a forerunner to the modern pop valve. They had a long arm, like some weighing scales. The weights on the arm determined the amount of steam carried in the boiler.

He said that he was firing an engine one day when they came to a slight grade. They had a full head of steam, but the train gradually slowed and finally came to a stop with the throttle wide open and the Johnson bar in the extreme front corner. He looked up at the engineer, wondering what was to be done. It was a warm day. The engineer talked about other things, not of their predicament. He took off his hat and casually hung it on the end of the arm governing the pop valve. He took out his handkerchief and began wiping the sweat off his brow. He had made no effort to shut off the throttle.

After a little while the engine started to tremble, then slowly started to move the train ahead. When the train was well underway and over the slight grade the engineer reached up and retrieved his hat. The additional weight of the hat on the extreme end of the lever had slightly raised the boiler pressure. Bartlett said that he had used additional weights himself, when he needed a little more steam pressure. He shuddered slightly when he told of this. It was a very dangerous practice, he said, the worst result of which could have been a boiler explosion.

In an emergency I have seen engineers do many things that I considered extremely dangerous. They have usually remarked afterward that they would never do that again. They didn't—until another emergency arose.

7

Old Heads, Rails, and Boomers

*A*strange thing to me is the seeming fact that a man always holds fond memories of his days on the Rio Grande. I have seen this demonstrated time and time again. It's the same with me now. I still consider myself a Rio Grande man. But since the steam locomotive has gone out and the diesels have come in, the Rio Grande, and all the other railroads, seem to have lost their glamor.

I would love to stand once again at the depot at Helper in the early morning and see no. 1 come into town off the eastern desert. There were always two "monkey" seven hundreds double heading that train into town. That was before they got the bigger power. The best engines were assigned to the Desert Division on account of the bad water in use there and the fact that the Salt Lake shops were the largest between Salt Lake and Denver and conveniently available to the west end.

You would see no. 1 come into Helper with the fireman of each engine standing proudly in the gangway like a soldier standing at attention. The pops would be wide open as a rule and the exhaust from the stack would gradually diminish in volume as they eased to a stop.

The reason you could depend on the pops roaring was partly the result of the situation of track gradient at that location, but also it was due in no small measure to tradition. Those enginemen would always be wanting to show off to the hill men of the west end. In this they were helped greatly by the alignment of the grade.

That grade, after being more or less flat over most of the desert, rose sharply for the last three quarters of a mile coming into Helper. If a man had the water well up in the boiler at the yard limit board he could shut off his injector and come into Helper with a full boiler and a blazing fire due to reducing speed on this increase in grade. So it became customary when getting close to a stop at Helper to shut off the injector and partly coast to a stop with the pop blasting off into the air. It was quite a sight to see those two engines double heading to a stop with the pop valves roaring wide open. It was almost a ritual.

Of course it wasn't advisable to let the pops open too often over the road. It was a waste of water while the pop was open, and besides, it irritated some of those old enginemen to hear the noise too often.

I once heard an old time fireman remark concerning a certain engineer, "He wants a hundred and fifty-nine and three-quarters pounds of steam, always; no more and no less."

Of course he was speaking of the little Rome passenger engines. They popped at one hundred and sixty pounds. I fired for an engineer once who, in speaking of this same man, said that while firing for him he let a little Rome pop while drifting down the Price River Canyon. That cranky old engineer put the reverse down in the front corner and worked a heavy throttle to get rid of the excess steam.

This engineer in question was a man by the name of Dickerson. It was said of him that he would climb on the engine, take out a white handkerchief, and rub the corners of the window glass. If he got the handkerchief dirty, he asked for another fireman. That may be an exaggeration, but it was one of the tales that circulated.

I was once sent up to Ogden to relieve a passenger fireman when I was on the Salt Lake extra board. After several trips the regular fireman reported for work, and I was released back to Salt Lake. I was down at the roundhouse at Ogden. The engine crew of the train that I was preparing to deadhead home on were getting the engine ready. I climbed on to do a little visiting with the fireman. His name was Adams. The engineer was Dickerson—the same. He was down oiling the pig around.

I told Adams that I had been released at Ogden and was going to deadhead home. He told me that he would like to lay off a trip or two and that if I would stay in Ogden 'til he returned I could take his place while he was off. I was just a young fireman at the time and having heard of this man Dickerson's reputation I was very much afraid of him.

This was in the days when a fireman had to keep the engine clean and spotless above the running gear and when an engineer could pretty nearly hire or fire his fireman.

When Adams proposed that I stay at Ogden and take his place for a few trips, I protested long and loudly. No Sir! I wouldn't stay and fire for that old so and so. No Sir! Not Me! I had heard all about that old so and so. I used many adjectives in giving my opinion of him. All the time I was spouting off I was standing in the gangway facing into the cab. Adams was standing in front of me on the deck. All the time that I was giving my opinion of this engineer, Adams was trying to shush me up. But I wouldn't shush. I kept right on telling what I thought of this engineer in lurid terms.

Finally I felt a little nudge between my shoulder blades. I turned and Dickerson was standing in the gangway behind me wiping his oil can with a bunch of waste. That was the reason why the fireman was trying to shush me up. I stepped aside and the engineer stepped into the cab. He didn't give me a look or say a word. You can bet that I climbed off that engine without delay. I never did fire for engineer Dickerson. Whether he was the ogre he was painted to be I have only say-so to go by.

About engines popping I have several other remarks to make. An engineer named Slim Wilkins told me this one. He said that General Manager Welby's private car was staked out on a spur track at Thistle one night. Wilkins came down the grade on a train of coal, and when he stopped his engine was right beside that business car. He and his fireman, a man named Joe Westbrook, got off and went to the Beanery to eat. After a while that pop on the little hog let go with a wild bang. Pretty soon it would blow down and the pop would seat and be quiet. Then as the pressure built up again it would bang out on the summer's air. Intermittently that pop would blast off and then close again. When they came out of the Beanery the first thing that attracted their attention was a short, fat little figure in a white union suit jumping and scampering around that hog trying to find someone to put water in the boiler and close that d—— pop valve.

Mr. Welby was quite annoyed, it appeared, and was on the verge of firing everyone at Thistle. Slim said that they lost no time getting water in the boiler and silencing that pop.

I once fired for an engineer named Blocky Welch. We had an engine that was a wonderful steamer, the 1152. It was the first engine I fired that I could "blow the dome off of," as the saying went. Blowing the dome off meant making her pop anytime. I was a very young fireman at the time, and when I found that I could make her pop at any time, I did just that. Not realizing what I was doing I kept that pop open until the engineer got angry and told me to let it come down. He explained to me that I was popping that water away faster than his injector would supply it. Those were the only words we exchanged during that eastbound trip.

This engineer, Blocky Welch, liked to play poker. One winter I fired a little hog for him on an ice train on the Park City Branch.

Every winter they cut and loaded ice at Gorgoza, at the eastern foot of the grade in the valley between Altus and Park City. Every morning in the cold weather two trains of empties would leave Salt Lake for Gorgoza. We were on the point of the first train. There would be a little hog pusher on the rear to Altus. When we arrived at the ice ponds, I would stay on the engine and set the empties for ice loading. The head brakeman and I would make up trains of loads to return to Salt Lake. The rest of the crew would be in the caboose playing poker.

When the second crew arrived we would arrange a train of loads for them to take back to Salt Lake. This went on all winter. The ice cutters on the ponds would cut the ice in oblong shapes and the loaders would load them in the cars. After the second crew left we would make up a train of loads for ourselves. We usually left late in the afternoon. It was said of Blocky that he made many trips for nothing, as he lost his wages in the poker game.

Every night those ice ponds froze over for the next day's cutting. That ice was stored in sawdust to be used for icing fruit cars the following summer. Of course that was before the day of electric refrigeration.

Henry Hanagan, whom I fired for, had a brother who was a brakeman on the Western Pacific. This brother was killed in an accident.

Henry laid off when this happened. He didn't return to work for several months. He put in most of his time grieving for his brother at the Cosy Corner Saloon at Sixth West and Second South in Salt Lake. During this time he did considerable drinking, trying to drink up all the whiskey that was made. The trouble was that they could make it faster than Henry could drink it.

Most everyone on the railroad knew of his condition. I think that was the reason, when he was forced to return to work or give up the job, that I was chosen to fire for him. I recognized the fine hand of our traveling engineer, Jack Snyder, in this. When I heard that Henry was to be the engineer I was just a little bit worried. I knew he was in a very poor condition—nerves and otherwise.

I went up to see my mother before appearing on the engine. As I passed the Cosy Bar I thought again of my engineer. Something prompted me to go inside. I think I was looking for Henry. He wasn't in sight so I started to leave. I glanced behind the bar at the rows of bottled whiskey. At that time you could get a pint bottle of what was called "bar whiskey" for thirty-five cents. Several times in my early career as a fireman I had left town with a pint of this whiskey in my traveling bag. This was one of those times. I took that pint of liquor, and when I reached the engine I climbed on the back of the tank. There I hid it inside one of the marker lamps. I didn't tell anyone it was there.

In due course of time Henry showed up at the ready track. He looked much the worse for wear, as the saying goes. His eyes were bloodshot and he had a dilapidated appearance. He went ponderously through the routine of getting ready.

Our train, as I remember, consisted of about forty empties. On our way east we headed in several times to meet westbound trains. One of those meets was at Lehi. We had quite a long wait at that place. I could tell by Henry's actions that he was getting pretty restless and nervous. He had already been four hours away from the Cosy and the whiskey bottle. At last our meet arrived and we started to leave town.

The head brakeman went ahead and lined the switch to let us out on the main. He stepped across the track to the right hand side of the engine. As the engine went by him, this brakeman looked up into the cab. I think he must have recognized Henry's condition. With that peculiar cruelty born of comradeship, he hollered up at the engineer, "How would you like a big slug of whiskey now, Henry?"

Then he laughed loudly at his joke. Henry turned his head inside the cab and muttered something that sounded like, "You so-and-so!"

A short time later we were rambling down through the sag at the Lehi Sugar Works. I stepped across the cab and jabbed my finger in Henry's side.

"Henry," I said, "did I understand you to say that you would like a little drink?"

He gave me a look that spoke the answer more plainly than words.

"If you climb the coal pile up onto the back of the tank," I said, "you will find a bottle in that right marker lamp."

I never saw a man act so quickly. He lost very little time in scrambling up over that coal onto the back of the tank. When he returned to the cab he was an entirely different person. Gone was that fidgety nervousness. He seemed much more alert and alive. So there must be something to that old belief of taking a bit of the hair of the dog that bit you.

I believe Henry would have given me anything he owned after that night if I had asked for it. Many times later he would recall that incident to mind almost every time we met in the long years that followed. Needless to say we got Henry over the road that first trip and rehabilitated in his job.

Another time I recognized the fine hand of Jack Snyder was when I was called to fire for a man named Lydick. Lydick had been night roundhouse foreman at Salt Lake for several months. Previously he had been a boomer engineer. His last job in that capacity had been on the Copper Belt, a subsidiary railroad of the Rio Grande up around Bingham Canyon. He had never been over the Rio Grande mainline. The only reason he was called for the run that night was because there was not another engineer available.

Lydick had no conception of mainline operation. I coached him all the way over to Helper on the eastbound trip. The same procedure was followed coming back. All the way over the road he kept asking me questions, mostly about train handling on the new line down the west slope off Soldier Summit. This grade had only been in operation a few months. It had the old heads guessing.

On the old grade it was mostly a question of holding the train and not letting it get away. On the new grade the trick was to keep from stalling and breaking the train in two or more pieces. Where on the old grade twelve or thirteen heavy loads was a train, on the new grade, if it was coal, a train was usually sixty-five loads. These long trains were quite a problem for awhile. If a man got down without stalling or breaking the train in two or three pieces he considered himself lucky.

When we were ready to leave Soldier Summit, Lydick proposed that I take him down the mountain. He said that he had been talking to several mainline engineers at Helper, and they had advised him to turn the train over to me at Soldier Summit. His voice was almost pleading in tone when he asked me to take it off his hands.

This is conceivable only to those who understand the conditions under which we operated at that time. We didn't have the modern brake equipment that was to come later. The rolling stock was generally in very poor condition compared to what it is now. Most of the draft gear was timber. It was very easy to jerk out a drawbar or two and to have the road tied up for several hours while you put the train back together.

I was not at all loath to get over on the right side. That mountain didn't scare me one bit. For this I had Toby Sheldahl to thank. His coaching was to pay me well that night and later.

I took that train down the mountain smoothly and without incident. When we stopped at Narrows for inspection we had a hot box about half-way back in the train. The conductor and rear brakeman spent some considerable time doctoring it. Lydick went back to see what was what.

When he got back to the engine he told me about it. He said he suggested to the conductor that maybe we were going a little too fast.

The conductor replied, "No, the speed was just right."

He asked how the caboose was riding behind that long train. The conductor said it couldn't ride smoother or better. He added that he and the brakeman had remarked about it.

He said, "Any man that can come out of the roundhouse and handle a train down this mountain like that should be given a better job on the road than roundhouse foreman."

Lydick told me, "I couldn't take it any longer. I had to tell them that the fireman was handling the train."

I received nothing but praise from that conductor and train crew. The conductor's name was Coombs—Johnny Coombs.

That man Lydick didn't stay on the night roundhouse foreman job very long after that trip. Business picked up and he landed a job running a switch engine in the Salt Lake yards. He never made another trip on the mainline but ended his days right there on the yard goat.

Johnny Coombs was a little Welshman. He was not much bigger than I was, although he was several years older. Like all active little Welshmen, he thought he could lick any man twice his size, and he came pretty close to doing it, too.

That Cosy Bar was quite a hangout for Rio Grande rails. One of the backrooms was fitted out as a gymnasium. I worked out with several fighters there after this little yarn I am about to tell on Johnny Coombs.

I was firing out of Ogden at the time. One afternoon I was on my way to the Bamberger depot to catch a car up to Ogden in order to come out on no. 4. I intended to visit with my mother a little before going on, so I left my house a little early. I had to pass the Cosy Bar on my way to Mother's place. As I went by the Cosy Bar, a brakeman by the name of Turner came out and called to me. I knew him well.

He said, "There is a little guy in here that says he can lick any Welshman in town—especially if his name happened to be Gould."

Of course I knew he was just trying to kid me along, but I followed him into the backroom of the saloon. There I found about six or eight Rio Grande men—some trainmen and some enginemen. I knew most of them.

Johnny Coombs was among them. I had never, up to this time, had any dealings with him, although I knew who he was. These guys were having a good time. They had a set of boxing gloves and Johnny had proved himself the best man of the bunch. They needed another sucker, so they had me put the gloves on with him.

Boy! I was right in the pink of condition just then. At first I fully intended just to box a little with Johnny. But the way he came at me I had no choice but to fight back to keep from getting my head knocked off. After his first wild rush I met his next one with a straight left right in the face. This set him back on his heels, but Johnny was game and came at me again. By this time I knew I could reach him with a straight left anytime I wanted to. Every time Johnny flew at me I just stuck my left straight out, and he rammed his face into it. He started to back up, and I followed him, jabbing that straight left into his face. From wall to wall we fought. I used only that one punch and didn't miss. Johnny was game; game as any little Welshman could be.

When the others finally stepped between us and stopped the match, Johnny's face looked like hamburger. But he was still grinning and fighting back. He did not know me then. He thought I was just some tough punk whom Turner had brought in to lick him. That was before the trip with Lydick. We parted friends.

There was a time in 1912–1913 that the Industrial Workers of the World became very strong in the West. They were called the IWW. Some interpreted those initials to mean I Want Work. Others said they meant I Won't Work. I think the latter term was the more appropriate. They traveled in gangs. All freight trains carried them, and there were always too many for the train crews to cope with.

One night we were coming east on a train of empties. This was at a time when most of the Rio Grande between Midvale and Tucker was single track. Sy Perkins was our head brakeman. At Provo the coal was quite a ways back in the tank. Sy began looking for a hobo to pass coal up to where I could reach it.

The first car behind the engine was a box car. There were about fifteen or twenty IWWs in that car. It was a warm summer night and they were all asleep. Sy went back to that car and woke them up. He told them that we needed a couple of them up on the engine to pass coal. They told him to go to h———. Further, they said that they were going to ride and didn't intend to pass coal for no S.O.B. They chased Sy out of the car and back to the engine.

Sy was quite angry. The old grade rose sharply after leaving Springville. (This is now the westbound mainline.) With a full train one of those eleven hundred engines dragged very slowly in some places. At one place where we were barely moving Sy said to me, "If you will help me, we'll fix those IWW so and sos." I agreed to help.

We dropped back, first on the right side, and closed and locked the side door. We then did the same on the left side. Then there was only the little door in the end that was open. Sy climbed up and closed that door also. We put the lock pin in the staple when that gang inside suddenly became aware of what was taking place. If you ever heard a gang of hard-boiled IWWs you should have heard that bunch. They didn't scare us anymore, though. We knew that tightly sealed box car would hold them.

At that time the eating house at Thistle consisted of a couple of old grounded box cars. The regular eating house had just burned down. We spotted that first car close to the eating house, and after taking coal and water we went inside to eat. All the while we were in there we could hear that angry bunch voicing their threats about what they were going to do when they got out. I'll admit that I was afraid. There were too many to be turned loose in Thistle at night.

My engineer was named Chancelor, a man whom I admired and respected greatly. As we came out of the Beanery he engaged in conversation with that wild bunch. Never one to raise his voice was Art Chancelor, but he could, if the occasion warranted, express his thoughts in blistering, scathing terms. He sure had that bunch mad when we left town.

At the upper end of Thistle we stopped, cut off that head car, set it out on the top end of the passing track, and left town. For myself, I was much relieved to get rid of them. I never did hear what eventually happened to that car load of bums.

In the annals of the Salt Lake Division, they tell a story on one Speedy Grump. He was called one morning at Helper to help a westbound drag. He came up to the roundhouse and seeing an engine that appeared to be waiting for a crew he proceeded to get it ready for the trip. He oiled it around, got it ready in all other ways and wondered if a fireman had been called. After a long time of waiting he was approached by another engine crew and a brakeman who thanked him for getting their engine ready. It developed that he got on the wrong engine. A new superintendent gave him a bunch of brownies for indifference, whatever that was.

They also tell about Speedy coming east one morning. It was in 1909 during the boilermaker and machinist's strike. The power at that time was in very bad shape. It was hard to keep those eleven hundred class engines from leaking about the flues and elsewhere. Also the machinery—the running gear—was in poor condition. If the engine wasn't dying from leaky flues, you could expect an eccentric to slip or some other mechanical breakdown to occur.

On this morning of which I relate, Speedy had gone as far as Lakota, about three miles west of Provo. He had a meet with a westbound train there. He headed into the long passing track. After the train he was to meet arrived Speedy discovered that the flues had started to leak and he didn't have enough steam to start the train. They tried blowing up boiler pressure but to no avail. Pretty soon the engine was standing in a pool of water, and the pointer on the steam gauge registered zero.

Speedy informed the dispatcher of their condition. After several hours a light engine appeared. They took the train and left Speedy and the fireman there in the passing track with a dead engine. It was assumed that some westbound crew would stop and pick them up and return them to Salt Lake. But nothing like that happened. Several westbound trains went by without noticing that dead engine.

After a while Speedy and his fireman flagged an eastbound train and rode to Provo where they had a big meal. They then rode a westbound man back to Lakota. Twice a day for four days they rode back and forth between Provo and Lakota for eats. Finally the dispatcher tumbled to the fact that there was a dead engine in the passing track at Lakota, and had a westbound train stop and pick them up.

For a while it looked like there would be an investigation, but those rumors didn't bother Speedy. He had notified the dispatcher of the circumstances in the beginning. The dispatcher most assuredly knew of it, because he had dispatched a relief engine to take the train on over the road. It was not really up to the engineer to remind him. Speedy and his fireman drew pay for four days and nights work, when they didn't do any work. How is that for featherbedding?

About 1910 or 1911 Speedy bought a couple of automobiles and started a taxicab business in Salt Lake. I believe he was the first cab driver to operate in Salt Lake City. He drove one of those cars himself. When he laid off to do this he was running an engine on what was called the "Provo tramp" job. This job worked as much as sixteen hours a day going various places on the mainline east and west out of Provo and up the branches. With those hours it paid very well.

After he had been driving a cab for several months the men on the extra board started to complain. They thought he should either go back on the engine or resign to drive cab. They hoped he would do the latter. Instead, after finally yielding to the pressure they put on him, he sold the taxicab business and went back on the Provo tramp job. There was no mileage agreement at that time. The Provo tramp jobs were about the highest paying jobs on the road. So Speedy went back, and for a year or more he didn't lay off one trip. That bothered the extra board too.

He said, "They wanted me to return to work—well, here I am."

Someone asked him if he didn't get tired and weary riding that engine night and day.

"What? Me get weary riding that seat box? I should say not!"

We had two shanty Irishmen, Pat and Rodger Reynolds, running engine on the Rio Grande. They were always doing crazy stunts.

Rodger had been promoted after block signals were installed on the east end. He left Helper one morning on the "Sunnyside tramp." About two miles below Helper is the Blue cut. The track curves to the left through that cut and is visible to the fireman but not the engineer. There was a block signal midway in the cut.

The fireman, looking forward at the block signal called out, "clear block."

Rodger "big holed" the train. That is, he set the brakes in the emergency position, the "big hole" on that long train of empties. This really shook things up—especially in the caboose. He shouted at the fireman, "What did you say?"

The fireman answered, "I said 'clear block.'"

Rodger said, "Oh, I thought that you said 'big rock.'"

Then he did a foolish thing. He returned the brake valve to release position. Then all heck broke loose. After an emergency application of the brakes it is better to let the train come to a stop before attempting a release. Otherwise you are liable to tear the train in several pieces. And that was just what happened to Rodger. When he finally stopped, the train was in about four pieces.

One night while I was firing no. 4 and no. 5 for Art Campbell, we were double heading east on no. 4. Dudley Gallagher and Clarence Rawlins were on the head engine. In a case like that the man on the head engine always handles the brakes. We were rounding a left hand curve at Cold Springs, just below Castella. In those days a high board fence separated the highway from the railroad tracks at that point. This fence stood up off the ground about a foot and a half.

We were stepping along right smart. I had been leaning over my seat box with my head out of the window to get a breath of fresh air. I was about to get down and put in a fire when I saw a faint gleam of red on the inside rail. I waited a moment and saw a brakeman stepping off a caboose with a red fusee in his hand. I hollered at Art and got down on the gangway steps.

About that time Clarence Rawlins on the head engine shut off steam. I heard the brakes slam into emergency. I looked up at Art. He had shut off and was calmly dragging the Johnson bar into the back motion.

Looking ahead, I had a glimpse of Dudley Gallagher down on the step before the smoke rolling back cut off my vision. We were still making about twenty-five miles an hour when I let go and jumped. I hit the snow-covered ground rolling. I rolled under that elevated fence clear over onto the highway. That train ahead of us was slowly heading into the siding at Castella. Number 4, the train I was on, rolled up to within a car length of making a coupling with that slow moving caboose before it came to a stop.

When we had all gathered at the point of near collision, I asked Gallagher if he had gotten off. He said "no," but I believe he did. Anyway, he didn't have the smoke rolling back in his face as I did. He could see where he was going. But being the storyteller he was, he just loved to tell this one on me, and it got better with every telling. He said that when I came out from under the fence I was digging snow out of my ears and complaining about the cold. None the less, that was just another time to be glad you were still alive.

Gallagher was another who could be classed as a character in our little railroad society. He used to tell of a time when he was on a train going west into American Fork. The curve into town was on his side, and he was firing for Eskimo John Larson. John looked like an Eskimo, both in face and figure, which produced the nickname.

They had a scheduled meet at American Fork with an eastbound train. The eastbound man had orders to take the siding. John Larson was coming into town pretty fast. The eastbound man was coming in from the other direction around the curve with his headlight fully on.

The mainline coming west into American Fork follows a long sweeping curve to the left. A train coming east and heading into the pass cannot be distinguished from one on the mainline by a westbound man unless the eastbounder turns off or covers his headlight when he is into the clear. It was general practice to do this. That headlight was burning brightly and coming down against Gallagher and Larson, and they couldn't tell whether he was in the pass or on the main. At last Gallagher decided he was on the mainline, screamed a warning at John, and got down on the left gangway steps to jump. He then decided the eastbounder was in the siding so he hung on in the gangway.

After doing all he could to stop the train, Larson came across the cab. He took one good look and concluded that the westbound train was on the mainline. He hollered at Gallagher to let go. Gallagher tried to tell John that he thought they were in the pass. John Larson weighed about two hundred and eighty pounds. He wouldn't wait. He jumped straddle of Gallagher's neck, and they both went rolling in the snow.

When the westbound train had stopped it was found that the eastbound man was where he belonged—in the pass. However, he had confused things by having his headlight still lit. Those trains had passed each other safely on parallel tracks, before John Larson's train came to a stop. However, had it been otherwise there would have been a serious collision.

I have seen many cases like that where it was impossible to be sure, until almost opposite each other, where each train was. The worst place for this sort of thing was a stretch of track about five miles long just north of Salt Lake going toward Ogden. The Oregon Short Line and the Rio Grande run side by side there on a long, gentle curve. When you would see a headlight there you couldn't tell for sure whether it was on the OSL or the Rio Grande track. This problem was a contributing factor to one of the nastiest wrecks I can recall on the Rio Grande.

Number 62, running late with a high-wheeled mogul on the point, collided with a Salt Lake switch engine on the easy curve. Someone called up the Rio Grande dispatcher's office in Salt Lake and told McLease, the Rio Grande second trick dispatcher, that no. 62 was on the ground at Wood's Cross. McLease, without further investigation to learn the facts, pulled the silliest stunt that a man in his position could commit. He ordered a switch crew to go out to Wood's Cross and help rerail the engine on 62.

They met in about the middle of that long curve. Three switchmen and a fireman, all on the switch engine, died. Number 62 that night consisted of a deadhead coach, a car of grain, the caboose, and one of the 950 class engines.

I fired that job many times myself, and I can easily believe that under those conditions, 62 was making much better than sixty miles an hour at the point of collision. On that long paralleling curve, neither crew knew what railroad the other headlight was on until it was too late to do anything about it. Each thought the approaching train was on the Union Pacific tracks.

Mickey Coffery was firing the mogul on 62. Blue Beard Bert Kestler was the engineer. When Mickey at last realized that the opposing headlight was on their track, he jumped down from his seatbox and started to climb the coal gate on the tank. He was smashed up against the back of the boiler head by the shifting coal in the tank. He was in the hospital for several months.

Bert Kestler didn't have time to do anything, but miraculously he escaped with a few bruises. The fireman on the switch engine and the three switchmen were killed instantly. One of the switchmen was almost cut in two by the apron on the switch engine tearing loose and hitting him with the edge, worn sharp on the tender sill.

What caused all the trouble in the first place was an Oregon Short Line engine on the ground at Wood's Cross. Whoever called McLease—they tried hard to find the man who made the telephone call but were unable to do so—got the wrong railroad. Rio Grande 62 was not on the ground at all, but right where it should have been—on Rio Grande rails tearing along toward Salt Lake.

Chief Dispatcher McLease was fired for his mistake. He finally landed a job as dispatcher on the Bingham and Garfield Railroad. In the middle twenties he came to the Utah Railway as chief dispatcher at Hiawatha. He only held that position for a few years. He died in the insane asylum at Provo. That wreck continued to prey on his mind until the end of his life.

Pete Mistler was a man, I would judge, to be in his middle fifties, and he had only been promoted to the right-hand side a short while before. So he came to the position of engineer a little later than most.

Those trains descending that steep grade out of Welby on the Bingham Branch were very heavy. They consisted of ore, mostly out of Cuprum, just above Bingham. They had to be held down to a very slow speed in order to keep them under control. It was quite a ticklish job of railroading. If you let them roll a little too fast you would have a hard time getting them under control again. If you slowed them down too much they would hang up and stall. A speed of between ten and twelve miles an hour was just about right.

Old Pete had a habit of confiding aloud to himself. He would seriously coach himself all the way down the grade. I listened with amused interest to him one trip. It went something like this as he started the descent.

Now Pete, watch yourself, Pete.... Set the straight air gently and bunch 'em up a little.... that's the way, Pete! ... That's the way! ... Now watch yourself, Pete! ... Don't let 'em roll too fast!

Now give 'em about seven or eight pounds.... Watch yourself, Pete! ... Give 'em a little more now.... That's the way, Pete. Now let go of 'em.... Let go now.... Watch yourself! ... Now make another application....

You've got the retainers charged up now, Pete, so don't give 'em too much this time.... Better give 'em a few pounds more, now.... Ah! That's nice.... Let go now....

You're doin' all right, Pete.... You're doin' all right now.... Cut loose your driver brakes now, Pete.... You don't want to loosen a tire!

Now check 'em again.... Not too much! ... Just a few pounds.... Give 'em a little more now, Pete.... Not too much! ... You're doing all right.... You're doing fine ... Better give 'em a little more now, Pete.... Not too much! ... Just a little ... Don't get 'em down too slow.... Maybe you'd better give 'em a pound or two more now....

That's the.... Oh ... Oh ... Oh ... not too much, Pete.... Oh! ... G—d—you, Pete! ... You gave them too much that time!

The last I saw of Pete Mistler he was running a switch engine at Soldier Summit. I don't know if he still coached himself or not.

There was another engineer named Bill Haymond. He was a man with a college education, yet he was always in some kind of trouble. The wags made up a story about him also. They claimed he would go up on back of the tank, lift the manhole cover, and look at his reflection in the water. Then he would tell himself how good he was—in his own opinion.

"Bill, you're there! You're there, Bill! You're the most successful young runner on the D & RG. Don't let anyone kid you, Bill. You're there!"

Then he would take a last look, close the lid, and return to the cab. Bill, I think, considered himself better than the average rail. At times he would assume quite an arrogant manner in his dealings with others. For this reason he was held in ridicule and contempt by the rank and file. I fired several trips for Bill and had no trouble with him. We got along fine.

We once made a trip with a little Rome passenger engine in freight service. By firing four scattered scoops to a fire, I had that little Rome sizzling all the way over the road. Bill paid me a very nice compliment. He told me I was the best fireman on the road. I took a good look at myself reflected in the water in the tank the next time I took water!

Bill had a brother, but try as I may I can't think of that brother's name right now. When I first went firing he was district superintendent at Tucker. Later he held the same position at Welby on the Bingham branch.

When the Bingham and Garfield Railroad (B & G) started to lay track around the foothills between Bingham and Garfield, they borrowed an engine, an engine crew, and train crew from the Rio Grande. The engine was a little hog and Bill Haymond was the engineer. They used this train and engine crew in work train service. After they had been on the job a short while, Bill let the water get too low and burnt the crown sheet. It's a wonder that little hog didn't blow up.

The Rio Grande fired Bill for this offence. He made no effort toward reinstatement. The reason became apparent after awhile. Bill Haymond's brother went to the B & G Railroad as general manager. When the B & G started operations Bill went to that railroad as the number one engineer on the blue print, the seniority list. I could have gone with him as the number one fireman. Bill got off the B & G business car to ask me to join him as we were standing in the Welby yards. He was riding over the road with his brother at the time.

Several times in my life I have wondered what would have been my lot if I had taken the well-meant advice of others. When it later became known to the Rio Grande officials that Jack Johnson and I were set on leaving to go to the Utah Railway we were told that they had made other plans regarding us. I wonder what they were, and what course my life might have taken if I had listened.

The B & G, after trying unsuccessfully to get the Rio Grande to double track their mainline between Cuprum and Garfield, finally built their own road on the other side of the mountain and forced the Rio Grande out of the territory.

I have told so many times of how I kept an engine hot where others failed. I am now going to tell of occasions when I wasn't so lucky.

There was a time when I was firing freight out of Salt Lake. It was Christmas, and I was laying off for a trip. I knew I would not have to go out, so we were doing a little celebrating. All morning I had been nibbling fruit cake and sipping wine.

About three o'clock in the afternoon the telephone rang. It was the call boy; he started to call me up for no. 2. Number 2 at that time was made up at Salt Lake with interchange off the Western Pacific connection. I interrupted to inform him that I had permission to lay off.

He just laughed over the phone, "Don't make any difference. This is an emergency and you're it."

The more I tried to beg off the more determined he was that I was going. At last I gave up. That's just one of the nettlesome aspects of railroading in those days. If an emergency arose, and you were elected, you went—or you went looking for another job.

Grumbling, I climbed into my work clothes and trudged up to the passenger depot. The 783 was sizzling on an off-track. The engineer was giving her a final looking over. He turned to grin at me.

"They got you too?" he inquired.

Big Ed Rhienhardt was the engineer. He too had been laying off from his freight job. Ed was a big Swede. He stood about six-foot-four. To some he appeared taciturn and morose, but he and I usually got along. I could even make him laugh where others failed.

I was still feeling a little light headed from my morning's imbibing when I climbed on the 783. But when I opened the firedoor to look at my fire, all my insides seemed to run down into my head and overbalance me. That firedoor looked about the size of a silver dollar. However, I managed to orient myself after a fashion.

We took off bravely, and soon we were stepping through the dew right smart, as the saying went. But not for long. The hand on the steam gauge seemed to have all the starch taken out of it. Instead of standing straight up like a good soldier, it wanted to recline more and more. Big Ed kept glancing at the steam gauge and then at me. His anxiety increased as the hand on the gauge slanted more and more to a horizontal position. We were losing time on the Scenic Limited. We arrived at Provo way off our schedule.

All the while we were standing at the depot the blower was rasping loudly, trying to bring up the steam pressure and proclaiming the humiliation of the fireman. Nothing that I can think of is more humiliating to a fireman than to stand up on back of the tank taking water near a passenger station and listening to the loud buzz of the blower telling the world that you're short on steam. We did pick up a little more pressure while standing there, but only while we were not moving. As soon as Ed laid his heavy hand on her she started to wilt again.

In freight service, if a fireman gets his fire clinkered up he can always find time to do a little cleaning while standing in a passing track or even stopped in yard limits. Not so on passenger! As long as you have enough steam to move the train you've got to keep going. But when you can't go any further, you have no choice. You must stop, and like a plodding freight, take time to blow up.

This happened to us that Christmas afternoon at a point where the railroad slants away from Spanish Fork to enter that deep cut on its eastward grind before entering the canyon. We managed to come into Thistle about thirty minutes late. At that place a large mallet was attached to the point. Still that humiliating sound of the blower announced our condition. With that mallet on the sharp end we made Soldier Summit about forty-five minutes late. Of course we made a little of it back on the downgrade into Helper.

I expected to hear about this from the authorities, but they contacted the engineer instead. Ed told me about it later on. He said that Joe Stevenson called him on the phone a day or two later.

He inquired, "Ed, you lost forty minutes on no. 2 yesterday."

"Yes, we did," answered Ed.

"What was the trouble?"

Ed said to me later, "I didn't know just what to do; there was nothing I could say except that we had no steam."

"No steam?" cut in Joe. "Who was the fireman?"

"I told him it was Gould."

"Gould? And you had no steam?"

"Yeah."

After a moment or two of silence, Joe had said, "Well, there must have been something wrong." And he hung up the phone.

How right he was; there sure was something wrong, only he never found out just what it was. I didn't hear a word about it, only what Ed told me.

I can remember several other times when I didn't do so well.

I came out of Salt Lake one night on the 1184. Charley Showacre was the engineer. We had a hot shot fruit train. The 1184 was a good steamer. If she hadn't been, she wouldn't have been on the sharp end of that fruit train. I had never in the past had any trouble in keeping her hot.

We left Salt Lake this night, and try as hard as I might, I couldn't get that gauge hand up against the peg. Those fruit and bullion trains were heavy, and they had to be put over the road. After zooming through Midvale I managed to regain a few pounds on the steam gauge. Still I was having trouble. That hand just wouldn't stand up as it should.

About a quarter of a mile before reaching Riverton there is a slight letup in the grade. At that point I was sweating desperately, trying to get that gauge hand up against the peg. When we hit that letup in the grade, Showacre hooked the Johnson bar back a nick. Before we had gone a dozen car lengths, that pop let go with a loud bang. I walked over and tapped Charley on the shoulder.

"There she is, Charley. Use her!"

He laughed loudly as he turned to me. "What's the matter Gouldie? Did you get off on the wrong foot?" He went on, "I've been watching you ever since we left Salt Lake. I knew you would catch up after a while."

That remark about getting off on the wrong foot was standard. Whenever a person experienced trouble from the start, he was getting off on the wrong foot. I got off on the wrong foot more than once in my career.

I recall one time when we came up out of Helper on no. 5. I was firing the 768 for Art Campbell. I had trouble trying to keep my old pet hot. We had an eleven hundred on the point as a helper. Joe Stevenson was riding that helper engine. He could tell by the weakness of the bark of old 768's exhaust that we were not doing our stuff. I knew that as soon as we stopped at Soldier Summit he would drop back to see what was the matter. That fire was all clinkered up, but I must not let him know it. Just before Art shut off at the Summit, I bounced about a half dozen scoops of coal right in front of the fire door.

Sure enough, as soon as we stopped Joe climbed up on the 768. He grabbed the scoop and opened the firedoor. He placed the scoop on the fire ring and looked over it at my fire. Of course he couldn't size up that fire because the coal that I had dropped just in front of the door was in full flame now.

He turned to me and said, "I can never see your fire, Gouldie."

With that he got off the engine and we left town. On the long descent down into Provo, I had plenty of time to straighten out my fire.

On several other occasions I didn't do too well, but I think I was a pretty good fireman, anyway. When a man goes running and sees other firemen perform, he gets an idea of how good he was. I once got a letter from Billy Cook, the general road foreman of equipment. It made me feel so good I learned it by heart. I can still repeat it word for word:

Mr. W. G. Gould, Fireman:

In looking over the Traveling Fireman's report I notice he shows your service as a fireman as excellent. It pleases me greatly to get such reports, and it certainly should be a credit to you.

Signed,
W. B. Cook
General Road Foreman of Equipment. Burnham, Colo.

I wish I had kept that letter. It would sure bring back the warm glow of pleasant memories.

Two engines, the Denver & Rio Grande 955 and a seven hundred, "blowing the dome" to show off. Photo from the W. J. G. Gould collection, photographer unknown.

Railroad Hazards and Wrecks

When I look back through the years, I truly believe someone up there must have been guiding me. Someone up there must have been watching over me and directing my movements. When I think of the many slight incidents or variations in timing or setting that have meant the difference of life or death to me, I sometimes marvel!

There was the time when I was a very young fireman and was firing an eastbound drag. We were in two reverse curves between Mill Fork and Tucker. It was in the small hours of the morning and Goose Neck Johnson, my engineer, was half asleep over on his seat box. We were beginning to come out of a left-hand curve that circled the low foothills. I was keeping a watch ahead as best I could between fires.

Just as we were about to enter the long tangent, I thought I detected a flicker of light dancing along on the polished inside of the rail. I waited a moment. Then, as we straightened out on that single tracked mainline, sure enough, there was a pale oil headlight dancing along down the track against us. I awakened Goose Neck, and he lost no time bringing our train to a halt. We watched that headlight getting closer. We knew instinctively that someone was trying awfully hard to get that train stopped.

When only a few car lengths separated us we heard that engineer reverse his engine and start to work steam in the back motion. We could hear the roar of the exhaust as the drivers started to spin frantically in the opposite direction. That headlight seemed to shiver and shudder crazily. Only a few feet separated us when the other headlight came to a stop.

After stopping, that other engineer wasted no time. He quickly jerked three blasts from his whistle, and to our astonishment he started backing up to Tucker at a very fast speed. He was a Thistle helper engine returning light. We followed cautiously.

Just into the clear of the mainline on the pass at lower Tucker we caught up with him. He had covered his headlight and was out in the center of our track waving us down with a red fusee. He climbed on our engine and crossed over to the right side to speak to Goose Neck.

I heard Johnson say, "Sure, sure!"

The other engineer started to get off. I was sitting on the left hand seat box. He pressed down on my knee and said, "Don't say anything about this, will you?"

I told him I wouldn't, although, as I was a young fireman, I didn't really know just what there was to say about it. Later when we had plenty of time, my engineer told me how it all came about.

Kid Needham was the engineer on that helper engine. He was returning light to Thistle after making a help to Soldier Summit. He got an order at Lower Tucker to take the siding and meet us at that point. He failed either to read his orders correctly or at all. He just climbed on his engine, a large consolidation, and started for Thistle. He was well on his way when he saw our headlight circling the foothill. It then suddenly dawned upon him that he was supposed to meet an eastbound extra at Tucker. He was making pretty good time down that straight track and he was quite busy getting stopped.

It seems like when a man grows older he analyzes previous incidents more carefully than he did when he was younger. At the time I thought little about it, but in later years I have often thought what little difference there is between life and death situations.

Just think what could have happened if Needham had been about thirty seconds earlier—or if we had been about thirty seconds later. We would have met in those two reverse curves where there would have been no chance to see each other until it was too late. It could have been disastrous, because those light engines returning from making a help on the hill lost no time between Tucker and Thistle on their way home. They literally just fell down that canyon.

A few years later I was firing for this man Needham. He had come to Salt Lake to work in the pool. We were going up past the Dog Ranch just before entering those reverse curves. All the way up from Thistle, Needham had been telling me of his experiences. The old head telling the new.

I walked over to him and said, "Needham, did you ever come down that straight track up ahead and see a headlight coming around this mountain?"

He looked at me kind of foolishly and said, "Yes, but who told you about it?"

I told him I was firing for Goose Neck Johnson that night. He fell into silence and didn't tell me anymore of his experiences for a few trips.

Goose Neck Johnson met an awful death. He was going west on 61 with an eleven hundred engine. The fog was so thick he could only see a few car lengths ahead. At a point about a mile and a half east of Midvale, a westbound work train was dogging along trying to find the switch to head in on the pass. They failed to get out a flag or even a fusee. Goose Neck came bowling along through the fog on the sharp end of 61, a carded fast freight. I don't believe he ever knew what happened to him. I don't think he had time to even see that work train before he hit it. His head brakeman died with him.

The rear brakeman on the work train was pinned in the wreckage of that burning caboose. They couldn't get to him to release him. As the flames grew closer he begged for a gun. No one gave him one. I am not sure anyone around had one to give. It was not an item normally carried by railroaders. The poor fellow died in awful agony.

To use a dramatic, or more properly, a morbid phrase, death was rampant on the rails in those days! I wonder if I could go through it again; maybe—if I were younger. I'm content now to sit at home and wait here for the grim reaper.

When the mainline was a single track between Provo and Thistle, two miles below Castilla there was a piece of straight rail about three-quarters of a mile long. At the west end of this tangent was a house where the attendant of a dam on the river lived. This place had a few lights around it all night. One of these lights was right in line with the end of this straight track.

In those days of the old oil headlights on locomotives, a crew coming west down this tangent could easily be fooled by this light. It was just about the height of a headlight and just about the same brilliancy. Many times I nervously watched that light, wondering if it was what I thought it was or if it was a headlight coming up against us. Things like that could sure bring out the goose pimples. However, no one would ever admit to being scared.

I was working in the pool out of Salt Lake firing freight. Henry Hanagan, an engineer I had worked with for some time on the Bingham Branch, came to Salt Lake to take a mainline job. I was firing for him on his first trip out of the Salt Lake pool. We had made the eastbound trip with no trouble due to my coaching. On the return trip leaving Provo, Henry asked me how far we should go for no. 2. We had a train that was not too heavy, so I told him we could make Geneva. If our train had been of the usual tonnage I would have said Lakota. No one would head in at Geneva going west with a heavy train. If he did, he would not be able to get them rolling fast enough to make American Fork without doubling the hill.

So we started out from Provo, intending to go to Geneva for no. 2, an eastbound passenger train. Somewhere around Lakota it started to snow quite heavily. Henry and I hadn't exchanged a word since I had told him he could make Geneva. After we passed Lakota, the snow really began to fall.

About two miles east of Geneva, Henry became panicky. He shut off steam and began to set the air brakes. I asked him what he was doing. I could tell by his voice that he was going to pieces. He said he was going to cut off the engine and run ahead and flag no. 2 as we didn't have time to make it into clear with the train. This was the usual procedure in case you were caught on short time to make a station for a timed train. You would cut off the engine, run ahead with the engine to the place you intended to meet that opposing train, leave a man to flag, and then go back and get your train.

When I realized Henry's intention I started to take stock of my flagging equipment. I didn't have a red lantern. I didn't have any torpedoes. I had just one red fusee and a white lantern.

When we got to the east switch at Geneva I told Henry to let me off and go back and get the train. He did just that. When I hit the ground it was really snowing with a brisk wind whipping it in every direction. The first thing that happened to me was the light in my white lantern went out. There was no chance to relight it in that weather.

Henry started back for the train, and I opened the switch so that he would be able to head in on his return without stopping. I then started running down the track to meet and flag no. 2. In exasperation I threw the useless lantern as far as I could off the right of way.

I was running down the mainline in a wild snow storm to flag no. 2, and all I had to do it with was one red fusee. It was snowing and blowing so hard you couldn't see twenty feet into the storm. I stopped running for an instant to listen for no. 2. All I could hear was the shrieking of the wind. I kept on running and praying that no. 2 would be a little late.

I could fancy what would happen if no. 2 got by me. I could hear the shattering of glass and the sound of that terrible impact when that passenger train collided with Henry at top speed. I wondered if that fusee would really light up when I needed it. I had no way of knowing. I could only wait until I could hear the rumbling of a passenger locomotive or catch the glow of a headlight. Then I hoped that fusee would blaze long enough to flag no. 2.

By this time, I knew no. 2 was off schedule. I hoped he would be a little later still. Pretty soon I heard the sound of an engine. I couldn't tell if it was Henry or the passenger train, and I couldn't see a headlight in either direction on account of the storm. If that was no. 2 I could hear I had better be cracking that fusee. I held off a little longer. I still could not tell from which direction that sound was coming. My mind was in a terrible state. If I was sure of that fusee lighting everything would be okay. If it didn't? Much as I hated to, I couldn't help picturing the result.

I had now arrived at the west switch of the passing track. The wind and snow seemed to be dying down. Soon it quit snowing and I could see the faint glow of a headlight to the east and discern an engine rumbling slowly toward me. I was sure that our train would soon be into clear on the pass. It suddenly quit snowing altogether and paradoxically the moon, a big, round moon, lighted up the countryside.

I was still holding tightly to that damp sodden fusee when I heard Henry call me in with those five blasts of the whistle. I knew then that he was into clear on the passing track. I saw his headlight go out. What a relief! Number 2 could come anytime now. I looked to the west. Under that bright moon shining on the snow I could see almost to American Fork. And I could not see any sign of that passenger train. I contemplated the fusee in my hand. Then to ease my mind, I tried lighting it. After all that worry the fusee blazed out the first try!

I was firing for Kid Needham one night. We were going east on a fruit train. We had a good old eleven hundred—220 class—engine. The best of the power at hand was saved for the fruit and preferred runs. There were no better engines anywhere than those 220 class consolidations when they were in good shape.

We were rolling furiously down the long tangent track east out of American Fork to a meet with a westbound coal drag at Geneva. We had superior train order rights, so he had to take the siding for us at that point.

At the west end of Geneva the mainline makes a slight curve to the right if you are going east. If you are going west the track turns to the left. An engineer going east can see down into and for quite a distance east of

Geneva. An engineer coming west cannot see past the west switch due to this curve.

As I was saying, we were rolling east on that long down grade out of American Fork. Two miles west of Geneva Needham called to me.

"Come here," he said looking straight ahead.

I went over to the right side to see what was holding his attention. The night was very dark. About a mile east of Geneva we could see an oil headlight shivering along the mainline toward us. We knew the fireman was down on the deck spading the coal. He was flashing the door. When he opened the door to put in coal the sky would light up around the engine. We could almost distinguish the engine cab and the clouds of smoke mingling with the steam sizzling around the pop valve and rolling back over the train.

Knowing, as we did, what all this meant, it was a chilling and frightening sight. They had no idea of heading in to meet us at Geneva, according to orders. We could see them coming, but they couldn't see us. That engineer couldn't see us due to the curving track. The fireman was down on the deck shoveling coal into that blinding firebox. If the head brakeman was on the engine, he must surely be asleep, which was not unusual. Already my engineer had shut off what little throttle he was working on the long slight downgrade.

On came that trembling headlight. Intermittently the sky would light up and then darken as the fireman continued to flash the firedoor. We knew now that they were intent on making the run for the American Fork hill, for they had already passed the east switch where they should have headed in for us. The engineer and I both prepared to leave our perilous positions on the engine. We were still rolling along about twenty miles an hour. Needham had made a heavy application of the brakes. There was nothing more that could be done. I got down on the steps on the left side. I could see that headlight just straightening out onto the tangent. There was no sense in waiting any longer. I stepped off the engine.

When I hit the ground I was soon aware that I hadn't improved my position. About three feet from the right of way was a large swamp, a deep pool of stagnant water choked with growing cattails. I had to line up beside those towering boxcars. I couldn't get away on account of the swamp. I wondered if on the pending impact those cars would turn over on me. I looked ahead at the approaching headlight. It was now facing us on the straight track. Behind it I could see the wheels of the train still on the curve. Every wheel, as far as I could see, was a round circle of fire thrown out as the brake shoes bit deeply into the revolving surface of the wheels.

Our train had already stopped, and I knew from those fire-encircled wheels of the other train that somebody was trying desperately to stop. Would that stop be made in time? That headlight was getting closer, although its approach was considerably slower. I began to feel a little better about my chances. If those engines did come together, It wouldn't be hard enough now to topple a boxcar over on top of me.

At last there was much loud screeching of brakes—then absolute silence except for the panting and wheezing of the air pumps. Both trains had come to a stop. I moved ahead as fast as I could along that narrow path between the swamp and the cars. When I got to the engine on the left side Needham was coming up on the right side. We both arrived about the same time. There was a space of three car lengths between the two engines!

Needham went up to the other engine. The engineer was a man named McCall. He was a little old man, as I remember, with a little gray Charlie Chaplin mustache. He had been on the Rio Grande about four years. He had come as a boomer and had stayed.

Although he was very bright and intelligent he was always getting himself into some trouble of his own making. I never talked to a man so well informed on air brake operation as he was. He could diagnose any trouble in the air brake system. But when it came to handling it expertly, he just couldn't do it. He could talk air brakes all day, but he couldn't handle them very well.

His excuse in this case was that he had misread the orders. He read the name Gravan instead of Geneva. Gravan was a little side track down in the bottom of the Jordan Narrows used mostly for storing cars. I never heard of anyone getting a positive train order meet at the place. A railroad company tries to have the names of its stations differ as much as possible in order to prevent any mistake in the reading of train orders.

The conductor, it developed, had pulled the air when he saw that the head end was intent on going up into American Fork. That's what stopped their train.

This case was covered up, as we would say. It was never reported. If it had been maybe that engine crew would have had to attend an investigation and would very likely have been fired.

As those names did, in a way, look a little alike, in the hurried reading of train orders, it could very well be that he spoke the truth when he said he read the order Gravan instead of Geneva. I had a bad experience once myself, after I was running an engine, when I misread a train order.

We had another harrowing experience on this eastward trip. Coming into Provo from the west is a long sweeping curve into town. It is also on a slight downgrade. The yard limit board is about a mile west of the depot. This curve that I speak of is to the left. The engineer must depend on the fireman to inform him of any obstruction. All trains, except first-class (passenger) trains must come into town through yard limits prepared to stop in the distance that they can see. There is no flag protection in yard limits except against first-class trains. That means that if you are on anything but a first-class train, you must travel through these yard limits prepared to stop anywhere.

This night we were rambling into Provo right smart, to use a favored expression. I think Needham had something on his mind. Maybe he was still thinking of that experience a few miles back at Geneva. I had never seen him come into town that fast before. I was staring fearfully ahead from my side of the cab. We had traveled almost the full distance of that curve when I saw a glint of red on the inside rail. A moment later I saw a red fusee burning on the rear platform of a caboose.

I hollered to Needham, "That will do!"

We had a heavy fruit train and Needham set the air in an emergency application. Without looking across the cab I heard the slam of his brake valve into the big hole. As those brakes started to take hold and slow us down, I watched that caboose get closer and closer. Soon I saw that it was moving ahead. Our brakes were doing a good job of slowing us down. We got up to almost a car length of that caboose before it started pulling away from us. Then we stopped.

I then turned around to face Needham with a deep sigh of relief. He wasn't in the cab. I looked up on the coal pile. He was no where in sight. I wondered what had happened to him. In a moment or two he climbed sheepishly up the right hand gangway.

I said, "Where have you been?"

He answered, "I got down on the steps to see if the drivers were sliding."

I remarked that the gangway steps were a poor place to be if the drivers were sliding. He turned aside without another word. The truth of the matter was that in approaching Provo he must not have realized exactly where he was. He was probably preoccupied with other thoughts. If he had been he wouldn't have been coming into town so fast in the first place.

As I hollered, "That will do!" he normally would have waited for me to set the example before he got off, because the reason for stopping was in my vision. But in his preoccupation or nervousness he big holed the train and unloaded, as the expression goes. That experience at Geneva was apparently still with him.

Another time I was firing for another Swede, Ollie Johnson. We came out of Salt Lake on the house drag. This train set out loaded cars at different points along the line. On arrival at Thistle what was left of the train usually went down the Marysvale branch. So the house drag crew was usually turned around and sent back to Salt Lake or was assigned to some other service.

As it happened that morning, we were told to turn our engine, take our caboose, and back up to Gilluly. We were to get a westbound train of coal and take it on into Salt Lake. We backed up as ordered, put our caboose on the rear end of about sixty-five cars of coal, came around, and backed our engine onto the head end.

Those eleven hundreds had only one eleven-inch air pump on them in those days, and as it was a cold morning in the middle of winter, we were quite some time pumping up—"charging"—that train with air. Before we started, if we had been living up to the rules, we should have made an air brake test. This, my engineer failed to do.

We had been standing there quite a while pumping that train line up to pressure. We knew from the way the pump was working that the train was getting the air, but even at that Ollie should have tried his brake valve before starting the train. He didn't do it.

We took off from Gilluly and started rolling down the grade. When the speed reached about twenty-five miles an hour Ollie started to make his first application of the brakes. I heard him bring his brake valve around to the service position. I then heard the preliminary exhaust port open— and that was all. There was no corresponding sound from the train line exhaust as there should have been. Ollie moved his brake valve to the service position again. And again there was only the sound of the preliminary exhaust. We were now sliding down that grade pretty fast, and I was all ears and eyes. Something was wrong! Ollie brought his brake valve again to the service position and left it there. Still only the sound of the exhaust from the preliminary port (equalizing reservoir) was heard!

I jumped across the cab and looked up at the air gauge. Both hands on the gauge were falling together! Ordinarily the hand representing the train line—or brake pipe, as moderns term it—should have lagged behind the preliminary exhaust. As it was, the condition shown by the hands on the gauge would indicate that we had a very short train line. Not more than one or two cars. Behind us were sixty-five cars loaded with coal that were not responding to the braking system.

By now we were really rolling! There was nothing I could do. On the big curve just above old Tucker I decided to leave, and got down on the tender step. I looked back along the train. Two car lengths back of the engine the head brakeman was already down on the stirrup step of the car. He was holding on with both hands, and standing with one leg on the bottom rung. He was tentatively and fearfully feeling with the other foot for the ground sliding by him so swiftly.

I turned away and made a careful jump. I lit over against the outside eastbound rail. Half stunned, I grabbed hold and slid along on that rail for about two car lengths before I could stop myself. When I did stop there was quite a weight on top of me. It was the head brakeman, Bobby Davis. When he saw me let go he had waited no longer. He had let go, too. We ended up together in one lump, and in one lump we slid along together on that eastbound rail.

The train went by us with a rush. We picked ourselves up and watched that caboose rolling along around the curves and out of sight. Already it had held the rail longer than we expected it to do. Then, the last look we had, it was still rolling swiftly along, but didn't seem to be rolling any faster. We started walking down the track. My right elbow was giving me quite a bit of pain, but you don't notice that too much when you are young.

Bobby Davis and I continued on down the track. When we got to Detour, to our great surprise, we could see that caboose standing right side up about a half-mile away.

That train had been giving the original engine crew trouble right out of Soldier Summit. At Gilluly the engineer, Toddy Magee, had complained about it being a hard train to hold. He had told the brakeman to get the conductor up to the head end. He wanted to talk to him.

The conductor, Lew Combs, had come out of the caboose and walked up to the engine in the cold of that early winter's morning. That could not have been helpful to his Welsh disposition. When Toddy started to tell him of his having trouble holding that train, he interrupted to tell the engineer that the only trouble was on the right hand seat box of that engine. That did it! A Welsh-Irish argument was in full swing.

Finally Lew had threatened to cut Toddy and his engine off the train and send them to Thistle light.

Toddy said, "Go ahead. Cut me off!"

Lew said he would.

"Go Ahead," said Toddy again. "Cut me off!"

If it weren't so comical it would have been ridiculous. Both of these hot tempered little game cocks were trying to bluff the other into making a move. But Lew had deliberately strode to the back of the tank and closed both angle cocks. He gave Toddy a highball signal with his lantern. Toddy called his bluff, whistled two short blasts, and took off. He didn't stop until he got to Thistle. I often wondered what Lew thought when he saw that engine fade away around the curve and head for Thistle on his highball.

That was the reason for our crew having to back up to Gilluly to get that train off the mainline.

When Bobby and I got back to the train, we were subjected to a lot of good natured censure and ridicule for having left the train. I know though that the reason that some of the others didn't get off was their fear of the result. That ground was really rushing by when we let go.

You may wonder how that train finally did stop. I can explain that. I have observed conditions several times in later years when it was possible to get air into the train line and charge it up, but very difficult to get it out to set the brakes. The pressure in the train line after charging must be reduced to set the brakes.

If the inner lining of an air hose is ruptured the air may flow past the rupture or flap into the train line if that rupture is near the head end of the train. However, that rupture or flap of lining will choke off the flow of air in the opposite direction when an attempt is made to reduce the pressure through the automatic brake valve.

Or, if a chunk of ice forms in an air hose it will, due to the flow of air in the two different directions, roll itself into a ball until it gets big enough to choke off the passage, usually up against a metal fitting of reduced diameter in the train line. This will act as a check valve, allowing air to flow into the train line, charging it up; but the ice will not allow it to flow out to reduce the pressure as is necessary to set the brakes.

There is no question that one of these two conditions was operating with this train that morning. It was probably a little marble of ice. If Ollie Johnson had made the required air brake test before starting, this condition would have been detected immediately. No doubt Toddy Magee suspected it when he was having the original trouble, but apparently he couldn't get Lew Combs to inspect the train. As it was, that train line was fully charged with air when we left town, but due to the ice plug near the head car that pressure could not be reduced through the engineer's brake valve.

However, with the engineer's brake valve in negative position no additional air was getting into that train line. There are always a few leaks in a long train line. Those leaks reduced the train line pressure slowly. By the time the train had run three or four miles those leaks would have reduced the pressure and gradually set the brakes, and by the time that train had reached the flat rail below Detour those brakes had set hard enough to stop the train.

If this incident did nothing else, it taught me the importance of making an air brake test before starting after standing around for any great length of time.

I had one experience in my days on the rail that would be hard to forget. That was the time we ran away down the old Soldier Summit grade.

At the Summit in those days there was a long snow shed. If the wind was blowing or if the weather was bad, trains would be pulled into the shed for inspection. The inspection was rigorous and exacting. The train line, that is the brake pipe, and all connections, including triple valves, auxiliary reservoirs, and such, would be gone over thoroughly in quest of leaks after the pressure had been pumped up to eighty pounds. This was very important, as the pumping capacity of those engines wasn't what it was in later years.

The largest pumps on the road were the eleven-inch pumps on the eleven hundred class engines. All other engines, including those in passenger service, were equipped with nine and one-half-inch pumps. The size in inches referred to the size of the air cylinder bore. The eight and one-half-inch cross-compound pump, later standard equipment on almost all engines, had a capacity two and a half times greater than the eleven-inch pump. When the Utah Railway engines appeared they were the wonder of the road, for they had two eight and one-half-inch cross-compound pumps on each engine. All the pumping capacity in the world!

We had the little old 951 that night we ran away. She had one nine and one-half-inch pump. It was necessary that all leaks be taken up before attempting the descent of that heavy grade. After charging the train line and reservoirs to eighty pounds pressure, the car men would go over every joint and connection with a flaring torch. If the flame on the torch wavered when held against a joint that proved that there was a leak at that point. This had to be made tight. That was the leakage test.

After that the brakes would be set with the retainers in holding position. Any piston travel over seven inches would have to be shortened. The brakes were then released, and the holding condition of the retainers was noted. All this information had to be conveyed to the engineer before he started down the grade.

The usual comment would be like this: "You've got one a little long and one not holding," meaning that on one car the piston travel was over seven inches, and that one retainer was not retaining. This was the maximum deviation from perfection allowed in any one train.

If the engineer decided it was a safe train he would whistle off, put his brake valve in full release, and gently ease his train out onto the grade. With the brake valve in release position instead of running position, twenty pounds more air would be pumped into the train line. So before he got ready to brake the train he should have one hundred pounds in the brake system.

Some engineers, a little overly confident, would neglect to return the brake valve to release position. This would cut down the braking pressure from one hundred to eighty pounds. If the train was a good holding one this would work all right. If not, then eighty pounds would not be enough. The events of the night of this story proved that eighty pounds was indeed not enough.

This night we had an engineer by the name of Bill Boucher. He was a very capable engineer and a very fine man. I liked him a great deal. After going through the ritual described above, we started down the hill. The first application of the brakes took hold okay. However, instead of returning his brake valve to release position to get that extra twenty pounds pressure, Bill elected to stop at the running position. When he next made a brake application it had little effect, and by this time we were rolling merrily along.

He made several more reductions of air with no appreciable effect. As things were he didn't dare release to get more air and he couldn't get more air pressure until he did go to the release position. Too late he cut in his driver brake. That is the brake on the driving wheels. We were by this time indeed rolling too fast, much too fast.

Although he hadn't said a word to me, somehow I knew we were running away. When I saw him fumbling along the inside of the cab for the driver brake cutout, I jabbed the torch into the firebox for a light and held it so that he could find the valve.

We were now rolling along right smart. Finally Bill reached for the whistle cord and one long appealing moan split the night air. It was the ultimate in the drama of a railroad runaway—that urgent call for brakes. The call that would send the trainmen out on the tops of the cars, out on the "hurricane deck," to tie down the brakes by hand and brake club. The driving wheels on the little old 951 were now turning faster with every revolution.

In my short career as a mountain rail I had often pictured such a condition. I had often wondered how it would feel to be running away down this steep grade. I don't know if those thoughts had prepared me for this occasion, but I will say, more truly from pride than braggadocio, I was cool and in full command of my actions. This was it, I thought. This is a situation that I have been wondering about. Would I now end up in a hospital, the morgue, or would I live to tell about it? The very next few moments would tell. I seemed to glory in it!

I walked the gangway, first from one side and then to the other. Bill Boucher didn't say a word to me. He again sent that appealing moan from the whistle out onto the night air. The sound seemed to fill the canyon. He was again calling for brakes. If that whistle could be translated into words it would say:

"Tie 'em down, boys, Tie 'em down!"

"I've done all I can do now!"

And those brakemen riding out on top of those rocking cars with their brake clubs would try to get one more nick, one more notch, in the brake staff ratchet. One more nick just might do the trick!

During the early seconds of our roaring descent I had walked from one side of the engine to the other. The thought had been in my mind: I can still get off. I can still jump. I would look at the engineer for direction. He weighed about sixty-five pounds more than I did, and he was about twenty-five years older. If he could stay with the engine and take a chance, then why couldn't I do likewise?

Now as I looked down at the ground swirling by the thought came to me: you've waited too long! You can't get off, now! You've missed your chance!

Three and a half miles below Soldier Summit a derailing spur took off from the mainline and led up the mountain side. The switch to this spur was always lined for the mountain. An elderly woman and two grown daughters tended this switch twenty-four hours a day. A stop board a quarter of a mile above the switch commanded all trains to stop. After a full stop was made, four loud blasts from the whistle brought one of this trio of women out to line the switch for the mainline.

The train could then proceed on its way. But only if the train came to a full stop would that switch be lined for the mainline. Immediately after the train had passed, the switch would again be lined for the derailing spur. Where this spur ended against the mountainside was a pile of wood. It was the remains of shattered slats from the wooden pilots in use in those days. That pile of wood was a grim reminder of others who before us had smashed up against that mountain.

I was now standing in the right gangway as we flashed by that stop board. I thought, it won't be long now!

In those last few seconds of our flashing descent Bill Boucher had cut out his driver brakes. Opening his cylinder cocks he managed to get the Johnson bar over into the back motion. Now he cautiously fed steam into those cylinders. The wheels turned hesitatingly backwards, slipping on the sanded rail, but to no avail.

Just before we entered the spur Bill stepped down onto the deck. I was standing in the right gangway watching the crazy world fly by me. He then spoke his first words to me since leaving Soldier Summit: "You better get off now, Kid, before she turns over."

Reluctantly with my foot I felt for the gangway step. I wanted to wait a little longer. I thought that when that train felt the upslant of that spur the speed would decrease slightly, and I would be able to get off with less danger. I could look across the deck and see my engineer duplicating my position and actions on the left side. Oh, how I wished that train would slow down just a trifle!

We had just entered the derailing spur. It was early in November, and there was a light snow on the small rail. The engine was in the back motion, the cylinder cocks were open, and she was working against her own forward motion. Then she hit the snow-covered rail, and those high driving wheels started to spin crazily backwards.

I thought she was on the ground. It was now or never! I couldn't wait any longer. I leaned into the breeze and let go. I never made a more careful jump in my life, but that hard snow-covered ground didn't wait for me. The earth flew up to meet me. It hit me a dazing blow in the forehead, and head over heels I went. Vainly I spread my arms in an attempt to stop my pinwheeling gyrations. At last I came to a stop about thirty feet off the right-of-way.

Funny what thoughts pass through a person's mind in moments of stress. As I was doing cartwheels over the snow my thoughts were: I wonder if anyone is watching me? I'll bet I'm a strange sight rolling around in this snow.

When I left that engine I made a trail in the snow. The head brakeman was riding the first car. When he saw me make that jump he let go too. The trails we left in the snow paralleled each other for about thirty feet away from the track. I had hardly gotten to my feet when the caboose lurched to a noisy crashing stop just a few car lengths from us.

What a contrast was the absolute silence that then prevailed for a few moments. Suddenly I heard hysterical chattering and quavering laughter from the region of the caboose. We all converged there sizing each other up, trying to find out what injuries we had sustained.

Bill Boucher limped painfully up over the bank. The rear brakeman and the conductor rode the caboose to a stop and were in good condition except for hysterics. The head brakeman had a few bruises but no broken bones. Bill had a badly sprained knee and some back injuries. And me—I was sure a bloody sight, but luckily no broken bones.

It developed that the engine had stuck her nose up against the mountain, and it appeared that she had tried to climb it. If she had gone another car length I believe she would have laid over against the first car. As it was she needed only a little help to get back on her feet, minus her cowcatcher.

We all considered ourselves lucky. If I had any assurance that I wouldn't sustain injuries I wouldn't mind going through it again. It was for a few moments a thrill never to be forgotten.

There is no sound in all the world quite like that appealing moan from the whistle when you know it's a call for brakes—a monster in distress, calling, pleading despairingly for help and for sympathy. He who has heard that appeal ring out on the winter's night air will never forget the sound of it or fail to feel the utter helplessness it conveys. He will waken from a troubled sleep to hear it again and again.

While we were standing there five helper engines running light back down to Tucker came down the hill in succession and stopped behind us. We let one of them go on down the mainline and stop just clear of the spur switch. The rest of them got behind the caboose and yanked us out onto the mainline. The one that had cleared the spur then backed up and coupled onto the head end. After going through those tests again we proceeded down into Tucker. The little old 951 needed a little work. Then we proceeded to Salt Lake with the train we had. There was no filling out to normal tonnage at Tucker that night.

We were all out of service when we got to Salt Lake. After four days' delay we were ordered to attend an investigation. At this investigation the only member of the crew that could be censured was the engineer, although I got a big bawling out from the master mechanic.

Old Honest Bill Boucher might have saved his job if he had been willing to tell a couple of small lies. But he told me before the investigation, "I wouldn't lie to save my job." That was the way he was. The instruction in handling trains on that grade was to put the brake valve in the full release position between applications of the brakes so as to charge the brake pipe to the higher pressure. Also the driver brakes must be cut out and the water brake used on the engine. Bill had violated both instructions and admitted that he did. There was no possible way that they could have checked on him if he had wanted to lie. He knew it, and he also knew what the penalty was to be. Still he refused to lie about it.

I had fired for old Bill quite a bit prior to this time, and I liked him a great deal. He was as honest a man as you would find in railway service.

At that time I had been firing an engine about two and a half years. I was not looking for promotion until I had at least four years of service.

Consequently I was not as well posted on air brakes as I would like to have been. When it came my turn for questioning the Master Mechanic posed a few routine questions, then asked pointedly, "Do you know how much main reservoir pressure your engineer had?"

I answered, "No, Sir."

He went on, "How much train line pressure did your engineer have?"

I said, "I don't know."

He was beginning to get angry. "Do you know how much excess pressure your engineer had?"

I said, "No, Sir."

He leaned over and looked me full in the eye. "Do you know your engineer was on that engine?" he shouted. I was getting angry too and my cockiness was showing.

"Yes, Sir!" I shouted back.

"Oh! You do know that, do you?"

Then he began tapping on the table with the end of his pencil. "Young man, this railroad does not want just coal shovelers. It wants bright, intelligent young men. Young men who can become engineers, and don't you forget it."

He made several more remarks that were not flattering to me, then he said, "You go back and mark up on the board, and don't forget I'll be watching you."

They fired old Bill for those two violations. Notwithstanding his own misfortune, he did his best to console me.

"Don't mind what he said, Kid. Just let it pass. If you had tried to answer his questions he would have tangled you up. So what!"

I thought that was pretty decent of him. He waited around for several months in the hopes of reinstatement, which was refused him. After about six months, the Bingham and Garfield Railroad was just about to go into operation. The superintendent had held that same position at Welby on the Bingham Branch of the Rio Grande. He was more than glad to hire Bill Boucher as an engineer.

When the Rio Grande heard of it, they offered to reinstate Bill. He simply and directly told them to go to Hell!

There is never a time when I travel up the old grade to Soldier Summit in an automobile that I don't look over when we pass the former location of Media and size up the markings of that runaway spur leading off the mainline. I see the distortion that marks the culvert location under the track. In recent years it has begun to fill up. But you can still put an X there and say, "X marks the spot where Gilbert Gould took his chance! Where he made that jump!"

Yes, give me back my youth and health, and I'd like to do it again! It's one event I shall never forget!

I did go back on the board, and I did take notice of myself. I obtained some books on air brakes. I took a course in locomotive running with the International Correspondence Schools. I studied diligently, and when I did take the engineer's examination I was glad to see Master Mechanic Bennett sit in and listen. He listened for about an hour. Then without a word he took his departure.

One day I was firing an eastbound drag of empties. There was a preferred job (a hot shot) coming along behind us. We headed into the pass at Gilluly to let him by. This preferred job was a train of bullion out of Midvale. We both pulled up and stopped at the upper water tank about the same time. We, being the inferior train, let the engine on the bullion job take water first. We sometimes showed a little courtesy—especially when the rules demanded it.

I was on the ground ready to swing the spout over to our tank when they released it. Their head brakeman stepped down beside me to stretch his legs. We entered into a friendly conversation. He was a boomer. I had never seen him before, although he had worked on the Rio Grande at several previous times, in both the capacity of a brakeman and a fireman. He had a very pleasing and friendly personality. I took quite a liking to him during our brief gabfest there at the tank spout.

When their tank was filled, and they were about to leave town he climbed aboard. The engineer blasted two ear-splitting blasts from the whistle. Like a long, delayed echo came the same sounds from the helper engine back in the train. They took off on up the hill.

My new-found friend waved at me from the gangway as the train started to move. "I'll see you at Helper," he shouted.

Well, I saw him at Helper alright, but I don't think he saw me. He was lying on a slab in one of the lower unused rooms at the railroad YMCA. He was killed at Castle Gate a couple of hours after his promise to me.

At that time all bullion trains had to stop at Castle Gate ten minutes to cool the wheels and to give the brakemen a chance to look over the train. It was there, either in stopping or starting, that this happy, carefree, boomer brakeman got his among those jostling cars. It was never known exactly in what way.

There used to be a big arc light at Castle Gate just above the coal tipple from the mine. It was at this point that the heavily loaded eastbound trains stopped for inspection and to cool the wheels. There was a slight curve to the left at this place.

One night I was firing an eastbound bullion train for Ole Johnson. Coming down out of Royal I felt a slight jerk on the engine. Ole looked inquiringly across the cab at me. Neither of us spoke. We continued on our way. At Castle Gate the usual stop was made for inspection.

It was a warm summer night. I listened a moment to the sizzling sound of the electrode and carbon in that arc light off to my side. For a moment I contemplated it. Then my gaze wandered back along our train. What I expected to see was a long line of box cars over their smoking wheels, maybe also the brakeman's lantern moving alongside. What I actually saw was just one box car behind the engine!

It developed that when we felt that little jerk in the sag at Royal, the train had broken in two. That is, a drawbar had pulled out of its connections to the car. The automatic brakes had stopped the rear portion of the train. With the brake on only one car, we had drifted down into Castle Gate to stop with the straight air at the inspection point. The head brakeman was still getting his rest on the back of the tank. We got him up and very cautiously backed up to Royal for the rest of our train. Anything can happen on a railroad!

Let me talk a little bit about the state of mind that we frequently observed where a man was afraid of being afraid.

I was firing a little Rome one day on the eastbound local. We were just leaving Salt Lake, and I noticed a wash-out plug sizzling down where the deck rubbed up against it. I called the engineer's attention to it. Reluctantly he glanced down and took a look.

"Oh, that's all right," was his verdict.

But I didn't think so. I was very careful when I got off the seat box to put in a fire. I knew that in spite of what the engineer said he too was more than a little worried. He kept glancing down at the plug. I got up on the seat box as far away as I could after every fire.

All at once the engineer started to holler, "Look out! Look out!"

That plug started to spew out scalding water and steam. I was glad that I wasn't down putting in a fire when it let go. We both got as far out the window as we could get. That wash-out plug was actually jiggling under the stress of a hundred and sixty pounds of steam. After we stopped (we had both injectors going by that time), we got down on the ground and let her gradually die. That engineer was afraid of that plug on the first look, but he would not admit it. He was afraid of being afraid.

I believe the best example of this condition of mind that I ever saw took place on the branch that ran from Provo to Heber Valley. It was in the early spring of 1915. I had not yet been promoted. Business was very slow on the Rio Grande. I couldn't hold a regular job anywhere, so I was working on the extra board out of Salt Lake. There was a snow slide up around Vivian Park on the Heber Branch.

I was called off the extra board to fire the rotary snowplow. We went up the Provo Canyon with two little hogs pushing us. Al Baxter was operating the rotary. On the first pass we made at the slide we knocked out a cylinder head on one of the rotary's engines. It could be that I had too much water in the boiler or Al Baxter didn't have his cylinders clear before he gave her the gun.

We disconnected the damaged engine just as you would disconnect one side of a locomotive that blew a cylinder head. We then proceeded to operate with only one side connected. As you would expect, there was excessive vibration when the rotary was operating on just that one side.

We would get the rotary wheel turning as fast as we could with only one engine. Then Al would give two toots on the whistle. The two little hogs would then ease us into the snowslide. As long as the wheel kept turning those hogs would keep shoving us further into the snow. When the wheel stopped, Al would whistle three toots and the hogs would drag us out. After several hours, we had cut a neat square slot into the snow on the mountainside. It towered way up over the rotary. We would look up at it fearfully, especially when the rotary was vibrating vigorously.

High up the mountain on the other side of the canyon a man heavily clothed and armed with binoculars and a shotgun watched the snow up over our heads. If the snow started to move he was to fire the shotgun. We would then get the hell out of there. At least that was the idea.

That snow on the mountainside was high and heavy. If it did come down with us in the slot it would bury us. We all knew that, but we kept on working. Time after time those little hogs would push us into the snow with the rotary blades spinning and vibrating. Then when those blades quit turning they would drag us out until they started spinning again. The snow thrown by the rotary up on the bank of the slot grew higher and higher. No one gave voice to his thoughts. Everyone was silent. The tension was great, and we were all scared, but no one would admit it.

I know what my thoughts were. I was greatly relieved every time we were dragged out into the open. Each time we went in I thought, this is it! This is the last time. We will never come out again! That snow can't hang up there any longer.

I remember looking back at the fireman on one of the little hogs. His face was expressionless. He shook his head slowly and held up his hand with his fingers crossed. I believe everyone on that crew felt as I did. If one man had said, "I'm not going in there again," that slide would not have been cleared as soon as it was. We were just all afraid to say we that we were afraid.

So we kept on. In we would go! We pressed up against the snow as long as the rotary blades turned, then we were out again. We finally made it through and the snow still stood, sheer up on the mountainside.

In a way this illustrates a paradoxical outlook on life. You will hear men say after relating some dangerous experience that they lived through safely, "I would never do that again!" Maybe they would and maybe they wouldn't. It's hard to tell. But just put them up against the gun and the odds are they would do it all over again!

I sometimes wonder when I think of some of my experiences if I could go through them again. I just don't know—maybe yes, and again, maybe no.

Curley Dyet, the engineer who first took an interest in me, was originally an engineer on the Park City road when it was an independent narrow gauge outfit.

He used to tell me about bucking snow on that road. He said that you couldn't get one of those little hogs stuck in the snow if you used your head. The idea was that when you rammed into a snow bank as far as you could go and were dead stopped, the first thing to do was to swing the Johnson bar over into the back motion. If you delayed doing this the snow would settle down in the links and you would be unable to move.

I saw this demonstrated several times, once very clearly on the Eureka Branch. We had come out of Salt Lake on the "house drag," all the freight loaded during the day for near points. It was always called for around midnight. After setting out the eastbound consist of our train at Thistle we had been ordered to take a little hog engine and the flanger and go down to Springville and flange out the Eureka Branch ahead of the mixed run. We had the flanger between the little hog and the caboose.

Whoever ordered this operation was surely not correctly informed of the situation. A flanger is for use against a moderate fall of snow. It is useless when up against deep, snow-filled cuts such as we encountered.

We left Springville ahead of the mixed job and were progressing nicely until we got to within about a mile and a half of the top of the hill above Eureka. It was there we ran into those cuts. What we needed was a rotary or at least a wedge plow, and ahead of, not behind, the engine. We made very little progress after that.

We would lunge at the snow, and as soon as we got stuck we would back out for a fresh start. Fifteen car lengths down the grade, we would stop and stand still. At that time a half a dozen section men, who were riding the caboose, would start shovelling all the snow we had loosened. They would throw it as high up on the bank as they could.

While we were waiting for them to do this we would be filling the firebox with coal and the boiler with water. The deck of a little hog engine was no place for the fireman to be while charging the snow bank. We would have the blower rasping out of the stack, so the steam pressure would be high when we charged. The further we went into the cut, the deeper became the snow.

My engineer was quite an old man named Daley. Several times we almost became stuck in the snow on account of him not being fast enough in getting the Johnson bar over into the back motion after our forward lunge was stopped. I had to help him after awhile. When we started ahead I would be standing up in the right side of the cab behind him. When we were almost stopped I would reach over and unlatch the Johnson bar. Together we would get it over in the back motion and back out.

Daley was a sort of a person who was contemptuous of others. It irritated him that he had to have help to get that reverse lever over. As the work progressed he had several run-ins with the roadmaster, Chris Nelson, a fine old Swede who had come with us out of Springville. After awhile, due to Daley's irritable disposition, I would not help him unless he asked me to.

After we had been slamming against the snow for several hours and making little progress, the mixed run came up behind us. We cut off the two little hogs that they had on the head end and put them behind our caboose. Then we had three little hogs to smash at the snow.

We would back down about fifteen car lengths or more and get those engines hot and full of water. Then, after the section men had gotten rid of all the loose snow, Daley would blast twice on the whistle. Each engineer would repeat the signal, and away we would go. As soon as we got stopped each engineer would reverse his engine and wait for three quick blasts from our engine which was the signal to back up. They would then repeat the signal, and we would back up.

This was the procedure. Once Daley couldn't get the reverse lever over quick enough. Chris Nelson, up on the bank, shouted down at him, "What's the matter, Jim?"

Daley stopped tugging at the Johnson bar and looked up at him. That irritable contempt was in his voice:

"What's the matter?" he echoed. "Why we're stuck in the snow! He screamed. "Just as we have been all day."

Much profanity passed between them for a few moments.

"Why the hell don't you whistle 'back-up' and let them pull you out?" said the roadmaster.

Much against his will Jim Daley blasted three times, and the two hogs behind us jerked us out.

We worked on that snow bucking job until our time was up, and we still had about a hundred feet to go before we would be through. In the meantime, Joe Stevenson, the traveling engineer and a trainmaster showed up on the scene. Joe relieved Jim Daley, and a section man took my place. Daley and I walked into Eureka, and after a feed we took on a little "hay."

When our rest was up we were back on the job. We had a few cuts to knock the snow out of between Eureka and Silver City. We were out of coal and needed the fire cleaned. There was an engine watchman stationed at Silver City to watch the passenger train's engine and to coal it. It was there the trainmaster came very close to firing me.

While the engine watchman and I were getting the fire cleaned the trainmaster had the brakeman and a couple of section men filling our tender with coal from a car that stood alongside. He looked down in the cab and saw us both down there cleaning the fire. He ordered the engine watchman to get up on the car and help coal the engine. He told me to finish cleaning the fire.

The fire was almost cleaned then. He told me to finish the job. I told him it wasn't part of my job. We had quite a chewing match, and I finally finished cleaning the fire. If he had fired me I have no doubt I would have been reinstated in time. But I couldn't afford to lose that time. In order for a man to stay on the job in those days he had to do lots of things that were not specifically included in his job. So I did.

That trainmaster afterward became my friend. He was among those who strongly advised me against going to the Utah Railway when I was considering it.

Incidentally, that was the first time I saw snow used for boiler water. We were out of water before we left the engine. Every time we stopped, there would be section men up on the snow bank shovelling snow into our tank. We would blow steam back into the tank to melt the snow. That's how we continued to have enough water to operate.

By the way, this was one of the examination questions for promotion to engineer: "If you should run out of water in a snow bank would you kill the engine?"

One of the highlights of my career was the time no. 15 stubbed her toe at Colton.

In the spring of 1915 the Rio Grande put on a fast express train between Denver and Salt Lake. When I say fast, I mean just that—fast! It was really too fast for the track, roadbed, and signalling we had at that time.

Departing Denver, this train was just an ordinary local passenger run, but at Grand Junction it was made over into a different one, consisting of four express cars and a coach. And from there it literally took wings and flew. Out of Helper there would usually be two monkey seven hundreds on the point all the way into Salt Lake. The running time between Helper and Soldier Summit was fifty minutes. That was much too fast for the condition of the roadbed at that time, considering the curves and such.

The night before this wreck I was firing the 774 on the sharp end of no. 15. It was customary to take a pool crew at Helper to man the second engine. This second engine was always on the point. Due to the curvature of the tracks at that time between Helper and Kyune, the train usually lost time on the schedule. This was made up across the flats between Kyune and Soldier Summit.

I have watched this train from the vicinity of the depot at Colton come around that sweeping curve east of town. You could remark leisurely to yourself, there she comes! and before you could hardly get those words spoken, you could say, there she goes!

I had noticed what seemed to be a soft spot in the track as we went by the water tank. The night before, as we had hurricaned through Colton with the 774 on no. 15, that soft spot momentarily gave me a sickening feeling. I don't know what I could liken it to. It seemed like the engine was suddenly sinking from under us, then just as suddenly finding its feet again.

On the night of the wreck the 774 was the lead engine, with Frank Ladd as engineer and Jack Johnson scooping the coal. The second engine was either the 771 or the 773, with my old friend Art Campbell at the throttle and Dutch Shafer firing. Art did not have his regular engine, the 768, that night for reasons I do not know.

A year or two earlier, Dutch had told me that if he was ever in a serious wreck, he would take it as a warning and quit railroading. It wasn't long after that I helped get him out of a smashed engine and carried him back to the baggage car when no. 19 smashed into the local in the Jordan Narrows. Poor Dutch! He didn't heed his own advice. He continued on the railroad and had the bad luck to be firing for Art Campbell that night.

The sequence of events surrounding the accident was simple. Number 15 roared into Colton as usual doing probably seventy-five miles per hour. Right where the soft spot was at the water tank the second engine seemed to turn a somersault and crashed into an eleven hundred-class engine that was tied up on the passing track. There were nine hoboes on that engine warming themselves. All of them were killed. Art Campbell was killed instantly and Dutch Schafer died a few minutes after they found him.

The lead engine, the 774, broke loose from its tender and went clattering up the mainline. They got it stopped between the west leg of the wye switch and the stock yards. Neither Frank Ladd or Jack Johnson were hurt. It was the opinion of the officials that the trailing steam hose on the first engine got caught in the frog of the crossover switch to the passing track and thereby derailed the second engine. That may be so, but I still think that soft spot under the water tank spout had something to do with what happened.

The night of that wreck I was firing an eastbound preferred run for engineer Charley Sorenson. We got to Provo and spotted at the water tank. The stop board was out for orders. After taking water I climbed down into the cab. We had not received orders yet. After a few moments of waiting, Charley went back to the telegraph office to see what the delay was. After a while he came back to say, "Number 15 went in the ditch at Colton. Art Campbell is dead and Dutch Shafer is badly injured."

How feeble is the effort to convey the real feelings that come over a person when he hears news like that concerning men that he has known so intimately. As a boy I had watched old Art Campbell going through town on those little Rome passenger engines. "Old Silver Tip," we had called him. He had a profuse head of hair, and it was white—white as snow. And now he, too, was gone! That white hair is what had singled him out to me as a boy. And after I was grown I had fired for him—a consummation of my dreams.

And Dutch Shafer! I thought of his words regarding a warning—a warning he had failed to heed.

As soon as the mainline was open we went on through to Helper. It was the middle of a warm afternoon when we passed through Colton going east. From my side of the cab I had a good view of the wreck. That it was awful is very much understating the case. I could see a foot sticking out of the piled-up wreckage, clothing and blankets of dead hoboes, and other little reminders of lives snuffed out. There was a heavy stench in the air—a stench identified with dead bodies not yet recovered. I thought of the words of an unknown railroad poet:

> *Great God above, Who rules,*
> *And Who, amidst Thy might of justice,*
> *Holds man's destinies.*
> *Spare us these awful scenes of blood,*
> *On running wheel; on blades of steel,*
> *When engines crash!*

Can you imagine the feelings of men in the railroad game when accidents of this nature collect their toll of friends and acquaintances? You know that there will be more of the same, and you know that there will be more violent deaths. What you don't know is where they will occur, or when. Partiality is unknown on the railroad. The old head is just as susceptible as the youngest on the road. Is it any wonder then, that some who are a little weak or are less imbued with the love of the rail may desert to less hazardous means of a livelihood? This happens to some degree in every case.

In those days the trend of life, it seems to me, was less hazardous than it is today. To the ordinary lay people, railroad life was a glorious, romantic, devil-may-care existence. Those in the game were a people set apart. But in these days people pick up a newspaper and read of the commonplace slaughter on the highways; they note that a plane has gone down taking scores of passengers to their deaths. They read of gun battles between outlaws and law men. They shrug it off as something common and usual because every day the papers recount such violence. They view such things as something unavoidable. They take this aspect of life for granted.

If you will allow a reflection of mine, it was not that way when I was a boy. There was not so much violence in the world. Incidents that now occupy a few paragraphs in the newspapers were front page news articles.

Heroes and martyrs were made overnight. And the railroad contributed much to this way of life. A railroad accident furnished news, adventure, glamor, and incidents of bravery in the telling of it. An engineer in those days presented the same picture of courage and daring that the airplane pilot does now. So you see, most of the young, red-blooded kids of those days wanted to be engineers. It was a profession a little above the others.

What I mean to convey in simple words is that life was more tranquil, more serene and quiet then than it is now. There were fewer hazards, and life was more simple. In the small towns people with nothing else to do would stroll leisurely down to the depot to see the passenger trains come into town. What hazards and violence that did exist were mostly on the railroads or in the mines. So when anything out of the ordinary did occur, the newspapers gave more space to it than they do now.

Engineer

Dear Bill:

> *I could hear the wind—hollowly howling,*
> *And the deep river dashing below.*
> *I could hear the forest leaves rustle;*
> *As the trees by the tempest were fanned.*

Have you ever read that railroad classic "Asleep at the Switch?"

Your mother has gone to bed and I am sitting here at the kitchen table getting ready to continue "My Life." The wind is rustling the trees outside. It moans softly down the stove pipe and intermittently it increases in volume and tempo. I am just in the mood to be enchanted by that sound. I haven't heard the wind sighing down the chimney for a good many years as it is tonight.

It reminds me of the stanza quoted above. It is from that poem. As a small boy I learned that poem from beginning to end. And as it breathed of the railroad I was always reciting some part of it to myself when alone. Not only was I reciting it, I was singing it. I could sing those words to most of the popular current tunes.

So you will understand what the railroad has always meant to me. I knew from childhood that my life was going to be tangled in some way with the railroad. I always wanted to be an engineer.

The Denver & Rio Grande Western 1200 and 3404 double heading up a mountain grade.
April 24, 1938 photo by R. H. Kindig.

Engineer on the Rio Grande

It was not uncommon for a man to be approached by slickers, who for a few dollars would furnish a certificate declaring that the bearer had passed the mechanical examination for locomotive engineer on some little-heard-of railroad. If a man could appear at some master mechanic's office on a railroad that had a sudden increase in traffic and was in great need of enginemen, the theory was that he would be hired with very little in the form of examination. The important thing was being able to show that you were experienced.

I had a man follow me from the roundhouse at Ogden clear up to Twenty-Fifth Street where I roomed. I had just removed my work clothes when there came a knock on the door. There stood the man who had followed me. He was quite an old fellow. The boomer look stood out all over his person.

He began by asking if promotion was fast or slow on the Rio Grande. He then asked how long I had been firing. His talk got around to how I would like to be promoted. Then stepping inside, he told me he could fix me out with a service letter showing that I was an experienced engineer, having worked several years in that capacity, and was now cut off on account of a decrease in business.

That service letter would be from a railroad away down in the deep South where a general office building had burned down, destroying all records of former employees. A man's service on that railroad could not be verified or denied. A letter like the one he proposed would cost about twenty dollars—asking price, no doubt. If no interest was shown by the prospective buyer, I am reasonably sure the letter could be had for five dollars or less.

I told him I had no desire to change railroads. He became quite insistent, and I finally had to order him out of my room. I doubt that a mountain road such as the Rio Grande would hire a man for engine service without some form of an examination.

I was ready for the engineer examination any time for two or three years before it came my turn to sit for it. I had put in many hours of study getting ready. Then, about two weeks prior to the scheduled date of the exam, Pokey Cowan, my old enemy, approached me. By this time he had been made a traveling engineer. He notified me of the coming event, and asked me how I felt about it. I told him I was ready.

He then reached in his inside coat pocket and brought out some folded sheets of paper. They were the lists of questions asked at the examination.

He said, "You take these and study them and when you're through with them, bring them back to me."

That was the first friendly gesture from him toward me in over eight years. I was dumbfounded.

Ten firemen were ordered to appear at the examination car at nine o'clock, January 10, 1917. Five of us showed up. The rest were on the road or away from Salt Lake. Before the examination started the other four candidates told of having been caught suddenly and by surprise by the scheduled test. They would have liked a few more days to study up.

Clarence Rawlins was the chief examiner. I had fired for him quite a bit when he was running an engine. His title was now general air brake instructor. When the others asked for more time he looked at me and said: "What about you, Helen?" (Helen was one of my nicknames on the Rio Grande. It was taken after Helen Gould, the daughter of the infamous Jay Gould. At that time Helen Gould was the major shareholder in the Rio Grande.)

I told him I wanted to take it.

He said, "Do you realize that if you take it alone that you will get every question yourself?"

In the procedure of the exam the questions were asked in rotation. If there were five of us taking it and each man in turn answered his assigned question correctly, then I would get every fifth question. If I took it alone I would have to answer every question on the list. Obviously the odds favored taking the exam in a group. Nevertheless I told him I still wanted to go on with it.

He smiled and said, "Okay, here we go!"

When the others saw that I was going to take it alone they all made another request: Could they stay and listen? After Clarence conferred a moment with Jack Snyder, he said, "All right, sit down." It was then about 10:30 or 11 A.M. Clarence started asking questions. What did I know about combustion? I had done some mighty good jobs of firing, that he knew; so before I could give him my answer he passed over that question.

Hour after hour he kept asking questions, and I answered them rather well. About two-thirty in the afternoon, a hired man came in the examination car. He was a boomer. He sat in to take the exam to qualify to go to work as an engineer. From then on I should have received only every other question. But that boomer missed most of his questions, so I was not much better off than when I was the lone candidate.

There were only two questions with which I had any trouble. Clarence asked me, "When does a brake hold the best: when the brake shoe is hot or when it is cold?"

I answered, "When it is hot."

Clarence looked at me with a doubtful shake of his head. It was the first question I had stumbled on.

I hastily said, "I have heard the old timers tell of how up at Bingham on the Copper Belt, they would drag a car backward and forward with the brake set tight to warm up the shoe and get the ice and snow off it before descending the grade."

Clarence looked at me and then at Jack Snyder. Then he said, "You're right, Helen, to a certain extent. In all cases the ice and snow must be off the shoe before it will take good hold. So after that explanation we will have to give you a 'correct' on that one."

A little while later we were talking about automatic slack adjusters in air brakes. My question was: "When does the slack adjuster operate, when the brake is set or when it is released?"

Without giving it too much thought, I answered, "When it is set."

Again Clarence gave me that doubtful stare. I recovered by saying, "I will explain how it works."

I started by telling what the automatic slack adjuster was, what it was for, how it was built, and where it was tapped into the brake cylinder and at what point in the travel of the piston. I then went on, "When the brake piston moves out in the cylinder far enough to uncover the port where the slack adjuster pipe is tapped into the cylinder, air gets into that pipe. It moves up against a smaller piston. This piston moves a pawl over the teeth in the slack adjuster ratchet. The pawl slips over the first tooth in the ratchet and catches on the second tooth. Then when the brake is released the brake piston, by spring action, moves back, uncovering the port in the pipe. Air rushes out to the atmosphere. The slack adjuster spring then moves the piston back, taking the ratchet with it. This takes up the slack in the brake rigging to the amount of the two ratchet teeth."

Clarence looked over at Big Liz West, one of the firemen who was listening in on the session. Big Liz shook his head as much as to say, "It's all mud to me."

Clarence, with a wide smile, said, "That's exactly how it works." Then to me, "Now, when does the automatic slack adjuster operate: when the brake is set or when it is released?"

This time I blandly answered correctly, "When it is released."

Those were the only two questions I had trouble with in a full day of questioning.

Mr Bennett, the master mechanic who had been so disgusted with me at the investigation when Bill Boucher and I had run away down the old Soldier Summit grade, came in and sat listening for about an hour. A few minutes previously, Jack Snyder had left the car. They both came back in together. I will always believe that Snyder went out to get Bennett so he could hear part of the performance. Jack was always a friend to me.

About four-thirty in the afternoon the caller came into the car. He handed me the call book and I signed to go out on an extra east at 6 P.M. That was to be my first trip as a qualified engineer. It was January 10, 1917.

That boomer who came in and took the examination with me was hired on as a switch engineer. This is the point I want to make: No matter how much experience a man has, a mountain railroad such as the Rio Grande would be foolish to put him out on a mainline job unless he could show some knowledge of air brakes.

I had just finished with the air brake part of the examination when I was called for that extra east. I thought I would have to report for the machinery and the transportation examinations later on when there was more time. But I was never called in again. That air brake part was all I ever took on the Rio Grande. A year so later when I went to the Utah Railway I had to pass the transportation part, but that was the end of it.

When business began to pick up on the Rio Grande in the late thirties due to the approach of the Second World War, they called up a number of men for promotion. One of those men told me of a little incident that happened in that examination.

By that time the form of examining men for engineer had changed greatly from what it was when I took it. About six weeks before they were to be examined each man was given a book of questions to study and to fill in the answers. He kept this book and when all the answers were written out he was called in to talk them over with the examiner. Of course, under these conditions a man could leisurely look up the answers to all the questions and write them in without really knowing what he was writing about.

This man told me that Clarence Rawlins got pretty disgusted with the whole bunch on account of the poor manner in which they were displaying their knowledge. His disgust and anger increased as the session went along. Finally he really got mad. He had all the questionnaire books in front of him. He picked them up and slammed them against the opposite wall.

He rose to his feet and shouted, "This is the dumbest class I ever saw. Some of you guys have been firing an engine for fifteen years or more and you can't talk on the simplest question. What have you been doing all this time? What do you intend to make of yourselves?"

By that time he was stalking up and down before the class. He paused in mid-stride to say, "I had a man take this examination alone and he answered every question himself. He passed one hundred percent. And here you guys can't answer more than one question in a row correctly. That man is running an engine right now on the Utah Railway, and his name is Helen Gould."

I always thought well of Clarence. And apparently he did of me.

When I left that examination car and started home to prepare for that first trip I was walking on air. I felt like stopping every stranger I met to tell him I had just been made an engineer. My boyhood dream had come true.

My first trip as an engineer I remember well. I think an engineer always remembers his first trip better than any others that followed. I don't think that my first trip could have happened under more trying conditions.

As I have said, I was called out of the examination car just as I had concluded the air brake section. It was about four-thirty or five o'clock, and I was called for six or six-thirty. I had been out of bed from early morning preparing for the test. I was tired but eager. I would not have traded places with the president of the road. It was also the middle of a cold winter, and the fog hung thickly over the entire valley from Salt Lake south to a few miles above Springville. The single track mainline was overcrowded with traffic.

There were three eastbound crews called out of Salt Lake twenty minutes apart. We closed the gaps between us at Midvale. I was on the middle train. It was so foggy you couldn't see your hand *behind* your back, as I heard a brakeman remark.

When we all received orders to proceed over that single track we knew we would have to meet westbound no. 3 before going very far. There were no block signals or other safety devices as there are now, and that dense fog didn't offer help or comfort in any way. We all arranged between ourselves what procedure we would follow. It was like this:

Smokey Taylor, the engineer on the first train, would take off and go to Mesa for no. 3. I was to wait, as I recall, five minutes, and then take off. I was to go to Olivers for no. 3. The man behind me was to give me a five-minute start and then follow. He would go to Riverton for 3.

According to plan Smokey whistled off and left town. After five minutes I took off behind him. It was so foggy it was hard to distinguish the telegraph poles along the right of way. There was only one thing to do—just pound along as fast as you could go. Once in a while I would recognize some object that would give me an idea of where we were. I dimly noted the mile board at Riverton. A moment later I heard the echoing muffled roar as we passed the section house.

Now would come the most hazardous time for me. I must head in at the next station—Olivers. These stations were only three to four miles apart. I was watching ahead for several things. If that man ahead slowed down or stopped for any reason, he had better hurry and get a flag out. It would have to be done with red fusees. I would never be able to see his caboose markers in time to stop. In fog a red fusee lights up a large area when you are close enough to see it. There is very little chance to get by it.

My main concern after passing the station at Riverton was that I wouldn't overrun Olivers. While I was straining my eyes ahead for the flare of a red fusee, I was also hoping I would not miss the station mile board. After passing that board I would know I had another mile to go before heading in. If I missed that board I might continue on down the main in the face of no. 3.

I was beginning to wonder if I had gone by that mile board when its ghostly outline came rushing toward me. I now had to judge where to stop. When I finally made the stop I was just an engine length over the switch. I hurriedly backed up that distance, the brakeman lined it for the pass, and I hastily dragged those forty empties into the clear.

I had hardly stopped when we heard the subdued roar and the whistling of that approaching passenger train. That roar grew in volume, but as yet we could distinguish no headlight. Not until that engine was a very few car lengths away could we then see the faint white light that rushed at us out of the fog. I was surely glad that we had no trouble getting into the clear.

After no. 3's departure we again rambled out onto the mainline. The only thing that I clearly remember after leaving Olivers was how wonderful it was when a few miles above Springville we came up out of the fog into a land of clear vision. It was like a swimmer breaking out onto the surface into clear sunshine.

During the night the gaps between our three starting trains closed up again, but we plugged along as well as we could under the conditions that prevailed at that time. The forenoon of the next day found all three of us tied up at Colton on account of the sixteen-hour law.

I can remember that no. 5 came up out of Helper with dog catching crews to relieve us. I had tied up behind the caboose of the first train, and, gathering up my possessions, I went into that caboose to ride down to Helper. When I saw the relieving crew climb on the engine I had just left, I went out onto the back platform to see who they were. My brother Marvin was the fireman. He afterwards said that I came out on that platform to show them who the engineer was. Maybe so. I was very proud that I was the engineer, and I didn't care who knew it.

In those early days when I was a newly promoted runner it was necessary for a man to run an engine in freight service for a year before being qualified for passenger service.

I was called one morning at Helper for no. 5 shortly after I was promoted. I had one of those "monkey" seven hundreds. It was sure a thrill to sit up there on the right side of a passenger engine and speed over the road after dogging along in freight service for some time. It was sure pleasant to feel that engine eating up the miles. You had nothing to look out for except the schedule. All other trains were into clear for you. What could thrill a kid like me more?

I don't know how they came to call me at Helper when I was just a young newly set-up runner. It may have been that I was the only one available. And again, it was war time, so there may have been other extenuating circumstances. Anyway, I heard no complaints on my performance.

A week or so later I was being called on the telephone one morning for second no. 6. I heard the call boy say, "Wait a minute."

Then I heard him exchange words with the engine dispatcher. In a moment he came on the phone again, "You're not okay for passenger are you, Gould?"

I told him I didn't know if you could call it that but I had fired passenger a good deal and just recently I had brought no. 5 over the road.

The Denver & Rio Grande Western 779, a 4–6–0 ten-wheeler. June 12, 1938 photo by R. H. Kindig.

I also told him of having run the engine on no. 511 and no. 512 on the Marysvale Branch.

Again he turned and talked to someone in the office for a moment. I thought I heard the voice of my old friend Jack Snyder in the background. In a moment he resumed, "You're called for second no. 6."

That was the longest trip I was ever to make in passenger service. Everything went okay until we got to Thistle. There they coupled a big mallet on the head end as a helper. We were about to take off when the telegraph operator came out of the office waving his arm in a stop motion. As we hesitated he told us he had a message to hold us.

He took the conductor into the office with him. In about thirty or forty minutes the conductor handed me and the helper engineer a copy of the message. There had been a derailment in the Red Narrows and the mainline was blocked. We backed down, headed up the San Pete, Marysvale, Branch and backed the whole train down into the yard. We turned the engines and train over to the foreman at Thistle and were released from all responsibilities. This happened at about 1 P.M.

At nightfall we went to bed at the Gordon Rooming House. At about 9 A.M. the following morning we were called to resume duty. When everything was again ready we pulled up the San Pete Branch once more. We still had that mallet on the head end. We backed down the San Pete mainline to clear the coal chute. Both engines were in need of coal and water.

As we backed down the engineer on the mallet tried to spot for coal using the straight air. He stopped alright but in doing so he pulled the entire front end out of the head baggage coach. I was sure glad it was on him instead of me. He was an old head around Thistle. But like most of those old heads at that point on the road he had very little experience handling trains. He was primarily experienced in helper service.

If he had he never would have tried to spot for coal using the straight air while backing down with a big mallet. That mallet stopped right now, but the brakes on the train were all released. That was the first time I had ever seen a break in two in a passenger train.

Of course this caused more delay. We had to set the damaged baggage car over on another track. Then we had to back the whole train down on it. As the damage was on the east end of the car it had to be chained to the rear car in the train. It was about 2 P.M. before we were ready to leave Thistle. We had come into Thistle as second no. 6 on one date and left there as first no. 6 of the following date.

But that wasn't the end of the delay. When we arrived at the derailment in the Narrows we were held up for better than an hour as the wrecking crew finished opening the eastbound main. That was railroading in those bygone days!

A few weeks prior to this, several other young runners and I had been sent out to Thistle to work the extra board. There were several foremen at outlying points who liked to have a full extra board. There was one of this bent at Thistle: Old Bill Jones.

These men liked to have a large extra board. This condition made it hard for an extra man to make a living. Yet that didn't bother these roundhouse foremen. They had been up against a shortage of men at one time or another, and they weren't taking chances of being caught again.

For about two weeks the only work I could get was to help no. 2 with the old 1073, a broken down old mallet 2–8–8–2. This engine was long overdue for the back shop. That's the reason I was getting the work. This paid me fifty-nine miles a day, which was a little over a half day's pay. This did little more than pay my expenses, and I had a wife and two kids in Salt Lake.

Gallagher was there with me. About two every morning he would be called to help no. 20 with the 953 or the 955. Every morning we would wait on Bill Jones with a plea to release us to Salt Lake so that we could make a living. Every morning he would turn us down.

It was during my time at Thistle that I called myself for a passenger run. I had been promoted on January 10, 1917. The time was now early in April of the same year. So you see I had only been running an engine a few months. There were several of us extra men sitting on the baggage truck by the depot, just waiting for no. 18 to come into town. We were doing considerable bellyaching and "dynamiting," which is the same thing. The 714 was purring over on the San Pete mainline. When no. 18 came in the three rear cars would be cut off. The 714 would back down and couple onto them. That would then comprise no. 512's train down the branch. It would return westbound as no. 511.

The engineer on this run was named Baker. He was quite an elderly man. I had fired for him out of Ogden. He was supposed to be a very good man on an engine. That is, when he wanted to be. He had a little trouble with McKelvy before I fired for him. Something about McKelvy's attitude angered the old fellow. He started to "hammer" the engine—the 788. That is, he worked the engine at too long a stroke thereby burning more coal than was necessary.

McKelvy was a hot-tempered guy, and he got angry. Going up through Sutro he straightened up and grabbed old man Baker by the neck and forced his head down over the Johnson bar quadrant and told him, "Now you hook her up where she belongs, or you'll go down in the corner too."

Of course the old man had to hook that Johnson bar back a few notches. There was quite a fuss over that. Everyone thought that McKelvy would be fired. Why he wasn't I'll never know. That was an unpardonable offence.

(I fired for Old Man Baker on nos. 2 and 4 shortly afterwards with that same 788. I must say he was a smooth man with an engine. He used less coal than any engineer in passenger service. He kept telling me all the way over the road that he was handling the engine same as always when McKelvy blew up.)

Old man Baker had put in an appearance on the 714 and had her all ready for the trip. Then while he waited for his train to come in on no. 18 he looked across the cab and saw a student fireman climb aboard. The old fellow saw trouble ahead, and he looked for a way out.

A Thistle engineer who happened to be laying off crossed the track behind the 714 on his way to the depot. Baker saw him and called to him. This engineer's name was Dan Gull.

Baker told him, "I've suddenly taken ill. I wish you would hurry and get your overalls and go out on this job in my place." He added, "They haven't got time now to call a man." Dan was agreeable. He started for his home to get his overalls. As he passed the baggage truck where we were all sitting around giving up old head, he stopped to tell us what he intended to do.

I heard him through, and then I said, "Dan, I'm first out on the extra board. I was sent out here to work. I can get my overalls as quick as you can get yours."

I slid off that baggage truck and ran as fast as I could up to Effie Gordon's rooming house. I grabbed my overalls and ran back. By the time I got back, no. 18 had arrived and they had cut off the three rear coaches. Baker had backed the 714 down to a coupling and was dragging them up to the depot.

The conductor, a man named Stowe, was waiting for him. I told Stowe I would be the engineer. I took the orders out of his hand and climbed into the cab when Baker stopped. Baker eased himself onto the ground. I gave the orders a hurried once over, then whistled off. Conductor Stowe gave a puzzled high ball and the 714 started barking. I put my overalls on going up the canyon.

You might well ask who it was that called me for that job. Well, I called myself, and I was quite aware of it all the way down to Marysvale and back. I knew that I would have to make a successful trip or it would be too bad for me. Here I was, just a punk kid with the responsibilities of a passenger engineer tearing over a strange piece of track. I had been down that branch just once and then only as far as Richfield on a snow flanger. Not only that but I had a student fireman as well. His name was Jackson. It was the first time I had laid eyes on him.

Out of Thistle the grade ascends quite sharply for twenty-eight or thirty miles. It is necessary to work the engine hard. The pointer on the steam gauge began to lag. By the time we were at Indianola, about half way to the top of the hill, we were out of steam. We had to stop and "blow up."

Those 714 series engines had a long, narrow firebox. The boiler back head came clear back to the rear end of the cab. I felt sure that I could have kept that engine hot, but I had other things to do.

I had learned as a fireman that if I shoveled slowly and steadily and bounced the coal off the fire-ring they would steam well. I tried to tell this student how to fire her, but he couldn't savvy, as he didn't have enough experience to understand me.

After we had blown her hot and the boiler was full of water, we started again. We barely made it over the top without stopping to blow her up again.

From Hill Top it is downgrade most of the way, so I let her out a little although I wasn't familiar with the road. We came into Fairview forty minutes late. While they were unloading baggage and express the conductor came up to the engine and told me the track was in pretty good shape as far as Manti and that I could probably let her out and make up a little time going there. So I let them roll leaving Fairview.

It was a good thing that there were sign boards along the right of way one mile in advance of each station. These mile boards would tell you where the next station stop would be. These were my guides, although it was customary to stop wherever a party waved a hand to flag you down.

At that time the rail was very light from Manti to Marysvale. In fact, it had only been a short time earlier that the operating department had allowed engines the size of the Rome or the hog to go past Manti. The 714 was quite a bit larger than the Rome.

There were some very sharp curves too, especially between Sevier and Marysvale. In one place, you came out of a tunnel onto a very sharp curve and then immediately dodged into another tunnel. Practically all the way from Sevier to Marysvale the flanges kept up a constant squeal like a herd of pigs as they ground their way around the curves.

I know I came into Marysvale ten minutes late. That was pretty good, so the brakeman told me, considering the time lost blowing up on the grade. The conductor put us in, on time.

One thing that seemed funny to me was that the engine behaved as if it were downgrade both ways after we left Manti. On both the going and the return trip, after getting the train started, I could hook the Johnson bar up almost on center, just crack the throttle, and we would roll plenty fast. At least the line must have been very nearly dead level.

At Marysvale I met an old acquaintance. He was the engine watchman at that point. He and I had worked together at the cement works in Salt Lake for several years. To say that he was flabbergasted to see me come into town on the right side of that passenger engine would be a slight understatement. We talked over old times for quite some time, then he fixed us up a bed in the oil house.

I am sorry to say I did that engine watchman a nasty trick. It came about this way: I have told how precious valve oil was in those days and how scant was the measure doled out with which to make a trip. Most engineers had an extra tallow pot on the engine. I have seen engineers drain what valve oil was left in the lubricator into their private can upon approaching a terminal.

When Old Man Baker had realized someone else was going out on the 714 instead of him, he emptied all the surplus valve oil into his private can and took it with him when he left the engine at Thistle. This left me with no extra valve oil.

That engine watchman friend of mine at Marysvale fixed me up with an extra tallow pot full of valve oil on my promise that I would see that he got the tallow pot and the oil back. I am ashamed to say I disregarded that promise. Valve oil was just too hard to come by to give it away once you had it. In any event if I had tried to send it back with an engine crew I am sure they would have diverted it to their own supply. I never saw him again, and I am sure he never saw that tallow pot again.

That part of the country in those days was quite primitive and, I might add, quite desolate looking. There were lots of Indians settled on poverty-stricken farms. The government had built them small lumber shacks on these farms. I have seen whole Indian families line up alongside these homes to watch the train go by. What would make me laugh was that they would stare straight ahead as the train went by, never moving an inch as long as we were in sight.

That old seven hundred seemed to handle that train as though she were running light on the return trip. We were on time everywhere. At Fairview we were several minutes ahead of time.

As we started the climb to Hill Top the steam gradually got away from the fireman and we came into Hill Top a few minutes late. Before I found out how fast I could go down that grade to make running time I lost a few minutes more.

From somewhere I had obtained a cigar for the occasion. I had saved half of it all the way from Marysvale. I was determined to come into Thistle on time with that cigar stump in my mouth. As we lost time I grew desperate. I let them roll faster than I thought safe in order to pick up some of those lost minutes. To add to my troubles, it was Sunday morning and I had to stop to load passengers who were going somewhere for the day. Anywhere I saw milk cans alongside the track I had to stop and load them into the baggage car.

But by fast rolling I gradually picked up that lost time. I had my heart fully set on coming into Thistle OT—on time—with the last half of that cigar sticking out of my face. While yet a short distance from the depot at Thistle I could see our traveling engineer, Joe Stevenson, standing on the graveled platform. When I got closer I could see he had his watch in his hand—probably for my benefit.

So I played the game and came in with a flourish—with that cigar stump in my face. I blustered to a stop alongside of him. I did not give him a glance. With a casual and perhaps a little contemptuous look on my mug I withdrew the cigar stump from my face and deliberately but casually spit down at his feet. I tried hard to make it all appear as bored routine.

Out of the corner of my eye I watched his reaction. I can see it yet. He was quite a large man and no longer a youth by a long ways. He put his watch in his pocket, slowly turned his back on me, and without a word he walked away. Knowing Joe as I did I am sure he was trying hard to keep from laughing or at least to hide a smile. I will always, as long as I live, be able to see him as he slowly entered the telegraph office.

Joe Stevenson is dead and lying in his grave at Provo. When he died he was superintendent of motive power on the B & G. Some of the men on the road didn't like him. But I guess that was natural resentment of his official position. I liked him and always considered him my friend.

When I went up to Ogden to fire passenger we became better acquainted. He found out I was making a study of air brakes, and every once in a while when he would run up against a hard question concerning air brakes he would hand it to me just to test me out. When I left the passenger service to come back to freight at Salt Lake he didn't like it very well. One day he saw me on an eleven hundred freight engine at Provo with Needham.

He hollered, "Hey, Gouldie, why don't you go up to Ogden and take that job with Plum Haslet? He needs a good man to fire that 770."

Needham butted in, "Oh, he's doing all right here."

Joe gave him a look that silenced him. I had told Joe that I wanted to get a little experience on freight to prepare for promotion.

He had said, "There's going to be no promotion around here for a long time. Go on back up to Ogden; anybody can fire those freight engines."

It sure boosted my ego to have a traveling engineer come out and ask me to go up to Ogden and fire a passenger job. Usually it was the other way about. If you didn't do a good job of firing on those passenger jobs you were not only *asked* to leave, you were *told* to get off them.

I did go up to Ogden shortly thereafter. The call of the passenger work was too strong to resist. Plum Haslet had turned in his fireman, a big fellow named Christler, and they were having a hard time finding a man to cut the buck with that 770. I took that job with Plum Haslet on nos. 1

and 2, with engine 770. Number 2 was a particularly heavy train. It was always eight coaches. That was about all one of those little monkeys would handle alone. Those other eastbound passenger trains usually consisted of nine or ten cars, so they were double headed. Number 2 made fewer stops and was faster.

I remember my first trip with Plum. At Salt Lake Joe Stevenson got on the engine. I know I did a fairly good job firing that old 770. Somewhat to the amazement of Plum and Joe, we were making the time. Coming up out of the Jordan Narrows there is a long tangent about one mile long. It's on a slight upgrade.

Joe was standing alongside the engineer on the right side. They were both watching the steam gauge. I put forth an extra effort. I wanted that engine to pop. It had been reasonably hot all the way from Salt Lake but it hadn't popped. I thought that now would be a good time, and just before we got to the switch at Mesa the pop lifted. That pop let go with a loud blast! I can still see Joe Stevenson and Plum Haslet looking at each other as though dumbfounded. I stuck my head out of the left gangway to giggle to myself.

I thought when I was promoted that it would only be for a short time, and that I would be back as a fireman when the business boom that we were experiencing fell off. However, business did not fall off as long as I stayed on the Rio Grande. A score or more of men were promoted, and I began to accumulate a little seniority as an engineer.

One afternoon I was called to go out on an extra west to Ogden. I was twenty-six years old at the time. My fireman was a man named Rass Brown. He must have been sixty years old. He had failed to pass the engineer's examination twice, and was then set back in seniority to the youngest fireman with a regular job. He would have to work up again to promotion. Failing again, the company had the right to relegate him to some other service.

This rule was not enforced for a long time. Finally the firemen's organization compelled the company to comply with the rule. This was brought about by the fact that the first ten or twelve firemen on the seniority list were men who had turned down their chances at promotion to hold top seniority on the firemen's list. Consequently all the good short jobs out of Salt Lake were held by these fixtures, as they were called. A fireman could work up to promotion without ever being able to hold one of these preferred jobs.

The company's forced compliance with the relegation rule worked a great hardship on some of those old men like Rass Brown. But in the railroad game it couldn't be anything but fair. I felt sorry for those old fellows, but they knew the rules and had only themselves to blame.

One afternoon a young runner let Rass handle a train drifting down the Price River Canyon. Approaching Kyune, Rass got excited and set the straight air on the engine. Not stopping quickly enough, Rass, on top of the straight air, became more excited and hoisted the Johnson bar over into the back motion. The drive wheels picked up and slid flat spots on them so long that every tire had to be changed. After that the engineers were very careful about letting those old fellows play engineer.

There were three brothers in the train and engine service on the Rio Grande. Their name was Perkins. Each one answered to the name of Sy. One of those three was a brakeman and/or conductor, depending on the volume of the road's traffic. The other two Sy Perkins were firemen. They were all natural comedians.

Sy Perkins, the brakeman, was braking behind—that is, he was the rear brakeman on a train of coal that ran away down the new grade west of Soldier Summit sometime in October 1917. There were sixty-three loads of coal in this train. When they all piled up in the Horseshoe Curve below Scenic there were only seven cars and the caboose on the rear end still on the rail.

I was in a movie show over at Helper at the time. The caller came down the aisle calling for Engineer Gould. I answered him. He gave me a call timed as soon as I could be there to take the wrecker over to the Horseshoe Curve. I think I sometimes have the right premonitions. I asked him if there had been a runaway out of Soldier Summit. He answered, "Yes."

The Helper wrecker was by that time almost obsolete. It was not much good for use on modern heavy equipment. But as both tracks were blocked in the Horseshoe it was the only thing they had to work on the east end of the pile of coal and cars.

We pulled the cars on the rail back up to Scenic where we set them out on the passing track. We then worked on the east end of the wreckage for about twelve hours. By that time another crew had arrived with the Grand Junction wrecker, and I was relieved and deadheaded back to Salt Lake.

By the way, that wreck claimed one life. The head brakeman on that train was a new man. When the engineer realized he was running away he told that brakeman to go back on the train and set some handbrakes. What a hopeless, foolish task! Sixty-three loads out of control and a man is sent back over the top trying to stop them with hand brakes. The day for that sort of thing was past. He may have been able to do a little good on a lesser train on a lesser grade, but not on the Soldier Summit grade. If he had been an old head on the Rio Grande, he would not have tried. They found him on the third morning after the wreck under a small pile of coal where the coyotes had been digging during the night.

Fred Strosial, the engineer, and his fireman both jumped off just before the approach to the Horseshoe Curve. They were both badly injured and spent many days in the hospital. The engineer of course was fired. This was almost always the case in a runaway or in a rear-end collision. I never saw him again. When the fireman recovered, he quit the Rio Grande. He had enough of mountain railroading. The last I heard of him he was firing on the Oregon Short Line out of Salt Lake.

The eleven hundred class engine on that runaway broke off from the train in the Horseshoe when the first car derailed. It rolled around the curve and stayed on the rail. The driving wheel brakes were set and stopped it on the straight track above Gilluly with all the tires red hot.

Let's look at one humorous aspect of this unfortunate incident.

The conductor and brakeman, Sy Perkins, were, of course, riding the caboose on the rear end of the train. When they realized what was taking place they took the safe course, by uncoupling the caboose and applying the handbrakes. When they got the speed of the caboose under control they drifted slowly down to where the train had piled up and gently recoupled into the cars still on the rail.

A few days later the inevitable big investigation was convened. That part of the crew who were physically able to attend were there as were the carmen from Soldier Summit who had made the inspection of the train before clearing it to descend the grade.

One of the investigating officials asked Sy if he cut the caboose off from the train.

He answered something like, "And how!"

The next question was to be expected. "Why?"

As I have said Sy was a natural comedian. He grinned broadly as he answered, "Well, you know, Mr. Mayhan, I just had an idea that there may be a big investigation on that incident, and I wanted to be there! So I cut off the caboose."

There used to be a saloon just south of Second South on Main Street in Salt Lake. It was called the White House. It was the hangout of the rails of all the railroads. If you wanted to see a certain railroader, and if he was in town, your best chance would be at the White House. That place was usually full of rails, especially on pay day.

I was there on one occasion with one of the firemen Perkins. The place was full. Sy had imbibed quite a few drinks before I caught up with him. He was in a devil-may-care mood. He wanted to sing. He had several little ditties that would not stand the writing here in these pages.

He would get in with a rail off another road and sing one of these little verses. If the man liked it he would buy a drink and Sy would sing him another. After awhile Sy would get rather personal in the lyrics of his songs. They would gradually turn into criticism or ridicule and become disparaging of the other person's railroad. If he had been in a serious mood when he was doing all this, I believe there would have been some fighting, but as he was laughing and apparently being friendly, most of his listeners at the most just became a little irritated with him. I managed to get him out of there without any real trouble occurring.

After we left he turned to me. "I sure told 'em, didn't I? And made 'em like it, too!"

At that time there was some little feeling between the mountain rails and those working the flat country. A Rio Grande man just couldn't see a man whose only experience had been on a level railroad making a success on a mountain railroad.

There used to be a superintendent on the Rio Grande named Williams. He had risen from a conductor to trainmaster, then to superintendent at Helper. From there he went to Salt Lake as superintendent. He was a strict disciplinarian, especially regarding Rule G. If he suspected an employee of having taken a drink, he would get as close to that individual as possible and be constantly sniffing the air for the smell of booze.

His first name was Newton. He was called "Nifty Newt." He would fire a man for the smallest transgression. His pet phrase when doing so was, "The Pedro for you—one way," meaning the LA & SL, now the Union Pacific.

He was finally fired. He sold insurance for several years, then he finally landed a job on the Pedro. He went to the LA & SL as division superintendent at Salt Lake. When the UP finally took over the Pedro he continued to advance. When he died he was N. A. Williams, general manager of the Union Pacific.

All the men on the LA & SL knew of Williams's deprecating remarks concerning the Pedro while on the Rio Grande. At almost every stop on his first inspection trip with the Pedro someone would yell out at the top of his voice when Williams appeared, "The Pedro for you! The Pedro for you! One way!"

At first Williams tried to ignore the shouts, but when it happened at almost every stop, it began to make itself felt. Finally Newt contented himself with just appearing in the vestibule when a stop was made. Still those shouts continued, but he couldn't determine who was responsible.

In anger he started shouting back at his tormentors. "Who are you?" he would scream. "Show yourself, you so-and-so, and I'll fire you right now." Receiving no reply, he would reenter the car.

Immediately those calls started again. "The Pedro for you, one way."

Before that inspection trip was over Williams became quite reluctant to show up outside the inspection car.

I have to tell of a little experience that I had with Nifty Newt. I was firing nos. 61 and 62 for Blue Beard Bert Kestler between Helper and Ogden. One night our westward connection was late getting into Helper. We had our engine, the 952, spotted on an adjacent track waiting. Several others appeared and we were giving up old head—shooting the breeze, as you would say now—as we waited on the ground. Pretty soon Superintendent Williams put in an appearance. We were all a happy family as we waited.

At last our connection slammed into town. I started to climb up the gangway and on into the cab. Newt Williams, who was standing close by, reached up and pulled me down onto the ground. He said, "Where are you going, Kid?"

I told him I was going up on that engine.

He said, "And what are you going to do on that engine?"

I told him I was going to fire that engine.

He roared, "What, you fire that engine? Why, you can't fire that engine!"

I told him that I had been firing it for quite some time now. Blue Beard Bert, my engineer, spoke up, "Yes, Mr. Williams, he's my fireman."

Mr. Williams was silent as he turned and walked away, pondering my baby face and general youthful appearance.

During the month of September 1917 I was running the rod engine at Cuprum. There were two yard engines stationed at that point. One was a rod engine; the other was a shay. The shay worked the mines of the United States Mining Company. The rod engine crossed the canyon on a long and high wooden trestle to furnish empties to the copper company and bring the loads back to the Rio Grande yards.

The crews, working out of Welby, brought the empties up to Cuprum. The rod engine made up the trains of loads for the return to Welby. I was on that rod engine the full month of September 1917 while the regular engineer was in the Salt Lake Hospital.

This long trestle that I write of crossed the upper end of the canyon. As I have said it was of wood and was also quite high. To add to the tricky nature of the operation it was very shaky. When crossing it you could feel it sway. There was a standing order for a speed limit of five miles an hour across the structure.

That rod engine was a little hog. It would handle only five loads of ore at one time backing across. After the bridge the grade rose sharply. If you held the speed down to five or six miles an hour across the trestle you would not be able to get those loads up over the switch leading down into the assembling yard. It was quite a hazardous operation.

I would start backing across that bridge slowly with five loads. When I got to the center I would widen on the throttle. The bridge would sway as we pounded across. The track beyond the switch leading down into the yard and up to the end of this track was just long enough to hold that hog and the five loads. Moreover, the grade was such that when you reached the end of track your tank or tender was slanted way up in the air behind you. To make matters worse you couldn't see the switch leading to the yard from that point.

You just backed up to the extreme end of the track and stopped. You hesitated there the fraction of a minute to allow the brakeman to line the switch for the yard, then you started ahead. You didn't dare stand there too long due to the grade. That little hog was almost standing on its head. All your water was off the crown sheet and down in the front end of the boiler. So you only hesitated long enough to give the brakeman time to get the switch before moving ahead. If he got the switch over all right, you went down into the Cuprum yard. If he didn't you went back across the bridge, and the movement would have to be made over again.

One afternoon I was coming across with the usual five loads. I saw a man standing alongside the track on the Rio Grande end of the bridge. As usual, when I got part way across I started to pound that little hog. This man was watching the bridge sway. He started jumping up and down and waving his arms excitedly. I just turned my head and disregarded him. When we got down into the yard with those loads he climbed on the engine and gave me a bawling out about the speed across the bridge. It developed that he was an inspector sent up there to look at the bridge. The rest of the day, as long as we thought he was around, we went across with three or four loads.

10

Running the Utah Trains

Joe Stevenson, in charge of the Bingham branch, came out to Cuprum to speak in glowing terms of the jobs for enginemen on the Utah Railway, soon to begin operation out of Provo. He told of the fine big new engines that would handle the trains, and of how they would have rights over the trains of the Rio Grande on the joint track. He made those jobs sound very good, especially to a young man on the extra board.

Finally I said, "Joe, are you going over to the Utah?"

He was tamping tobacco into his pipe at the time. He just looked at me without answering. After he had left on a train of loads for Welby, I tried to figure out what it was that he was trying to tell me.

It was then that I remembered an occasion a month or so earlier. At that time I was deadheading east on no. 6 to relieve an engineer who was tied up under the hog law. Joe had come through the coach, and he sat down beside me. Going out of Provo we could see men, teams, and work trains breaking ground for what is now the Utah Railway yards.

I said, "What's carrying on there?"

Joe looked out the window. "That's going to be the Utah Railway terminal," he said.

We had heard rumors concerning the advent of the Utah Railway but that had been common talk for a couple of years. No one had seemed to take it seriously.

A few moments later Joe said, "If you get a chance to go over there, Gouldie, you better go!"

I had heard that the Utah would be a road of big mallets. I said, "Oh, I don't want to run a big old mallet."

Joe said, "The mainline power won't be mallets."

After that the talk had turned to other subjects. And now, thinking it over, I wondered if there was something for me on this new railroad.

The next time Joe came out to Cuprum I asked him point blank. "Joe, are you going to take me to the Utah with you?"

Again he was tamping his pipe. And again he gave me that half-furtive sidelong glance.

"Gouldie, you listen to me, and you'll have one of those fine new engines on a regular job. Just keep thinking about it, but don't say anything." He went on to paint it to me in glowing terms.

My wife came up to Bingham a day or two later to get my paycheck. I told her what I had on my mind—how I would soon have a regular job paying good money on this new railroad out of Provo. I would be able to make as high as two hundred dollars a month. No more skimping and scraping. We could live much better.

She said that if I had those prospects, why not start right now. Our kids were hungry at home. They were not getting enough to eat. When we left Salt Lake to move to Provo we left quite a large grocery bill which we soon paid up. The future looked rosy. I was walking on air. My hopes were high.

I will admit that I was a little reluctant to let go of ten years seniority to take a new job. There was so much talk that the Rio Grande men would have those jobs back again in a very short time that it took a lot of nerve to leave the "Dirty and Ragged and Greasy," as we sometimes called it.

I was sitting in the call room at Salt Lake one afternoon in November 1917. There were about a dozen rails there. Of course the talk was all about the coming of the Utah. I listened to those old heads give their opinions. Anyone who left the Rio Grande to go to the Utah would be out of a job in sixty days at the most.

This was very disheartening to a young fellow who had been promised a job on that new road. I afterward learned from Joe Stevenson that one of those guys, an engineer who was loudest in his faith that those jobs would revert back to the Rio Grande, had actually submitted an application for a job under Joe's front door.

I had not made my intentions known. One afternoon in late November I was again listening to the different opinions in that call room. They were anything but encouraging. I saw Bob Crosbie come in the door. After listening to the old head floating around the room he reached into his inside coat pocket and took out an envelope. He walked over to the slot in the door leading to the traveling engineer's office. He slid that envelope through the slot and turned to stun the gang into startled silence with a quiet remark.

"That's my resignation, brothers. I'll be going to the Utah in ten days!" As he started through the door he added, "There goes eighteen years' seniority!"

Eighteen years' seniority he was throwing away that easily! That decided me. If he could let go of eighteen years with no more worry than that, I could surely take a chance with my ten. I went into the engine dispatcher's office and grabbed an envelope and writing paper. I made out my resignation to take effect in ten days. I then got out of that place in a hurry.

Frank Deerman, an engineer on the Union Pacific, spent his last years of service on the Provo-Geneva run. He retired a year or more before I did. When we were both working he and I seemed to have something to talk about whenever we would meet down at the call room. The first time I saw him was when I was still on the Rio Grande.

The Utah Railway's 2–10–2s all came to the UP roundhouse in Salt Lake when they were first built. They were assembled (set-up) there and then taken to Provo light by a UP crew.

A few days before the Utah started operations, I was riding home on a street car down Second South in Salt Lake. When we got to Third West, the 102 was going south, light, over the crossing. Joe Stevenson had told me that the 102 was going to be my regular engine. When I saw it moving slowly over that crossing I unloaded from that street car and ran and climbed on the 102.

This Frank Deerman was the engineer. Of course Joe Stevenson was riding on her too. I rode with them from Salt Lake to Murray, just to see what it was like to ride an engine that size. Frank remembered that trip. He remembered me climbing on that engine at Second South and riding to Murray. He said he didn't know where or how he was going to eat that day.

They went on to Provo. He said that there Joe Stevenson found out about his condition and gave him a silver dollar. He said that dollar looked as big to him as twenty dollars has looked lots of times since. I guess that was a characteristic of a railroad man in those days. I wonder how many times I have been hungry and broke in my life.

The Utah Railway 100, a 2–10–2, at Martins. Photo by R. H. Kindig

The Utah Railway 101. Photo by R. H. Kindig.

The Utah Railway 102. Photo by R. H. Kindig.

The Utah Railway 108 at Helper. Photo by R. H. Kindig.

I brought the first coal train into Provo on the Utah Railway. Starting a new railroad is a pretty tough job. A new railroad starting operations is not prepared to meet all the situations that can confront it. Bob Crosbie was called to take out the first train of empties to the mines, but he didn't get out of town. He ran into the first set-back even before we had started. Being the oldest in seniority he was given the first call. For some reason or another there was no hostler on duty at Provo. Bob was called for the 103. The 103 was pointed in the wrong direction, so Bob had to put her on the turntable to get her oriented properly. When that monstrous piece of machinery put its full weight on that turntable the poor table gave a despairing sigh and settled down several inches. So Bob in later years was unable to say to his grandchildren, "I took the first train out of Provo on the Utah Railway."

They then called Bert Pumphrey with the 102, so he got out of Provo with the first train of empties for the mines. The 102 was also facing in the wrong direction. Bert took his train of empties to Springville or Thistle backing up. There he turned the 102 on the wye. After much hard work they got the 103 off the table, and Bob was called again. I don't remember what engine he had. That same afternoon I was called with the 100 or the 101. I am not sure which. It was a very busy mainline at that time due to war-time traffic and two railroads using the same track.

I do remember turning that huge contraption on the UP wye at Provo. This was a very slow job as the track was not built for engines the size and weight of ours. I remember I went around that wye very slowly. None of those curves on those wyes seemed ready to perform under the weight of those huge 2–10–2s. I know that in going around this wye I had to go very slowly. There were men walking beside me on both sides of that engine, watching every turn of the wheels to see how she held the rail. Several times I stopped at their command while they put oil on the rail to make her curve better. It was nerve-racking to turn on any of those wyes. But we got along all right and took off for the mines with, I believe, thirty-three empties. I was the third engineer to get out of Provo on the new railroad.

I left Provo on November 30, 1917. The next day, the official opening day of the Utah, December 1, 1917, I was called at Hiawatha to take the first Utah Railway train into Provo. I can tell that to my grandkids!

While on the eastward leg of the trip to Hiawatha, Joe Stevenson, our superintendent and master mechanic, was at Martin on the welcoming committee. The telegraph operator at Martin told me later that Joe made a remark to the effect that if any of them get through, Gould will. Of course that made me feel good, and I would have been something other than human if I didn't develop a slight case of swelling of the head.

Earlier at Utah Junction I had to wait while a Rio Grande crew came out of Martin with a Rio Grande train. I talked to an engine crew that was there to make a help on this train up to the Summit. I asked them how the track was up the branch to Hiawatha. They shook their heads dubiously and with some gloom.

They made remarks such as "I wouldn't want to go up there with one of those big engines," and "I'd hate to start across that Gordon Creek bridge with that thing."

This dampened my spirits somewhat. I hadn't been up that branch for three or four weeks. At that time the track was in anything but good shape. Derailments had been frequent. When one happened, while under Rio Grande management, the company would do nothing to clear the tracks for days. This had caused the shutdown of all the mines on the branch for lack of rail service. Such acts were what finally prompted the Utah Railway to take over the operation of this railroad themselves.

My orders on leaving Martin restricted the speed of the train to seven miles an hour. I asked Joe Stevenson how the track was. He answered that it was good. I rattled that slow order at him. He just grinned. I was in a quite fearful mood as I took off for the mines.

Holding my speed down to between seven and twelve miles an hour we made it to Hiawatha without too much trouble. But when I started across that Gordon Creek trestle I will confess my heart was in my mouth. I tried to remember that two of our engines had crossed that bridge already, and it gave me courage.

At Hiawatha we had more trouble getting around the wye, but we finally made it. Those wyes continued to give us trouble for some months. They were just not built for our heavy engines. That wye at Colton had to be rebuilt several times after we used it.

We were rested at Hiawatha and then called in time to get out the first train of Utah Railway loads. That train, I well remember, consisted of twenty-eight "battleships" (hopper cars) for Provo. Bert, the first engineer, took a train from Hiawatha to Martin. This was still Rio Grande tonnage. He got into Provo with only the caboose. Bob, who was second, took a Rio Grande train down the hill and set it out at Martin. With no Utah loads of coal available, he helped a Rio Grande drag to Soldier Summit. From there he also went caboose bounce to Provo. My train of twenty-eight loads was the first Utah Railway train into Provo.

On leaving Hiawatha I again received that seven-mile-an-hour slow order all the way to Martin. Of course I exceeded it slightly. It is very hard to hold a train down to that speed and I don't think the authorities really expected it.

I once heard an official giving instructions to the dispatcher over the telephone. He was talking about a piece of track which he wanted covered by a slow order.

He said, "Put out an order not to exceed, say, twelve miles an hour. That will hold 'em down to between sixteen and eighteen. That ought to be safe enough."

At Martin Joe Stevenson met me. He said, "Gouldie, have you got that slow order?"

I answered, "Yes."

He was fumbling with his watch.

"Well, Joe," I went on, "Can you hold a train of loads down to seven miles an hour for over twenty miles of grade like there is on that branch?"

He grinned slightly as he tucked his watch away. "Never mind now. Never mind," he said as he turned away.

At Martin, for a helper we picked up Gallagher and McKenna on that old Rio Grande hand-fired mallet, the 1073. Somehow we all made it up the hill to Soldier Summit. They cut off at that point and returned to Martin. I went on down the west side toward Provo. As we pulled into the yard at Provo Joe Stevenson again met me. I think he had run around me by coming in on no. 3.

He said, "Gouldie, you're bringing the first train of coal into town on the Utah Railway!"

I remember that our Utah cars (gondolas) had not arrived yet. But they did very shortly thereafter. The yards were full of our new all-steel coal cars. As fast as a train of empties left the yard the UP yard goat would jam some more in their place.

Compared to the consist of other trains, those fine, all-steel, newly painted cars made quite a contrast. Forty to forty-five of them, one after another, made a fine-looking train with one of those big 2–10–2s on the point. The equipment then in use on the Rio Grande could not compare.

I know that my picture is in many homes both locally and all over the country. There was always someone along the road unlimbering a Kodak to get a picture of us.

A few more words about those wyes: the one at Colton, I believe, was the worst of all. Although it wasn't much worse than the one at Hiawatha. One day we were making a Colton turn. That is, we set our train of loads out at Colton and returned to Hiawatha. These loads that we set out would be picked up by following trains. This day, after setting our train out, we had to turn the engine on the wye.

On the inside of those firedoors was a piece of sheet metal to deflect the coal into the firebox. This piece of metal was attached to the door by about a half dozen screws. This shield, as I will call it, had come loose. We had no screw driver on the engine with which to tighten it in place, so the fireman had removed it, and it was lying on the deck.

When we reached the stem of the wye and started to back around the other leg, the tank (tender) refused to take the right rail. Several times we tried but couldn't get it to track. I happened to think of the metal shield deflector plate lying on the deck. I told the fireman to get it. He brought it down and I fitted it in the frog so that the flanges would be guided by it. When we backed over it the wheels took the right rail, and we made the turn all right. That metal shield was all pushed out of shape and useless for its intended purpose. I don't know what became of it.

At Martin when we arrived I met Joe Stevenson, our superintendent and master mechanic. He wanted to know how we were getting along. I told him about our trouble getting around the wye at Colton. I told him how I had finally made it by using that door shield wedged in the frog to guide the flanges. He patted me on the back and told me that I was using my head. He told me that whenever a man got into trouble like that, if he would just use his head, there was always a way out. I began to think I was using my head.

A few days later I got a long letter from Joe. He noted that the shield on the inside of the firedoor of the 104 was missing. As this engine had been in my charge for several weeks, would I kindly explain what had become of it. I didn't answer that letter, but when I next met him I told him I had used my head and used that metal to guide the tank wheels over the frog on the wye at Colton. Joe told me that he hadn't dictated that letter at all. Ed Hall, the foreman at Provo, had told Tom Schott, the chief clerk, that the shield was missing. It was he who had written that letter over Joe Stevenson's signature.

I remember one occasion very early in my Utah Railway career that is worth mentioning. There were several westbound freight trains, Utah and Rio Grande, at Thistle. Something had happened to delay the westbound movement and traffic was piling up there. Besides that, two westbound passenger trains, nos. 1 and 5, were due.

They finally turned us loose. One man was to go right on through Provo to Lakota. The next man had cars to set out and pick up at Provo.

He was instructed to head in at Mapleton and stay there for the passenger trains. I had instructions to go to Provo—and fast!

I gave the man ahead of me a little start and then took off. These were the days before block signals, so I had to keep in mind that there were two trains roaring along ahead of me. When I came out of the canyon and could look down in the valley I could see the man ahead of me almost into clear at Mapleton. As we say on the road, "I took the bridle off."

As soon as the train ahead of me got nicely into clear the crews, both engine and train, got off and lined up against the right of way fence to get a better look at us as we roared by. They were making signs to me to speed up. That was one part of the road where you could really make time! And we did just that. We went rolling into Provo well ahead of nos. 1 and 5.

I was going east up through Mill Fork one morning. A flagman slowed me down. He pointed up ahead and made signs that I should blow the whistle and keep my eyes peeled. I rounded the curve at reduced speed, blasting the whistle. Up ahead another flagman gave me signs to come ahead slowly. In a cloud of black smoke I could see a slow-moving work train pushing material and work train equipment into clear on the passing track above the telegraph office.

When he was entirely into clear the flagman gave me a proceed sign. I blasted twice on the whistle and widened on the throttle. When I went by that work train I looked down at the engine. It was a monkey passenger engine. When the smoke cleared a little I read the number: 768!

I think I should be pardoned if I experienced a rising lump in my throat. A few miles further on I reached into my pocket and drew out a memorandum book that I carried to write down notes of the trip. With a stub of a lead pencil I wrote the following bit of poetry. I had it finished before leaving Soldier Summit.

> *Old Seven Sixty-Eight*
>
> *You're draggin a work train,*
> *   I'm 'plowing the main.'*
> *We're both getting old, but we're still in the game.*
> *   Old Seven Sixty-Eight, as I passed you today,*
> *A-shrieking a warning to stay clear of the way,*
> *   I glanced at your jacket, all musty with foam,*
> *And your greasy old side rods and rusty old dome.*
>
> *When I was a boy,*
> *   You were my toy.*

I polished your brass, and you were my joy.
   I've boasted with pride of how swift you could run,
And the sheen of your jacket out-dazzled the sun.
   When we charged o'er the line on old no. 3,
The way you would scamper was wondrous to see.

Now, you're sidetracked at last,
   Though back in the past,
You pulled the hot shots, the ones that were fast.
   I remember the time when your gleaming headlight
Was splintering the darkness as we crashed the night.
   You seldom did falter, you seldom did fail,
And I stoked your fire on the sharp end of the "Mail."

How I struggled and fought
   To keep you hot,
As we "stepped through the dew" on that fast "varnished shot."
   I've flung your door wide on a dark stormy night
When the glow from your furnace bathed the train in its flight.
   I've petted and curse, and petted again,
I've raved and swore at the stubborn old train.

Yes I fed you "slack"
   From your tank just aback,
Of that bright shining boiler and silvery stack.
   And the thrill of my life, how my hair raised my hat,
When that "crank" lined the switch that sent you out on the flat.
   In the swamps by the track where your nose took that dive—
Then—Oh boy! Wasn't it grand just to be there—alive?

Remember the Old Man—
   Old silver-haired Dan,
Who petted and oiled you with his trusty old can?
   He went to his God with a hole in his head,
When you stubbed your toe, east of the big snow shed.
   They picked you up, and brought you in, and built you anew,
But the soul of old Dan had flittered to the realm of the true.

On the side track there
   Do you wonder where
Are those who in the past your perils did share?
   They who have guided you on many a wild ride,

Are tottering now and dreaming by a warm fireside.
    They long to hear again your whistle's weird peal,
And the crashing and clanging of steel on steel.

You'll soon be junk
    And I just a hunk
Of clay, when this body and brain have shrunk.
    But tonight while the blood within flows free
Let's take up the battle on the stormy end of Three.
    Let me swing on your chain, fling open the "gate,"
And I'll give you some coal, Old Seven Sixty-Eight.

Sounds pretty good, I think, for a punk with a fifth grade education.

Several times I have recited this bit of doggerel when my fireman and I would get in a reminiscent mood. It always seemed to make an impression. Maybe it's the way I recite it.

There was a man named Young. He was, I think, manager of the Blue Hill Dairy between Helper and Price. He approached me one night when I was about to leave Martin. He said he had heard that I had a piece of poetry pertaining to railroading. He would very much like to get a copy. I hated to turn him down, but I didn't want it to get away from me. I told him also that it existed only in my mind, and I wanted to keep it that way; I wanted it only for myself.

There are several inconsistencies in that poem. The name Old Silver Haired Dan refers to old Art Campbell. Near the long snow shed means Soldier Summit. Also Art didn't have the 768 on that fateful night. Something had gone wrong with her at Helper, and they gave him the 771, I believe. Anyway, all those incidents are, I think, closely associated, and the poem pleases me.

Referring to the mention of the "silvery stack" in the poem, I have seen Art, at times when we were right on the advertised, take a bucket of paint he always carried on the engine and go out and paint the smoke box and stack. This paint was called Plumbago. When it dried it would glisten like silver in the sun. After three or four coats of this on the stack, when the sun shone on it, it would shine fit to knock your eye out. He did this usually between Lehi and Mesa.

The running time between Provo and Salt Lake was about an hour and twenty minutes. If you left Provo right on time it was pretty hard to kill the time on the schedule between those two points. It was customary in those days to lengthen out the running time on the last few miles into the terminal. This was done to allow the engine crew to make up a few minutes if you were late. Twenty-five to thirty minutes could be made up on the schedule between Provo and Salt lake. But if you left Provo on time it was pretty hard to kill that twenty-five or thirty minutes.

I refer to that "crank" lining the switch that sent you out on the flat. It came about this way. At Mill Fork at that time there was a section boss named Atwood. He had two boys. One of them went firing, and later fired for me on the Utah. I don't know what eventually became of the other one. He was the one I called the crank.

At the time of which I write the single track mainline was being straightened out considerably between Tucker and Thistle. One portion of about a quarter of a mile or less had been connected to the mainline at the west end. The other end ran out near where it would connect at the east end. This piece of track was not yet ready for service. Those ties and rails were just laid on top of the ground, and were not ballasted or lined in any final form.

This younger boy of Atwood's wanted to go up to Tucker. Number 4, the train we were pulling, did not stop at Mill Fork, so he got the idea that if he lined that switch for this unfinished piece of track we would stop to reline the switch, which would give him time to get on and ride to Tucker.

We came along with one of those little moguls on the head end for a helper. That mogul had an oil headlight. Its rays did not penetrate very far into the gloom. Besides that, Dutch Wiedman, the engineer, was having trouble with his injector, and the fireman was down on the deck flashing the door. So no one saw that the switch was lined for the spur. The result was that we went in on that unfinished piece of track at full speed.

I was down on the deck of the 768 putting in a fire. The first I knew that something was wrong was when that deck started to bounce and weave under me. I looked up at Art. He was staring ahead with a puzzled look on his face. That deck started to caper around more and more. I jumped up on my seat box, taking my shovel with me. Dutch, on the mogul, shut off. Pretty soon Art shut off also. We shortly jolted to a stop. The nose of the 768 was leaning slightly to the swamp on the right. The little mogul was leaning over in the opposite direction. The tank was almost at right angles to the track. No one was hurt, but there were several very scared people there.

The boy who lined that switch in hopes of getting a ride to Tucker afterward confessed. I saw him there that night and I had a suspicion he had done it. He was a very fresh young punk. A few days afterward a special agent—railroad policeman—got to him. He was sent away to reform school, as I recall. Anyway, we missed him around Mill Fork for several years.

The last time I saw him I was running an engine on the Utah. I was at Soldier Summit pointed west. A young fellow in about his middle twenties climbed into the cab. It was quite some time before I recognized him. He was dressed in western garb and had a six-shooter the size of a young cannon strapped around his hip. He wanted to go to Thistle. Who was I to tell him no? When I looked at that artillery he was carrying and recognized that he was something other than normal to be dressed the way he was, I let him ride.

He rode down to Thistle on the engine with us! Every once in a while he would blast off that cannon trying to knock an insulator off a telegraph pole. He was standing in the gangway when we passed the Mill Fork section gang. Mr. Atwood, the section boss, looked up as we passed.

He hollered at this wild-west punk, "Where are you going?"

"I'm going down here and get a guy," was the answer.

It was then that I recognized him. He was the punk who had lined that switch. He was now playing cop or desperado, I didn't know which. I was glad to get rid of him at Thistle. He went down the San Pete Branch, and that was the last time I saw him.

Gilbert Lathrop, the author of the book *Big Men and Little Engines* (Caldwell, Idaho: The Caxton Press, 1954), says that safety devices and modern conveniences have made the modern generation of rails soft. I heartily agree. It would be utterly impossible to get these recalled railroaders of late years to take upon themselves some of the tasks that we accepted as commonplace.

Take those old oil headlights. Do you think you could get one of these modern firemen to light one at a speed of thirty-five miles an hour or better? Of course, we are not plagued with oil headlights any more, and it's a good thing we are not. The electric headlight is such an improvement in so many ways. But to light one of the old oil headlights at the speeds I have mentioned required not only skill but nerve as well. I have, scores of times, hung on to the end of the hand rail that paralleled the boiler waiting to see if my efforts to light that headlight would meet with success.

Now, in my old age the very thought almost brings on a shudder. In those days if we were standing in a passing track with as much as two hours of daylight left, we would take advantage of the occasion to light the headlight. If that opportunity didn't present itself, we would just have to light it on the fly before it became dark.

We would take a few sheets of old train orders, of which there were always plenty in the seat boxes or stuffed behind the gauges. We would fold them into a long roll, go out along the running board, and stand with one foot on the little step on the left side of the smoke box holding onto that bouncing and shimmying hand rail with one hand. We would then open the side door of the headlight cage with the other hand. We would stuff that roll of train orders down the glass chimney inside the headlight. We would turn the wick up until it touched the bottom of those old orders, then light a match, touch it to the orders in the top end of the chimney, close the cage door, and hang on as best we could until the flame reached the wick. If it did, and if the wick ignited, you could reach in, turn the wick down to its proper position, and return to the cab.

If you were successful the first time, you were lucky. If you could get a match to stay lighted in the rushing breeze long enough to get those train orders burning, you were lucky. Then maybe you would have to return several times to see that the glass chimney was not smoking up. I've gone through this performance scores of times.

Now in these days of several units of diesel, it is too dangerous for a fireman to walk from one unit to the next while the train is in motion!

I had a Rio Grande engineer tell me that while they still had steam power he was called to take an eleven hundred engine light to Thistle from Helper. This engine was still hand fired. He said that fireman raised an awful fuss because he had to fire that engine light from Helper to Thistle with the scoop shovel. He was going to take it up with the firemen's organization and make a grievance of it. He would take it up with the railroad labor board if necessary.

By way of contrast I remember we once had a westbound train of loaded coke racks. These cars were quite a bit higher than the ordinary box car. They were boarded solid about half-way up the side and then racked the rest of the way with slats, like a chicken coop. When running along really fast, these cars would sway badly from side to side.

On this particular night, as we were leaving Provo westbound, the conductor came up and told the head brakeman to drop back to the caboose and eat (train crews did a lot of eating on the caboose in those days). That conductor took the brakeman's place on the head end on this occasion.

A little later we were rolling along at a pretty good speed between Olivers and Midvale when the conductor called my attention to a light coming over the top of those swaying coke racks. We watched that light for miles getting closer and closer to the engine.

Just before getting to Midvale that head brakeman dropped down into the cab with a lighted lantern in his hand. I wonder how many modern brakemen would have dared to walk over an entire train of swaying coke racks in the dark of night with only an oil lantern to show the way.

Of course, I know that it's better to be safe than sorry, and I know that the safety-first movement has saved lots of lives and injuries. But I do also believe that the modern railroader, just as that author says, has gone soft.

I was just a young runner newly set up when I was called one cold winter morning to deadhead on no. 6 to Soldier Summit. I had to pick up a train of coal that was tied up on the mainline due to the crew having run out of time on the sixteen-hour law.

I climbed on that engine when we arrived to await our orders to proceed. It was very cold. We pulled down the back curtain and tried to keep warm. It is always colder standing than when moving. The engine was hot and we opened the fire door. The pumps were chugging along, and everything seemed in order. The conductor finally arrived with the orders. We were ready to descend the mountain. The car foreman appeared in the gangway.

He said to me, "We have already worked this train; it's okay. Will you go or do you want a test?"

I was about to say, "We'll go!"

Then that party up there who has watched over me down through the years seemed to object.

I reflected a moment, then said, "we'll make a little test."

I whistled one long blast. I moved the brake valve to the service position. Nothing but the preliminary exhaust sounded. I again brought the brake valve around to service. Again nothing but the preliminary exhaust. I turned to the car foreman. No words were necessary. He took a doubtful look at the air gauge, bundled himself up and climbed off the engine. I put the brake valve in running position to keep up the air. The pumps jingled right along.

In a few moments that car man again appeared at the gangway. "There seems to be plenty of pressure in those reservoirs," he said. "Let's try it again."

I did, with the same result. There was then only one thing left to do: break every connection and see which way the air was flowing. This they started to do. They didn't have to go far. They found a nice little marble of ice in the hose connection between the tank of the engine and the first car.

How easy it would have been to have started that train rolling down that steep grade. The brakes were all released, and it was a continuous two-percent grade for fourteen miles. There were no let ups or flat spots to help

The Union Pacific 3619, a 2–8–8–0 compound mallet, ready to leave Cheyenne, Wyoming. Photo by R. H. Kindig.

the slow setting of the brakes from leakage to stop that train for all of those fourteen miles on that cold morning.

One winter, after I was running engines for the Utah Railway, the company was, due to the greater business, short of power. They rented a large mallet from the UP. It was the biggest engine I had ever seen up to that time. It was numbered 3636. As soon as it arrived at Provo, I was called to take it over the hill on the head end of a train of empties.

I believe that there was no railroad anywhere in the world that kept its power in the good shape that the Utah kept theirs. Old Jack Somo, our master mechanic, put all our power through the shop every summer when traffic was light so it would be in good shape for the rest of the year. But this old UP mallet was long overdue for the back shop. She was dirty and miserable inside and outside. However, she did handle that train over the mountain very well.

When we tipped over Soldier Summit I made an air test of the brakes. Everything seemed to be in order. But a little while later after leaving Kyune and entering the steepest part of the eastward descent, I noticed it seemed to take longer for the brakes to take hold. The exhaust from the brake valve didn't have that solid, healthy sound that it should have had.

At first I thought that maybe it was a peculiarity of the brake valve, but I didn't like it. The train line exhaust would blow faintly for a second or two and then quit. It would open and close several times before it blew down the desired amount. I thought that condition would improve with use. Instead it got worse. We were not as yet going very fast. But when I tried to set the brakes going down through Nolon all I could get was a sharp blow from the preliminary exhaust. The speed started to pick up. I thought several times, good bye, old UP mallet. Then after a short time I saw that the speed was not increasing, and I began to hope.

A short distance farther down I began to believe the brakes were taking hold—they were. I would not attempt to release them and let the train maintain momentum. I kept that brake valve in lap position until we finally stopped. I had been using the engine brakes as well, as much as I dared.

When we stopped I let go of the train brakes and set the engine brakes in full. I turned to the head brakeman. He was a boomer fresh up from California—low cut shoes and all. I tried to tell him that I wanted him to go back and see if he could find any ice in the train line. I don't think he had worked anywhere but in a warm climate. I couldn't make him understand.

I finally called the fireman over and told him to see that the engine brake valve was not moved. Taking a hammer to loosen the hose couplings I went back along the train myself. I broke the hose connections between each car, looking to see that they were free of ice. And there it was between the third and fourth car—a nice little marble of solid ice. It had rolled back and forth in that train line until it got big enough to block the outward flow of air. We were lucky to have been able to stop.

The colder the air the more leaks you will find in a train line. This condition helped us on this occasion. We were going down that mountain with only the engine and three head cars braking, yet we were still getting a little help from leaks in the train line.

Whenever you find ice in the train line it will be close to the engine. There is a certain amount of moisture forced into the train line with the charging air. This comes from the condensation of the cold air as it is compressed by the pump and not dropped out in the main reservoir on the engine. The wetness around a steam pump contributes to the moisture entrained as the air is compressed.

Another time at Soldier Summit we were headed west. My head brakeman was Speedy Martin, a former UP engineer. I can't remember now what the occasion was, but for some reason or another I felt that ice was forming in the train line. We were waiting to let no. 5 go down the hill ahead of us. I told Speedy to go back and break a few hose couplings to see if he could find any ice. He went back about a half-dozen cars and returned to the engine. He said there was no ice. I wasn't satisfied. The longer we stood there the more nervous I became.

Finally I got up on my feet and went back. Speedy followed me. I broke the hose between the tank and the first car, and there was what I was looking for—ice! I asked Speedy why he hadn't found it. He said he thought the engine was my responsibility, so he hadn't looked there. Yes, I think someone up there must like me.

The line from Mapleton down to Provo was a very fast track. I was tearing down this section one dark night, gazing into the swath of white light cast by the headlight. I was in a hurry, moving right along. I saw in the headlight's shaft a horse ambling slowly up toward the track. I made no effort to stop; it would have been useless. But I grabbed the whistle cord and yanked out a series of alarms. That horse paid no attention whatever, but continued to move slowly on up toward the track. It collided with the front end of the 108 as I watched helplessly. As I did so, a horse's head with two feet of neck almost brushed off my cap. If my head had been a little farther out of the cab window, I shudder to think what might have happened to the brave young engineer.

Another time I came down this piece of track with a mallet engine and was making good time. As I tipped down into the cut at the west end of this straight track the engine seemed to ride in a peculiar manner. I stuck my head out the window to look at the running gear. That low-pressure engine was intermittently running ahead normally and then reversing itself to turn in the opposite direction. It would also stop its movement for several turns and then pick up again. I saw this happen several times later in my career.

This time it happened from a different cause. A Rio Grande crew ahead of me had run through a herd of sheep. I have forgotten how many they had killed, but the rail was slick with mutton tallow and other liquids. That low-pressure engine with the back pressure building up in those large cylinders could not get traction. I have seen this happen on a dry rail at high speed with a mallet engine. Strangely, it doesn't seem to hurt the engines.

Speaking of sheep, Jack Johnson at this same place went through a herd of sheep with one of our 2–10–2s. The count was over two hundred and eighty dead and only the Good Lord alone knows how many were injured.

I followed a Rio Grande train up the Price River Canyon one summer night. I was making a Soldier Summit turn. That is, we were to set our train out at Soldier Summit and return to Hiawatha. A Rio Grande man went though a herd of sheep halfway between Kyune and Colton. I was following him pretty closely. It was a moonlight night. Where he went through this herd we could see dead and injured sheep all along the right of way.

After we set our train out at Soldier Summit we returned to Martin, caboose bounce. When we got to the sheep, we stopped and by the light of the torch we picked out several that only had their toes cut off. We loaded them in the cab and hung them up on the cross iron that holds the handles to the different valves. We butchered and dressed them there in the cab as we were going down the hill. At Hiawatha we put the meat in the ice house until we were again called. Somewhere we got a lot of thick wrapping paper and rolled them up in it and took them home to Provo.

Twice I have brought home deer killed from the engine. On one occasion deer season had just opened. We were going east just above Thistle. Hugh Brown, our head brakeman, was sitting across the cab on that little seat just ahead of the fireman. I happened to glance across and saw him sitting straight up on the seat. I thought this was a little unusual, because he would usually be asleep. It was just breaking day. I took another look at Brownie and noticed something else. He had a thirty-thirty rifle alongside of him. I knew then what that meant. As I have said, it was deer season. I let a nasty smirk cross my face.

"You poor bum," I sneered to myself. "You won't get a shot at a deer!"

That nasty reflection had hardly left me when I heard the loud crack of the rifle. I jumped across the cab to see a running deer going across the highway. Brownie had missed! He stood up now and took careful aim. Crack went the rifle. That deer's hind quarters seemed to raise in the air. Its head and front quarters slid along on the ground for several feet.

I jumped back to my side and eased off on the throttle. When we had slowed down sufficiently Brownie and McPhie got off. A little while later, when I was almost stopped, I saw them throwing the deer into one of the empty cars. I was the engineer, fireman, and head brakeman from there to Gilluly, while they dressed that deer back in the car.

About another deer hunt: Little Mickey Carter was our head brakeman this night, some time in the early 1950s. It was a very tough winter, and the snow was exceptionally deep. I had never seen so many wild creatures at the lower altitudes before. The deer all seemed to want to be down close to the tracks. The snow was so deep that they couldn't make much headway trying to move around.

It was almost pitiful to go by a deer a few feet from the tracks up to its belly in the snow. The poor things would look up at you as you went by with those big brown eyes as if asking for help. You couldn't help but feel sympathy for them. I have never pulled the trigger on a gun which killed one of these gentle animals. I have eaten venison many times that others have taken, but I was never able to kill them myself. In my younger days I may not have openly declared this in a world where it was a proof of manhood to hunt them down, but now I can say it.

We came up the canyon between Kyune and Colton. Mickey Carter had brought his rifle along. He had turned it over to the fireman, and he was up in the doghouse on the back of the tank, probably asleep. The fireman, a young fellow named Bryner, was holding the rifle in his hands. We were just starting to pick up speed.

All at once I heard a loud crack, and the fireman screamed, "I got him! I got him!"

I reached up and shut off the throttle. I set the brakes and brought the train to a stop. Mickey came out of the doghouse, and he and the fireman went back along the train. After a little while they came back dragging the deer. They hung it up and skinned it. When we got to Provo we brought it to our home and cut it up on our kitchen table.

I didn't feel right about this. Not only were the deer at a disadvantage in the deep snow, but it was also out of deer season. And what's more, our rear brakeman, a man named Sholes, was a game warden. I don't think he ever knew what we stopped for on that winter's night, although his suspicions must have been aroused. He made several funny remarks to me later.

One time *I* went through a herd. Only this time it wasn't sheep, it was cattle. I was working the mine run out of Martin. It was a Saturday night. Most of the crew lived at Provo. We were in a hurry to get tied up so we could catch no. 1 for home over Sunday. The last move we had made was to go caboose bounce to Hiawatha to get a few loads at that place. Bill McKelvy was my fireman. After crossing the Gordon Creek bridge you make a right-hand curve, follow a straight piece of track for a mile, then go into a deep cut on a left-hand curve.

I was running this old mallet about as fast as I dared to go when I entered this cut. All at once it felt as if the mallet was on the ground. You couldn't see for dust. There was a strong stench in the air as if from blood and warm meat. Before we could get stopped I realized we were into a herd of cattle.

The day work train had unloaded a couple cars of cinders. These cinders were warm and had attracted the cattle. They found it a nice place to bed down for the night. We counted fourteen dead. Off in the brush we could hear the bawling of the injured.

I told McKelvy to get the coal pick. I carried the torch while we put several out of their misery. One old bull was limping along and moaning most pitifully. I approached with the torch upraised. McKelvy lifted the coal pick. Then the old bull let out a deep roar and charged us. I'm glad he didn't have the use of four good legs, or we may not have beat it back to the engine.

We didn't try to relieve the suffering of any more that night. I am sure that was the biggest slaughter of livestock in which I was ever involved. There have been a number of times when I have killed one, two, or more animals as they wandered onto the track, and I found it impossible to stop. These are among the most unpleasant experiences a man has when engaged in this business of running an engine.

There's an old, shop-worn statement to the effect that anything can happen on a railroad. I think, and I have heard it said frequently by boomers, that nowhere was this more true than on the Rio Grande line between Helper and Salt Lake.

I can tell of a time when a westbound Utah coal drag lost a car out of its train and no one knew of it until the incoming train was checked at Provo. Bert Pumphrey was the engineer.

It was a dark, moonless night. Bert had just rounded those curves coming down out of Mill Fork. Shortly after coming out on that long tangent coming into Narrows with the brakes in the retaining position, the train brakes went into the emergency position and big holed the entire train. There is nothing that can be done under these conditions except to let the train come to a stop and examine each car in the train.

After the train had come to a stop, Bert sent the head brakeman back to see if he could find anything wrong. The brakeman walked back along the left side of the train. Everything seemed in order. However, when he was about fifteen cars behind the engine he heard, coming from several cars farther back, the intermittent blowing of blasts or puffs of compressed air. This was happening as Bert moved his brake valve from the lap to the service positions in order to see if the air pressure was building up in the train line.

The brakeman quickened his steps. A few car lengths further back in the train he found the air hose connections uncoupled. The drawbars were together with the knuckles locked in the closed position. The brakeman, thinking it was just a case of the air hoses coming uncoupled, recoupled them and went back to the engine. After building up the brake pipe pressure, Bert whistled off, got a highball from the caboose, and took off down the hill. When the car checker at Provo reported a car of coal missing out of the train they began to investigate. That missing car was on the ground, nicely clearing the right of way, on what would have been the right side of the train when it was stopped about a half mile west of Mill Fork.

It had happened like this: That car, for some unknown reason, had derailed and gone completely clear of the west-bound track to the right. The rear portion of the train, before both sections had stopped, caught up with the front section. The automatic couplers recoupled, and in railroad vernacular, the joint had been made.

When the brakeman saw the air hoses were disconnected he naturally figured that to be the trouble. All he had to do was to recouple the air hoses. The car was completely clear of the right of way on the right side of the train. It was dark, and the brakeman had worked from the left side and consequently had not seen the derailed car.

A few years after this happened, I read a railroad story in some magazine. The writer described an incident quite similar to the one above. Anything can happen on a railroad!

Jim "Fig" Newton was a conductor with the Utah Railway. His wife died very shortly after the Utah started operation. It seemed he had four or five children. What he did with them I'm not sure. I think his wife's folks took them. Anyway, Fig lived a very fast life after his wife died. He was slim and tall. I can't say that he was even good looking from a man's point of view, but he sure had something that appealed to the women. They flocked around him in droves. They weren't all single women, either. There were lots of married ones who thought Jim was the most charming of men. Everyone on the railroad either treated him with tolerance or with scorn.

One day we were coming west with a train of coal. Jim was my conductor. At Soldier Summit we met an eastbound Utah train of empties. Roy Palmer was the eastbound conductor. He and Fig met at the telegraph office. Roy thought he would have a little fun with Jim. He furtively called him aside. Speaking low and glancing cautiously around, he told Jim that before leaving Provo, a man came into the office. This man had a big six-shooter strapped on his hip. He seemed to be in an angry mood according to Palmer. He wanted to know if Jim Newton was in town. Upon being told that he was out on the road he wanted to know when they expected him to return. All this Palmer told Fig as though conveying some dreadful secret. He admonished Newton to be very careful on approaching Provo. Jim just laughed it off. He had nothing to fear!

At the east end of Springville was a derail in the track about twenty car lengths before crossing the Orem tracks. There were two block signals— a home signal and a distant signal—denoting the position of the derail. It was always desirable to slow down considerably on approaching this derail until sure of its position.

We came down on these signals about noon. A train length east of this derail there was an apple orchard in full bloom. As usual, I slowed down at this point until I was sure of the derail. When the caboose came by that apple orchard Jim jumped off. He hastily lost himself among the apple trees.

Our rear brakeman was Hugh Brown. When we stopped in the yards at Provo he delivered the way bills and did the necessary pencil work instead of Jim. He then hurried out and, without saying a word to anyone, got in Jim's car and drove out to that apple orchard above Springville and picked him up. I learned all this later.

Next trip out I had a new conductor and rear brakeman. I learned that Fig and Brownie were out of service. Everyone seemed amused, but no one seemed to know why.

When I returned to Provo after the next trip I received orders to report as a witness at the investigation of Jim Newton and Hugh Brown. How it ever got out I don't know, but Mr. Vaughan seemed to have all the facts. He fired Jim for deserting his train, and he fired Brownie for conniving with him. He asked me if I knew that I had come into Provo without a conductor. I assured him that I hadn't, which was the truth.

This was during the time of the Great Experiment known as Prohibition. Jim knew and patronized every speakeasy in the county. I believe he also knew who of almost all his friends were making home brew. He promptly landed a job as a revenue officer, and soon thereafter, one by one, all his beer-selling friends were raided. All of the joints he had patronized when he was working on the railroad were put out of business. That was Jim "Fig" Newton for you. He finally drifted out of sight, and many years later I heard he had died. Doubtless, numerous ladies, married and unmarried, mourned his passing.

There used to be an engineer on the road named Landers. At the time of this tale he was working out of Thistle. He had made a help to Hill Top on the Marysvale Branch and was returning light to Thistle. Somewhere up around Indianola his tank became badly derailed. For several hours he worked trying to get it back on the rail. He and the fireman were getting quite hungry, and they were not making much headway toward rerailing that tank.

Finally Shorty Landers decided he had enough. Their engine was a little hog, or a set out. They filled the boiler with water from the derailed tank. The fireman put in a good fire. They set the brakes on the tank and blocked its wheels. They then knocked the pin out of the drawbar connecting the engine to the tank and went down into Thistle on the engine—minus the tank. Anything can happen on a railroad!

Shorty Launders got his on no. 12 one night. He was deadheading from Salt Lake to Midvale on no 12's engine. At a point now known as Thirty-Third South an eastbound freight train was pulling out on the mainline in the face of no. 12. Number 12, with Scotty Grosebeck at the throttle, plowed into the freight. Shorty Landers was killed on the engine he was deadheading home on.

It was at this point that I came closest to getting mine. It happened this way. It was during World War I and I was pulling a westbound troop train. It was an extra, and I was moving along right smart coming into Salt Lake. Between Midvale and the yard limit at Salt Lake I mistook a switchlight for the home signal and big holed the train on nothing more than hunch.

After that switchlight went by the cab of our slowing engine, the fireman, who that night was Mike Maloney, and I were laughing about wartime jitters and an exaggerated fear of sabotage. When the engine stopped we looked ahead and saw a cut of box cars on the mainline just ahead of us with no lights nor flag! A local crew was working the area with no orders indicating our presence. When the conductor of the crew climbed into the cab his first words were, "Where in the h— did you come from? I have no dope on you at all!"

Obviously we were immensely lucky. Mike, a loveable guy and a devout Irish Catholic, said, "You know, Gilbert, The Lord Jesus was riding with us tonight!" And I rather think He was.

In my later days on the Utah Railway there was a time when I was working the helper job at Martin. One night I was on the middle helper of a westbound drag. The engineer on the road engine had pulled out of the yard with the head end of the train. I was backed down onto the rear section. After the usual preliminaries of connecting the air and testing, I pulled out of the yard. As I came out onto the lead track just west of the enginehouse, the conductor, a man named Nickerson, handed me the orders as I passed him. He then stepped back onto an enginehouse track adjacent to the mainline to check the rear portion of the train as I pulled it by him. This procedure was habit with him. He had done it this way innumerable times.

This night the hostler, a little fellow named Joe Pearson, was getting a mallet engine ready to make a help on a later train. He had the engine ready on the cinderpit track, and about this time he decided to back it down to the west end of the enginehouse. This took him past where Nickerson was standing checking the train moving by him.

Meanwhile, I had pulled the rear section up to a joint with the front section and waited. Apparently there was no one at the switch to line it so that the rear mallet with the caboose coupled behind it could move ahead and couple onto the rear car. Lining the switch and signaling the rear mallet should have been Nickerson's job, but he was nowhere around.

Those around the place started looking for the missing conductor. After about an hour or more someone started rehearsing Nickerson's habits how he always checked the train as it moved by him from the adjacent track. That mallet that had backed down off the cinder pit was contentedly sucking her ashes, as we used to say, just west of the roundhouse. I was up there in the middle of the train wondering what could be causing the delay.

Finally someone near the enginehouse had a bright idea. They looked around the running gear of that mallet, and there they found what once had been Nickerson. He had been run over as the hostler backed that mallet down off the cinderpit. His body was all cut up and tangled in the running gear under that engine. I was the last one to see him alive.

Apparently Nickerson was either so absorbed in doing his job of checking the train or the passing cars so drowned out the sound of the mallet backing down that he did not hear it and was taken unawares. In any event he was run over by the backing engine, moving as they usually did for such a short distance, without lights.

Joe Pearson, the hostler that backed that mallet over Nickerson, went all to pieces when he found out what he had done. Joe laid off for several months. When he did return to work it turned out to be only for a week or so until he quit altogether.

Although no blame could be attached to him, this incident did bring about a rule governing the procedure of hostlers moving engines in and around the engine servicing facilities, that any engine on the cinderpit must stay there while a train was pulling out or making up.

Then there was the case of Tim Devenish of Springville. He was a fireman on the Rio Grande. To start with, he was one of the loudest in his claims that the Rio Grande men would soon have those Utah Railway jobs back again.

One day the Utah Railway found itself short a brakeman on an outgoing train of empties at Provo. Tom Schott, who was the chief clerk to the master mechanic and superintendent at that point, called up Devenish at Springville and asked him if he would like to go out as a brakeman on the Utah. Tim accepted. Soon he was working for both railroads—as a fireman on the Rio Grande and as a brakeman on the Utah.

Tim was a social fellow, and I liked him very much. He was a husky, redheaded Irishman. One night he was braking ahead on our crew. We came out of Hiawatha on this trip with a boomer fireman, Tim Devenish braking ahead, Hugh Brown braking on the rear end, Jim Newton conductor, and me as the engineer. We were a jolly crew on the head end that night. Right out of Hiawatha the three of us in the cab started singing on our way down the canyon. By the time we reached Martin we had about exhausted our repertoire of all the current popular songs. Tim climbed off the engine as we drifted into Martin. It was to be the last I would see of him alive!

We had some switching to do on the head end of our train. After taking coal and water we backed onto the train and proceeded with the work. We had made several passes, that is, several switching movements, when I got a stop sign. I stopped and watched for the next sign. I peered back a long time in the darkness, but no signal came. I was beginning to think something was wrong. At last Bill Ralston came running up in the darkness. He was called as engineer on one of our helpers.

He scrambled up the gangway ladder, and without waiting to collect his breath, he screamed, "You have just killed Tim Devenish!"

Many times death has suddenly intruded into my consciousness. It is hard to remember what my reactions were at the time. I know I centered the reverse lever and locked the independent air brake valve in holding position. I climbed off the engine and silently accompanied Bill Ralston back to the scene of death. By that time they had carried Tim Devenish over to a little abandoned telegraph office and laid him on the floor. This man, who moments before was singing with us as we drove into town, now lay on this cold cement floor, stark in death, his eyes staring glassily at nothing.

No one ever knew how Tim got his. He had not been run over or cut up. There was no blood on him anywhere. His chest was crushed as though a mighty, giant hand had pressed the life out of him there.

After a long delay we received orders to set our train out at Martin and proceed, caboose bounce, to Provo. They loaded Tim's body into the caboose, and I received orders from the Rio Grande dispatcher to make no 1's time to Springville. All the way over the road I was worried about what I would see at Springville. I had visions of meeting Tim's family and witnessing their anguish on our arrival. However, I was spared that as there was only the undertaker and his assistant there to meet the train.

As I have stated, his death was and always has been a mystery. At the coroner's inquest which we all attended it remained unsolved. To this day no one has ever learned just what happened to Tim Devenish.

There was an old woman at Provo. She had the reputation of being able to commune with departed spirits. There were a lot of old women around Provo at that time who really believed her. Jim Newton, our conductor, roomed at her home. We all got together and decided to take her over to Springville where she could see the body and do some communing for us. We took her into the room where Tim's body lay. For a long time she stood silently looking through half-closed eyelids at the body.

Then she exclaimed, "He's calling; he's pleading with someone named Frank. Who is Frank?"

We were all momentarily startled. The only Frank we knew was Frank Branting. He was asleep in a caboose tied up on the caboose track at the time. Anyway, as that was the extent of her powers, we took the old witch back home and proceeded to forget about her. We really should have let her ride home on her broom!

The whole crew, along with several additions, acted as pall bearers. Every time I looked in Mrs. Devenish's direction, it appeared as though she was staring at me. It seemed as though she was saying to herself, "There's the man who killed my husband!"

Joe Loveridge was conductor on one of the mine runs out of Martin. Harry Clark was his engineer. Harry was the nervous type when on an engine. He carried it to the extreme. This crew had only a short time previously come down into town and set out a train of coal in the load yard. They had backed the engine and caboose down the eastbound main to clear the load yard lead. Then they had all gone to the Beanery to eat.

After eating they returned to the job just as another mine-run crew came into town with a string of loads. Harry and his fireman, a man named Henningson, climbed on their engine. Joe Loveridge and the rear brakeman, Sy Sorensen, sat down on the rail behind the caboose to wait for this second mine crew to dispose of their train.

When those cars of coal started backing into the yard, Harry Clark on the standing engine began to get nervous. He wasn't sure, after standing there all that time, that he cleared the load yard lead. Instead of investigating to find out, he decided to back up a little further. He did, and in doing so he backed that caboose over Joe Loveridge, who was sitting on the rail behind it.

I was just coming into town on a mainline drag when all this happened. They flagged me down and held me at the coal chute until they got Joe out from under the caboose. He was pretty badly cut up and he died after being taken to the hospital at Price.

Harry Clark may have had good reason to be nervous. Early in his career as an engineer his train had run over and cut off the legs of a small child playing on the track on the Spring Canyon Branch. He had also had several other pieces of extremely bad luck. Even so I know he was very nervous on an engine even as a fireman.

The train crews were all loud in their criticism of Harry in backing up without a signal. But if you will just stop to consider for a moment, what could have been more foolish than the action of that train crew in sitting on the rail behind a caboose with a live engine on the other end? This also violated all the rules of the railroad as well as the rules of common sense. Who was more to blame—Harry Clark or Joe Loveridge?

After they loaded Joe into the ambulance, I was standing at the desk in the roundhouse making out my trip report. Harry came in and walked up to the enginemen's register. He took out his lead-pencil, and with many a wild flourish he wrote, "H. W. Clark—All Through!" He quit right there. He had wanted to quit for a long time and was only trying to hold on till he could get a worthwhile pension. He never went back on an engine again. Yes, anything can happen on a railroad.

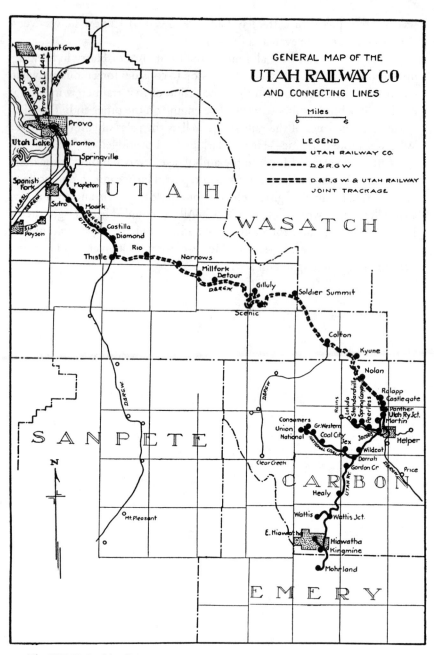

The W.J.G. Gould collection

Life on the Utah Railway

The Utah Railway officially started operation on December 1, 1917. Until about the summer of 1931 we were continually growing and getting bigger, handling more and more tonnage. During these years the Wattis Branch was built, then the Spring Canyon Branch. We also had a spur leading off the Rio Grande mainline just below Castle Gate which crossed the Price River to the United States Fuel Panther mine. It was after much agitation and argument with the Rio Grande that the three mining companies, Standard, Spring Canyon, and Peerless, built the Spring Canyon Branch. Then about 1926 the National Branch was built to serve the Sweet, Blue Blaze, and National mines. We operated them all as part of the Utah Railway.

For many years the talk was always that the Rio Grande was going to take over the Utah Railway. It would either be on the first or the fifteenth of the month that this change was to take place. There came a time when the Denver and Rio Grande changed its name to the Denver and Rio Grande Western. This change of name gave some of those Rio Grande men new hopes. This change of names would abrogate the existing contract. The Denver and Rio Grande Western would not be compelled to live up to a contract made by the Denver and Rio Grande.

About that time I went into the Beanery at Thistle for a quick cup of coffee. Across the horseshoe-shaped counter sat an old Rio Grande engineer. I always considered him a friend. He called to me to come over to his side of the counter. I crossed over. He had news for me, and I am sure he was sincere.

Did I know that the Rio Grande had added another word to its name? That added word changed the road's position regarding contracts made under the former name. If I didn't do something right soon I would be out of a job. He thought I should quit the Utah and try to hire back onto the Rio Grande to protect myself. I thought for a moment and then told him not to build his hopes too high on that change of names. I told him that I had been privileged to read the contract with the Utah before leaving the Rio Grande. I told him that in no place in that contract was either the name "Utah Railway" or the "Rio Grande" mentioned. It said that the contract was entered into by the party owning the eastbound mainline between the middle of the wye at Provo and the coal chute at Thistle, and the party owning the westbound mainline between those same points.

The party owning the eastbound mainline would be hereafter known as the "Utah Party." The one owning the westbound mainline would be known as the "Denver Party." Throughout the contract those were the names used to designate the two roads. As long as one road owned one mainline and one owned the other, the contract would stand. I don't know if I convinced him or not, but the more I thought about it, the higher my faith soared.

When we first started on the Utah Railway we were right in the middle of World War I. There was a general sabotage scare throughout the country. Consequently there were armed watchmen stationed day and night at the Gordon Creek bridge. They lived in a little cave-like shanty dug into the bank of the cut. It was reinforced with odds and ends of old lumber. They also had three or four barrels buried in the ground alongside the track for water.

All trains had orders to stop on signal and replenish those water barrels. We all hated this chore, although the procedure was simple. We only had to spot the engine right and prime the injector so the water from the overflow pipe would flow into the barrels. This was no task at all. Yet we all hated to be flagged for water.

If I thought I was going to have to fill those barrels I would try to approach the bridge as silently as possible so as not to let the guards know we were coming. I would work as light a throttle as I could. I would not blow the whistle for miles. Once I actually got away with it. We were half way out on the bridge before those poor thirsty guys realized we were there. Of course we couldn't see a signal then.

At first I was overjoyed to know that I had slipped one over on those guards. I was quite happy and proud of myself. After a while I began to remember how mother and us kids had suffered from thirst years before on account of such a feeling on the part of an engine crew. I began to rue my actions. I never tried to sneak up on those water barrels or ignore a signal for water again.

When we lived at Silver City Junction we had four big barrels buried in the ground alongside the track. The tops of these barrels just peeked over the level of the ground. These barrels contained our water supply.

Whenever the water got low in these barrels we would stick a white flag alongside the track. The 518, the mine-run engine that plied between Ironton and Eureka, would stop and fill those barrels from the tender. It was quite an operation. They would have to close the tank valve and disconnect the hose between the engine and the tank. With one man holding the hose, the tank valve would then be opened, and the water directed into the barrels.

It was quite a job to fill those four big water barrels. I think that is what caused that mine-run crew to be slightly blind. That is what happened many times when we needed water. They couldn't recognize that white flag. Many times we were without water for hours. As we had four to six section hands using water besides our own family, those water barrels needed refilling quite often.

It was always a mystery to that mine-run crew what we did with all that water, or so they said. I know we didn't dip it up and throw it on the ground, and we had no garden. Yet those guys thought we were wasting it in some way. If there was snow on the ground we could melt it for water. I have known many times when we all very badly needed a drink of water.

Years later, when I was coming out of Spring Canyon with my young son Bill aboard, people were lined up along the right of way with buckets and kettles. This was because their water came from underground sources in the mines and tasted heavily of sulfur. We stopped that night as I had done other times, and I took Bill down on the ground to fill their containers from the tank hoses.

Like all little boys Bill was full of questions. When we were back in the cab and rolling down toward Martin he asked me why we did it. When I told him the circumstance he asked if the water was all right for them to drink. I recall I smiled at his question and said something to the effect that it was good water and would only give them a mild laxative because of the boiler compound in it. I believe he thought that was a great joke.

Operation over that Gordon Creek trestle was quite exacting if you lived up to the rules. There was a slow board at the approach to the bridge from each direction. I believe the allowed speed was eight or ten miles an hour. This presented no problem to eastbound (up grade) trains, but it was very much a problem in the opposite direction with the down grade trains.

Coming down the grade with a long, heavy train of coal, all the retainers with the exception of five or six cars on the rear end would be in holding position. I think I have explained that a retaining valve is used to hold some air in the brake cylinders after a release operation and before the next application of the brakes. It could be likened to a plug held over the exhaust pipe by a predetermined weight. When the compression under the plug was greater than the weight, air would lift the weight and blow out to the atmosphere. When the weight was greater it would force the plug to its seat, thereby retaining what was left of the pressure in the brake cylinder. This was to control the train and to insure a recharge of the auxiliary reservoirs between brake applications.

On the east end of the bridge you came down a two percent grade. After crossing the bridge and leaving it on the west you had about a half-mile of level track. If you came down off the two percent stretch too slowly and with too much pressure retaining in the brake cylinders, you would always have to work steam to beat hell to get that train across the bridge and over the flat half-mile section.

I always tried to hit the east end of that bridge as slowly as possible and with as little pressure retaining as possible. I would most always work a little steam after leaving the bridge to get them over the flat. I always tried to live up to that speed restriction over the bridge.

There were some enginemen who were not so particular. Bert Pumphrey was one of them. Bert was always a little wild and reckless. There had been quite a lot of rainfall one year, and Bert was coming down the hill with a long train of coal. He let go of his brakes quite a distance above the bridge. By the time he hit the bridge he was going twenty miles an hour or better, and the speed was increasing. He figured on rolling them so fast that he wouldn't have to work steam across the flat beyond the bridge.

When the engine and about fifteen cars had left the bridge, Bert said he felt as though something was pulling back on the train. Something was slowing him down. He glanced back, then took a longer look. Those cars of coal were derailed and going in all directions. They zigzagged to a stop with that cut filled with coal.

I saw those rails in the cut afterward. They were twisted and kinked all out of shape like strands of bailing wire. I believe this was the first wreck we had on the Utah Railway. The Utah had an agreement with the Rio Grande to have the use of its wrecker when needed. I am sure the Rio Grande took its own sweet time in making it available, so I believe we were tied up for several days on account of this accident.

Compared to the Rio Grande we had very little trouble in the nature of wrecks, although we did have a few. I remember on one occasion we had the railroad tied up near Gilluly for several hours. A Utah westbound train had a car leave the rails just below the old station of Scenic. It stopped in such a position as to block both mainlines. I think that was the first derailment for the Utah on the joint track.

Johnny McKenna was firing for Gallagher in helping service out of Martin when we started to operate the Utah Railway. At the beginning of operations we had only received a few of the 2–10-2s we had on order. Consequently the Utah borrowed several engines from different railroads until all our power was delivered. Among the borrowed engines was one from the Rio Grande, the 1073. It was a mallet, a 2–8–8–2 and a very large engine. Not only that, it was hand-fired!

When the Utah engines came they were all equipped with automatic stokers. The first automatic stokers that I ever saw were on those Utah engines. All the Rio Grande engines on the west end were still hand fired. Even the big mallets.

Johnny and Gallagher wouldn't be very far up the canyon before Johnny would suddenly become sick. He described his illness as "one of them spells."

For a while the ruse worked all right. Gallagher would get down and take the scoop shovel and fire the engine. After a few times Gallagher got wise to Johnny. When Johnny would complain that he could feel "one of them spells" coming on, Gallagher would move the Johnson bar a little lower down. Then Johnny would remind Gallagher he was getting sick.

Gallagher would answer, "Yes, I know. I'm trying to hurry a little to get you to a doctor," And he would drop the Johnson bar down a little further. After awhile Johnny would get well. He didn't complain that he could feel "one of them spells" coming on anymore.

Johnny carried an old newspaper in the seat box. When he passed a Rio Grande engine, he would have his feet propped up against the boiler and be deeply engrossed in that old newspaper until the Rio Grande man had passed. Then the newspaper would be put back in the seat box. In this way he lorded it over his former fireman friends on the Rio Grande.

After a few years the Rio Grande's new engines also came stoker equipped. They then went back and put stokers on all the engines down to as small as the eleven hundred class. That old newspaper stunt didn't mean a thing anymore!

After going to the Utah Railway and while working as an engineer, Johnny McKenna was on the sharp end of a coal drag pounding up the canyon westbound toward Summit at Nolon. He had the 103 as his engine. He and his fireman had reached the west end of Nolon. It was dark. Around the curve and a number of car lengths above them they saw two red marker lamps bearing down on them at what looked like terrific speed. The fireman prepared to get off the engine.

Johnnie hollered at him, "Wait a minute! Wait a minute! Let's shake hands now ... so if we die.... Shake hands. I don't have anything but friendship for you. Goodbye now. Goodbye."

About that time a Rio Grande caboose plastered itself all over the front end of the 103. This caboose had gotten away at Soldier Summit and had come rollicking down the grade. The first obstacle it encountered was Johnnie on the 103 at Nolon.

I was called at Provo to deadhead out to Nolon and bring in Johnnie's train. Johnnie's time was up after the delay of scraping that caboose off the front end of the 103. Johnnie was still white and trembling when I got there.

It was quite an experience. When they saw those two red marker lamps bearing down on them they had no way of knowing that it was a caboose running light. It could have been a train of coal. In that case the result would have been different.

That old 103 carried the marks of that impact until they put her to the torch. The wheels skidded out from under the caboose, and their flanges were buried deep into the pilot casting. Parts of those flanges remained imbedded in that casting as long as there was an engine 103. This was a case of a caboose smashing into an engine, instead of the usual situation of an engine smashing into a caboose.

Very early in my career as an engineer on the Utah I had an experience that I shall never forget. I was coming west with a train of coal. My conductor was Lew Bayrell. The rear brakeman was Tommy Burk, who later died from injuries received in a tunnel wreck.

At Soldier Summit I got an order reading: "2nd. number 1 run 2 hours and fifty minutes late Soldier Summit to Provo."

That order, the way it was written, violated the rules regarding the way orders should be written. It started out by designating the word "second" in the manner of "2nd." This was not proper nor to be permitted.

"Second" should have been spelled out, as should all numbers, without abbreviations or flourishes.

I read that order as "Number 1 run 2 hours and fifty minutes late Soldier Summit to Provo." Every member of the crew read the order just as I did. We left Soldier Summit, and I dismissed no. 1 from my mind. The way I had read that order gave me plenty of time to go to Provo ahead of her.

I used the regulation time going down the canyon. About two miles above Thistle there is a straight piece of open track about a mile and a half long. We always turned to get a look at our train on this straight rail. This morning I casually turned my head for that look. What I saw was not only our train but no. 1 as well dogging along slowly behind our caboose.

Little Tommy Burke was out on a high car trying to get us to speed up. I reached for my train orders to reread them. It was then that I discovered that it was *second* no. 1 that was running 2 hours and fifty minutes late. First no. 1 was running right on schedule; or had been until they caught up with us. I lost no more time getting into Thistle and letting first no. 1 by us.

I was called up a few days later for investigation. It seemed rather odd that every member of our crew had read the orders the way I did. It just shows that the more orders you read, the less they seem in importance. Anyone asked to read that order out loud would have gotten it right the first time.

I was given fifty brownies. The rest of the crew were given the same except the conductor. He was demoted permanently to the position of brakeman. He spent the rest of his days in that capacity. What made it so tough for him was the fact that he was supposed to be all-wise on train orders. He had spent years on the UP conducting classes on the book of rules and train orders.

I believe that was the first really bad mistake I had made since going to the Utah, and I felt the humiliation deeply. In the few years that followed, without anything else against my record, I removed those brownies.

In the years that I worked as an engineer I can say more from pride than braggadocio that I have been called several times for some particular job that required extra skill. However, there was one incident that I recall where I fell down on the job with which I was entrusted. I will describe the circumstance.

Every so often the government would send out a specially equipped car to visit the mines. The object was to check on the mining company to see if they were living up to the safety rules and regulations.

Once, when this car had been at Hiawatha a couple of weeks, I was called to handle it together with a train of coal to Utah Railway Junction.

They held the switch crew on duty at Hiawatha until I showed up. I was asked where I would like to have this car placed in the train—on the head end or on the rear end next to the caboose. It was already on the head end so I told them it would be alright to leave it right there. We left Hiawatha with this coach right behind the engine and ahead of that train of coal.

There were two couples living in that coach. They were employees of the government. I gave them a very good ride from Hiawatha to Utah Junction. We set the car out at Utah Junction on a Rio Grande connection. We were returning to our train when the two brakemen decided that the car didn't clear properly.

After some discussion they decided to go back and nudge it down a little further into the passing track. We were moving slowly down against the car. It was very dark, and the brakemen were both walking down before me on an adjacent track. They were giving slow signs without paying any particular attention to where I was. All at once I crashed into the car.

The occupants were sitting at a table playing cards. A radio was going full blast. When the old 108 crashed into that car it upset the radio, knocking it to the floor and upsetting the card players. I was reprimanded for that. A reprimand is the lowest form of censure that a person can be given. The brakemen both got brownies, as did the conductor, for not being on the job. After that every engine was equipped with a back-up headlight. I consider this as another black mark on my record.

It was for a while tough on enginemen after the Utah started operations. It was difficult to find a place to sleep and eat on the layover at the far terminal of the run. The train crews, of course, had the caboose, their home away from home, that we carried with us.

You had to be at the Hiawatha boarding house during meal hours or you didn't get anything to eat. Most of the time there were no empty beds. Joe Stevenson finally cleared out an outfit car on the ground behind the round house. He placed several bunks and a stove in it. If you brought your own grub you could fry it on the stove, and then if there was an empty bunk you climbed in it. While you were in bed another engine crew would come in and start cooking. This made it very hard to sleep.

Joe finally had the section men unload a lot of used ties down the bank just as you come into town. Some crews dug into the bank and built dugouts with the ties.

Bob Crosbie had his eye on a little lumber shack that stood off the right of way at Royal, just above Castle Gate. Once when he came down the canyon in the small hours of morning he stopped and loaded that whole thing on the engine. When reassembled at Hiawatha he had the best shack of all.

I learned there was a dentist living at Provo who had two furnished rooms in a house at Hiawatha. It seemed that every so often he would spend a week or two at Hiawatha fixing up the townsfolks' molars. I went to see him at Provo to see if we couldn't occupy the place at Hiawatha while he was away. Early in our talk I thought I sensed the fact that he didn't seem to be anxious to revisit Hiawatha. Provo was growing fast at that time, and his practice was keeping him busy in Provo. He didn't know when he would be able to take care of his patients at Hiawatha again.

I cautiously put forth the idea of him selling out to me. After a little persuasion he agreed. I bought the whole outfit of his furnishings for ten dollars and took over the rental of the rooms. I paid five dollars a month for room rental, and from then on we were sitting pretty.

The biggest remaining problem was groceries. When we had groceries we had some real feeds. If you were in Hiawatha in the daytime you could always get canned goods at the store and sometimes a piece of fresh meat. If you tried to carry fresh vegetables or meats from home on the engine, they usually weren't fit to eat upon arriving at Hiawatha. After a while we finally got the train crews to carry our meat on the ice in the caboose.

I was burned out twice while we were working into Hiawatha. I had an old two-room lumber shack beside the mainline which belonged to the mining company. It was fitted out with an old coal cooking range. There was also a cupboard, dishes, cooking utensils and two sleeping bunks. Leon Smith was my fireman. Business fell off on the mainline with the approach of spring. Leon found that he couldn't hold a job out of Provo, so he went to Hiawatha to fire the switch engine. He had an interest in the shack so he bunked there.

One morning while I was at Provo the Utah Railway office called. They told me my shack had just burned to the ground at Hiawatha. Not a thing had been saved. It developed that Leon had let a brakeman sleep in my bunk while I was away. He said that when he had left for work that morning the brakeman was sitting on the edge of the bunk smoking a cigarette. The next thing he saw was the shack ablaze. No one made an effort to put out the fire, so it burned to the ground. I think the mining company was glad to see it burn, as it was an eyesore.

I arrived at Hiawatha the following evening. The switch engine had tied up. I couldn't see Leon Smith anywhere around. We took the engine around the wye and headed down onto the caboose. There was a train of coal on one of the yard tracks. We put the caboose on the coal train. It was to be our train to leave with in the morning.

Howard Hinton was my conductor. He came to the cab and told me that there was a guy in the caboose who would like to speak to me. I got off the engine and went into the caboose to see who it was. It was Leon. He had been doing a little drinking, and had a pint of liquor in his hand. As soon as I came in the door he shoved this bottle of whiskey in my face. I have always said that he wanted me to see the bottle before I saw him.

"I burned down our shack, old pal. It's gone—it's gone," he blubbered.

He had a room at the hotel, and I slept there that night. It was while I was there that I learned of the Provo dentist who had furnished rooms in a house on the main drag. I went to see him on my return to Provo. We soon came to an understanding, and Leon and I had a home again.

A few years later the railway company built an apartment house for the mainline engine crews. There were four apartments. McPhie was my fireman by then. We moved in apartment number 2. This structure was built on the high ground just behind the roundhouse. We only had to walk a few steps to or from work or for coal or water.

A year or two later the company built a house for the car man and his family, Jack Phillips, just a short distance from our apartment. Mrs. Phillips, Ma Phillips, served meals to the extra train and engine crews boarding house style. This arrangement went on for five or six years. Then one morning the telephone at Provo rang again to inform me that I was burned out at Hiawatha.

No one seemed to know how the fire had started, but it took the whole building. I have always thought I knew how it came about. Ma Phillips had a son. He was about six years old, the peskiest brat I ever knew. I have always suspected that he set that fire. Well, after that we had to rent and refurnish another set of rooms.

During the twenties the Utah Railway developed into quite a railroad. Business was getting better all the time. We served three big mines up the National Branch, three on the Spring Canyon Branch, one at Panther, one at Wattis, and three in the Hiawatha district. We ran more coal trains over the joint track than the Rio Grande did.

Westbound Rio Grande coal trains over Soldier Summit consisted of sixty to sixty-five cars. The Utah Railway handled up to seventy-five cars in a train. Mr. Vaughan, our superintendent, was desirous of handling even more. But there was one bad feature about handling long trains in those days. If the weather was cold over the mountain, as it is after the sun goes down, the brakes might operate well. But in the heat of the day a long train is apt to develop a "dynamiter."

A train that dynamites can cause all kinds of trouble in the triple valve operation. When a triple piston in the triple valve moves out on a service application, say five to twenty pounds reduction in train line pressure, it stops up against a post in the valve. This bumping post, as it is called, is held there by a spring.

In those days this spring had a tension of seven pounds to keep the piston from going all the way into the emergency position. The triple piston, when it begins to move, comes in contact with a small slide valve. Piston and slide valves then move out together until stopped at the bumping post. In this position the port in the slide valve is uncovered and connected to a port in the seat of the piston valve. This allows air to flow from the auxiliary reservoir to the brake cylinder.

When enough air has reached the brake cylinder to bring the pressure in the auxiliary reservoir down to just below what is left in the train line, the triple piston will then move back to lap position, shutting off the connection between auxiliary reservoir and brake cylinder until a further reduction in train line pressure is made. If the tension spring holding the piston bumping post is too weak to stop the movement, the piston valve will continue to move out until it reaches emergency position.

When one triple piston valve goes out into the emergency position it robs the train line of pressure, and every triple valve in the train will go into the emergency position. This is called "dynamiting" the train, when caused by a defective triple valve. If the sudden pressure reduction in the train line is at the engineer's brake valve, it is called "big holing" the train.

The reason a train was more apt to develop a dynamiter in the heat of the day than in the cool of the night was due to the oil or grease in the valve melting and running down to surround the slide valve. This would cause the valve to stick and move out in jerks, as the slide valve would be unbalanced. If the slide valve would not move at the first slight difference in pressure, but waited until that pressure differential was greater, the bumping post held by a seven pound spring would not be able to stop the piston valve at the desired service application but would continue to let it go on out into the emergency position.

This was getting to be quite a problem when we were trying to run longer trains with the old arrangement of valves and spring tension. When a train goes into emergency there is nothing you can do but let it come to a complete stop before attempting to release the brakes.

This undesirable condition was getting to be very annoying to Westinghouse, the manufacturer of the air brake systems. Someone back at the factory got a bright idea. They would equip a long train with a tension spring of fourteen pounds in each triple valve, instead of the standard seven pounds. The Utah Railway, way out west in Utah, was to them the logical place to try it out.

One morning I got a call for a westbound train of coal. I noticed a coach on the head end of the train right next to the engine. It was a Westinghouse dynamometer car. It had everything inside to register every move the engineman made with his air brakes. On the rear end was another such car. We had every load that the railway could scare up. We left Soldier Summit with seventy-seven cars. That was a long train of coal to descend that mountain in those days. Bob Crosbie, our traveling engineer, was riding the engine with me.

When we left Soldier Summit I made up my mind I would handle that train as I did all the others and try to forget its importance. Slim Wilkins, the Rio Grande traveling engineer, was also with us. I had fired many a trip for him when I was on the Rio Grande.

Those Rio Grande men had a certain way of coming off the Summit. They would try to hold the speed down by using the engine brakes and overcharging the head end until the entire train was on the grade. Under this method of handling, the speed would be about twenty-five or thirty miles an hour before the caboose came off the top.

Those two traveling engineers were watching every move I made. When the speed got up to about ten miles an hour I made a light reduction of about five or six pounds in train line pressure. I only held on a few seconds, not long enough for that reduction to reach the rear end. I then held the brake valve in release position long enough to release those brakes on the head end that had set.

When I started that first reduction Slim Wilkins was standing in the left gangway. When he heard the brake valve start to screech he started to cower against the back of the cab and protest loudly. He had never seen a train come off the mountain like that. He was sure we would break in two. But we didn't. Both he and Crosbie glanced apprehensively at each other when I started another reduction. I went through the same performance, again being careful to kick off any overcharge. They began to complain about my method.

I rose from my seatbox, and turning to Crosbie, I said, "Would you like to take 'em down, Bob?" That seemed to silence him, and Slim grinned out the gangway.

I made several more light reductions before the train was entirely off the top of the hill. The speed was never more than fifteen miles an hour coming off, and there were no jars or jerks. I held that train to regulation speed all the way down the mountain.

Before leaving Soldier Summit I was told that if I had a legitimate excuse to big hole the train to go ahead and do it so that they could see what would happen against those fourteen-pound springs. About a mile and a half below Gilluly there are two reverse curves. As I rounded the last one I saw a few rocks on the track that had slid down off the side of the high cut. Ordinarily I would not have bothered about them; there were not enough to cause concern.

However, having received instruction about trying out the fourteen-pound spring in the big hole situation, I thought this would be a good chance to do it. So I immediately moved the brake valve to emergency. Everything handled perfectly. That train came to a nice quick stop with no trouble at all. That test was all that the air brake engineers could hope for. From then on triple valves all over the country were fitted with the heavier spring.

I received a lot of compliments from those Westinghouse men on the way I handled that train. For several years I kept hearing remarks about it. The last time was when a Rio Grande man told me of Slim Wilkins's remarks to a student meeting in Salt Lake.

He was supposed to have said (regarding the speed off the Summit), "We don't know what happened back there, but that train came off that mountain as pretty as anything you'd want to see!" The dispatcher at Hiawatha told me of compliments going over the wire to Mr. Vaughan from Westinghouse. And the operator at Soldier Summit told me, "You didn't do yourself any harm in handling that train!"

That heavier spring in the triple valve did away with a lot of the dynamiting of trains. "Undesired quick action," it was termed.

Mr. Vaughan had his heart set on handling one hundred loads in a train down Soldier Summit. One morning he had set up to try it out. Claude Gillis was the engineer. When everything was right they assembled one hundred loads at the Summit. Everyone at the site was interested and carefully watching. Claude started the train. When it began to pick up speed on the down grade, Claude set the air brakes. I was not there so I can't say just how he did it, but the train broke in three or four pieces on that first application of air. I was at home in Provo at the time. They sent a hurry up call for me to get up to Soldier Summit as quickly as possible.

The rear third of the train was still up on the flat at the Summit. The bad order cars had been set out, and the train was ready to roll again. There were ninety-seven or ninety-eight loads in that train when I took charge. Mr. Vaughan and several Rio Grande officials were there as well as a half-dozen car men.

I started out bravely. That train came off the Summit without any trouble at all. I expected to have trouble with it, but I was agreeably surprised. It handled nicely all the way to Provo. When we pulled into the Provo yard, you could tell that Mr. Vaughan was relieved. He never did try to take one hundred loads in a train again, although we did handle as high as eighty-five on a routine basis.

I think I can safely say that up until the advent of the diesel locomotive I handled the heaviest train of coal that ever came down that mountain. And I smoked one of Mr. Vaughan's good cigars while doing it.

I remember a time when the coal miners at Spring Canyon were on strike. At that time McKelvy and McPhie were working out of Martin on a hill crew. I believe it was the only time the Utah Railway had a hill crew. In my opinion it could better be called the ping pong crew.

One morning they were called at Martin without being told where they were going. Mr. Vaughan appeared on the scene, and they received orders to go light to Castle Gate. Number 5 came into Castle Gate from the east and set out a coach-load of Mexicans.

Bill McKelvy grew suspicious, and upon inquiring, learned that the Mexicans in the coach were strike breakers destined for the mines in Spring Canyon. He refused to move the engine. McPhie and the rest of the crew joined him. Finally Mr. Vaughan fired them for refusing service.

A Spring Canyon mine guard named Webb, who happened to be an ex-Rio Grande fireman, volunteered to fire the engine. Mr. Vaughan thought he could run her himself, so they took off for Martin. At Martin, Mr. Vaughan tried vainly to get another crew to take that coach up to Spring Canyon, but no one seemed interested. He and Webb then decided to tackle the job. With Mr. Vaughan at the throttle and Webb at the scoop they took off. Upon emerging from the east end of tunnel number one, all hell broke loose. There must have been twenty or more striking miners with rifles blazing away at that engine and coach. From all accounts of the fray, when those guns began to bark the mine guard dropped his scoop and with his gun in hand started to climb the coal pile to return their fire. He never got off a shot, so the story goes, before a bullet went through his heart, and he was dead.

Mr Vaughan kept right on going. Instead of stopping to head up the Spring Canyon Branch at Jacobs, he went on up and stopped in the middle of tunnel number two. Leaving the engine and coach there, he walked to

Wild Cat and phoned for help. How he escaped being hit by one of those wild bullets is a mystery.

No one was ever arrested that I heard of in connection with this incident, and if anyone ever knew who the riflemen were that did the firing they kept it very quiet. The train and engine crews were not reinstated for several months. Meanwhile the National Guard was brought into Carbon County.

It was during the presence of the National Guard in the county that the Utah Railway had its nastiest wreck. Charley Johnson, with a train of coal, was coming down into Martin westbound. The Spring Canyon crew was pushing a train of empties with the caboose on the point up through tunnel number one. Charley, with the 102, met the caboose in the middle of the tunnel. The tunnel was timber lined and supported at that time. The caboose caught fire, and a serious fire raged in the confined space of the tunnel.

Tommy Burke, the conductor on the Spring Canyon job, was injured seriously. He never did fully recover. A brakeman on the same job was badly burned in the resulting fire. In fact, all they ever found of this brakeman after several weeks was a piece or two of charred bone.

Charley Johnson could hear Tommy Burke calling from his trapped position in the wreckage of that burning caboose. Amid all the smoke and steam that was making an inferno of that tunnel he walked around the wreck until he found Tommy, and then carried him out more dead than alive. The gas and smoke in the tunnel affected Tommy's throat and lungs so that he died several months later. I have often thought that Charley Johnson's persistence in that tragedy was one of finest acts of heroism I have ever known.

The fire in the tunnel continued to burn for several days before it was put out. It was feared the 102 would be damaged beyond repair, but she went back into service after a very short time in the shops.

During the time that the tunnel was blocked all trains to and from Hiawatha had to be detoured over the Rio Grande and down into Helper. From there they went up the Spring Canyon Branch to a place where a spur connected the Rio Grande with the Utah Railway mainline. There being room above the tunnel for about seven cars and an engine to clear the spur, all trains had to be cut in many pieces in order to get by the blockade. For a couple of weeks or more we juggled trains from one track to another in lots of six or seven cars.

The Utah Railway train dispatcher at that time had his office in the depot at Hiawatha. He had put out the orders that caused these trains to come together in the tunnel. Each crew had orders authorizing it to proceed. Neither train was informed of the other, nor a meeting point for them designated. When this dispatcher learned of the wreck he immediately packed his bag and left the country. After a few weeks he was located somewhere over in Colorado and brought back for the investigation.

The first thing the Utah did after this wreck was to install block signals on each approach to both tunnels. Block signals would have prevented that wreck had they been installed earlier. After that it surely felt good to come down toward Martin and see a big green light on the approach to those tunnels.

Business was getting better all the time on the Utah Railway. In the wintertime all the mines were working at full capacity. In the spring and early summer, activity would fall off a little, but toward September business would be booming again. In the winter you could go into the little call room at Martin and see boomers from all over the country waiting for a call.

Our master mechanic was a little Italian American named Jack Somo. If there was one thing he understood thoroughly it was engines. Our engines were in as nearly perfect condition as they could get. When business started to fall off in the early spring, he would take those engines in rotation and put them through the back shop. When business picked up in the fall all our power would be in good shape to battle through the winter.

Rio Grande engines in contrast would go up the canyon enveloped in a cloud of leaking steam so dense that it was hard to see from the cab to the pilot in the wintertime. By contrast, our power would be tight as a drum against steam leaks.

This reminds me of a story that I heard in my early days as a fireman on the Rio Grande. There were a bunch of us firemen in the call room at Salt Lake sitting around shooting the breeze. There was talk of the Rio Grande getting some of those double-jointed mallet engines for the Bingham branch.

One fireman asked, "What the h—— do they look like, anyway?"

Hardly anyone had ever seen one. One little Irishman named Pat Fay spoke up. "I'll show you what they look like," he said. He picked up a piece of chalk and went over to the black board. He smeared the black board up so that it resembled a big white cloud. He turned a sober face to the gang.

One guy spoke up and said. "That looks like a big cloud of steam. I can't see an engine in there."

"Well, you will," said Pat. "Just wait 'til the engineer shuts off and that steam drifts away; then you'll see the engine."

That's just about the way it was too. When those Rio Grande mallets were working you could hardly see the engine for the steam leaks.

Although we on the Utah kicked and belly-ached about steam leaks, we had nothing to worry about compared to the Rio Grande men. Our power was always in good shape. Our officials saw to it that they got the last pound of power working through their engines.

As I said, during those years our coal tonnage grew by leaps and bounds. Our railroad did too. We had at that time three big mines in the Hiawatha district, as well as Wattis. When the Great Depression of the 1930s hit we were running more trains of coal over the joint track than the Rio Grande. One of the Rio Grande officials made the remark that if it wasn't for the track rental that the Rio Grande was getting from the Utah Railway the Rio Grande would fold up.

There was a time in the late 1920s that the Rio Grande, being in bankruptcy, was sold at auction. At that time the Utah Railway was the highest bidder for the trackage between Grand Junction and Ogden. That was all of the road they wanted. But the bankruptcy court at Denver conducting the auction would not sell it piecemeal. It had to be all or none. I have often wondered what my destiny would have been if this sale had gone through.

Our railroad, and the mines it served, never did recover their former vigor after the depression. One by one our mines folded up due to the decreased demand for coal in competition with natural gas. A mountain slide closed the Panther Mine, and the rails to it were torn up.

When United States Steel located at Geneva near Provo there was no coking coal on our side of the coal fields in Utah. That hurt us, as the coking coal on Rio Grande trackage took away a lot of our business.

Since the Utah Railway never did recover from the depression the way the Rio Grande did, I have often wondered what would have become of me if I had stayed on the Rio Grande. I might have been better off in those later years—if I had survived.

As the Utah Railway business was ninety-nine percent coal, the introduction of natural gas for domestic heating made a big difference in our tonnage. On the other hand, the Rio Grande, through a program of extensive rehabilitation, gained a lot of through business. It is and has been for some time a real modern railroad. When I was on the Rio Grande it was far from that.

When the Utah Railway started building, the reports that went around would make any young fellow long to change to the new road. Although those reports proved to be mostly fabrication, still it was for many

The author in his later years as a diesel engineer for the Utah Railway. Photo from the W. J. G. Gould collection.

years a much better job than the one I left on the Rio Grande. Instead of being gone from home anywhere from ten hours to ten days or two weeks on a freight trip, as we were on the Rio Grande, on the Utah we were seldom gone more than twenty-four or thirty hours on a mainline trip. And those new engines were marvels compared to the Rio Grande power, which was held together, as we used to say, with bailing wire. For every year of the depression the Utah operated in the black while the Rio Grande was in receivership.

We had a wonderful railway through its prime years. In the fall and winter the boomers came from all over the western country. All were headed for the Utah. They were assured of good work up until the latter part of the following February. It was, I believe, the boomers' last stand.

Epilogue

This ends my father's writings of his life. Time ran out for him before he could conclude the recording of his Utah Railway experiences. On Monday, September 4, 1961 (Labor Day), he and my mother were picnicking at the Saratoga Resort on Utah Lake with their daughter, my sister Elaine, and her family. Here he suffered a heart attack which he did not disclose to any member of the family. At the end of the day he drove my mother home, all the while in great pain. Later that night, or more correctly, early the next morning, he was admitted to the Utah Valley Hospital at Provo as a cardiac case.

For a time he seemed to improve. Then on Saturday, September 23, 1961, while discussing with my brother John the prospects of returning home in the coming week, he fell asleep. His sleep appeared to be peaceful. At approximately 6:30 P.M. he groaned audibly several times but did not waken. A nurse was summoned, but it was then too late. He had already passed to his next great experience.

For his sake I do not mourn. In its own peculiar way life had been rich and full for him and had little else to offer. He was overdue for new experiences and growth elsewhere. But for my personal loss I do mourn. I loved this man beyond the usual love of a son for his father. He did much for me, and I did too little for him. In his life I found much excitement and interest which vicariously enriched my own. Much of this is recorded in his writings. This is my legacy and my heritage. For this I am truly grateful.

Gilbert Gould, in retirement, instructs his grandson Wayne in the anatomy of a steam locomotive. Photo from the W. J. G. Gould collection.

I tend to believe that his death was timely. By 1961, the year of his passing, the sights, the sounds, the smells of steam railroading had all but disappeared from the American scene. The sound of the steam whistle's mournful call across a nocturnal landscape had faded and died away forever, leaving the manufacturers of air horns for the diesel locomotive scrambling to try to duplicate it.

The institution of railroading was also changing. Like in much of corporate America, the infiltration of lawyers and Ivy League MBAs into the ranks of management was dehumanizing the corporate structure. The feeling of "family" was disappearing. The worship of the so-called bottom line was supplanting the dedication to service in the common need and in the public trust. No longer did anyone care about such things as on time arrivals and departures or the compulsion to get the train over the road. The railroad culture of earlier days was all but gone.

In the inevitable and necessary march of progress the diesel locomotive has done much to bring efficiency to American railroading. Its limitless power and immense flexibility of operation were highly prized in an industry undergoing renaissance. No one knew this more than my father who ran them in the late afternoon of his career. But these wonderful new machines also deprived the work force of their former pride in the demanding skills required to move trains over the rails by steam.

Almost anyone who could read electrical instruments, particularly the main power ammeter, could move cars with a diesel locomotive. It was no longer necessary to feel in the seat of one's pants the behavior of the train all the way back to the caboose. The fraternity of those who could finely tune the reciprocating steam machine to perform these tasks was no longer in vogue or needed. They were fading over the horizon with the sailor before the mast.

A remnant of this culture existed only in the minds of those who had lived through the high noon of steam railroadin'. And the dwindling ranks of veterans of those glory years could only gather to relive them in tale and legend. For ...

> ... *Each had a run that he made one day,*
> *When it took real nerve and a lot more skill,*
> *To make the time or climb the hill,*
> *Than it does today, or ever will ...!*
>   *(Anon).*

So it was indeed time for the mournful call of a steam whistle to sound a requiem for this man who had lived through it all and loved every moment of it.

I can hear it yet!

WILLIAM R. GOULD
LONG BEACH, CALIFORNIA

Index